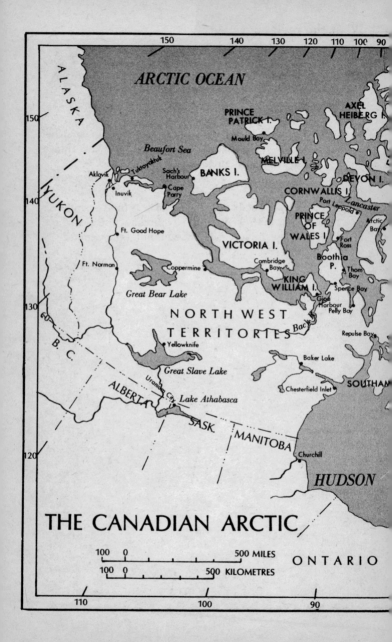

THE CANADIAN ARCTIC

To Mary Gurree.

Love. Michael (1985)

Ernie Lyall

An Arctic Man
Sixty-five years in Canada's North

Goodread Biographies

Published in 1979 by Hurtig Publishers
10560 105 Street
Edmonton, Alberta
T5H 2W7

Canadian Cataloguing in Publication Data

Lyall, Ernie, 1910-
    An Arctic man
    ISBN 0-88780-106-4

    1. Lyall, Ernie, 1910-   2. Canada, Northern —
    Biography   3. Arctic regions.   I. Title.

    FC3963.1.L92A31 1983   971.9'03'0924   C83-098342-2
    F1090.5.L923 1983

Published in paperback 1983 by Goodread Biographies
Canadian Lives series publisher: James Lorimer

Goodread Biographies is the paperback imprint of
Formac Publishing Company Limited
333 - 1657 Barrington Street
Halifax, Nova Scotia
B3J 2A1

Printed and bound in Canada

To the memory of Kavavouk—
and for Nipisha, and my family,
and all my friends in the north.

Contents

Acknowledgments

One of the things I found out about writing a book like this is that it takes a hang of a lot of people to get the job done, and for sure I never could have done it by myself, so I want to thank all the people that have helped so much.

There's people I've worked with in the north over many years, like Bill and Isobel Pringle, Chess Russell, Allen Thorburn, Jack Doyle, Alec Stevenson, and many many others; and friends in the territorial government in Yellowknife. Then there's the historians at the RCMP in Ottawa, and at the Hudson's Bay Company archives and museum and at the *Beaver* in Winnipeg, and also the Department of Indian Affairs and Northern Development in Ottawa. They've all lent a hand with information and pictures.

Nick Newbery, a teacher here in Spence Bay, helped me to put it all on tape, over thirty-five hours of it. Then the Ogles in Vancouver — Ruth Margaret typed up all the tapes, and she and Ed asked a lot of questions that stirred up more memories, and then they got it all organised and together.

Especially I want to thank Mr. Stuart Hodgson, former Commissioner of the Northwest Territories. He gave me a real lot of help and encouragement because he felt that my experiences would be kind of a slice of first-hand history of this north country.

I hope and believe that it's turned out that way, and if there's any mistakes in the book, it's not because a whole lot of people didn't try real hard to help me get it right.

Ernie Lyall
April 1979
Spence Bay
NWT

Foreword

I am delighted to have this chance to say a few things about this book of Ernie Lyall's. I have had an opportunity to read it in its entirety before publication, and I do indeed find it to be an excellent "slice of first-hand history", as Ernie puts it.

I am pleased that my old friend, Ernie, followed through on my suggestion that he do a book on his life in the North, and it is a source of satisfaction and pleasure to me that I had an encouraging hand in his project.

Ernie's unvarnished, straightforward account of his life in Canada's great north country tells it like it is with no punches pulled. As former Commissioner of the Northwest Territories, I feel this is the kind of book that should be found in every library and school in the NWT and, for that matter, in every library and school across Canada.

Although I think Ernie is right about the future Eskimo way of life, I think it is possible that he may be too pessimistic about the ultimate disappearance of the Eskimo language and culture. The government of the NWT has been at some pains for several years to reinstate the use of the language in its schools and to preserve and perpetuate many facets of the culture so that the young people may understand and feel a part of their historic identity.

The North is truly a land of growing opportunity, not just for the people of the North, be they Eskimo, Indian, or white, but for all the people of this great nation.

Men like Ernie Lyall have helped immensely to make it so.

Stuart Hodgson
Chairman, International Joint Commission
May 1979
Ottawa

An Arctic Man

Facts, fairy tales, and baloney

The main reason I decided to do a book about my life in the north is that I finally got fed up with all the baloney in so many books written about the north.

There's a saying up here that goes something like this — if you come up here from the south and you stop over at some place in the north for an hour, you can write an article for a newspaper; if you stay for overnight you can write a big article for a magazine; and if you stay for three days, you're an expert and you can write a whole book. There's a few places that have this kind of a thing printed up like a certificate to give to visitors, and it's signed by some local bigwig and dated for when you were there, and of course it's supposed to be all in fun.

But to be honest with you, it isn't all that funny a lot of the time, because there's people have been up here a lot longer than three days, they've even lived in the north for quite a while, and what they've written afterwards they've got wrong or mixed up. I don't know where some of them got their information, maybe they only got a little bit and dreamed up the rest of it to make what they thought would be a better story. But for sure, some of them, even some famous writers, should label their stuff "fairy tales" and not try to pass it off as the truth.

Now I'm not saying that even all northerners will agree about why some things have happened up here, about what's good and what's bad, or what's going to happen in the future, because some think one way and some think another. It's all according to how you look at it, and nobody can say for sure who's right and who's wrong about that sort of thing.

But what I am talking about is the people that don't get their facts straight, or the people that twist things around on purpose to fit some idea of their own, especially when they're about things that I myself happen to know about and had to do with personally. And that's the kind of thing that I wanted to set straight. I decided the best way to do that would be to begin right at the beginning, because I've lived my whole life in Canada's north — except for a few years in school — and my last forty-eight years have been north of the Arctic Circle, which is where I still live today in Spence Bay in the Northwest Territories. I've been in Spence since 1949 when I helped to found this settlement as a Hudson's Bay Company trading post.

A lot of people have thought I am Eskimo or at least part Eskimo, but I'm a white man. My name is Ernest Wilson Lyall and I'm sixty-nine years old. My first job was with the Hudson's Bay Company at a post in 1927 when I was seventeen. My grandfather, my father, and three of my brothers all worked for the Bay at one time or another along the northern Labrador or in the Arctic, and I was with the Bay most of the time until 1962 when I went with the government in Spence. Now I'm a local Justice of the Peace, and coroner, and game officer here, and I've known Eskimos all my life.

I began to speak the Eskimo language even before I joined the HBC, knew it pretty well by the end of my first year with them, and still use it all the time. My wife is an Eskimo, and my in-laws are all Eskimo of course. I lived the Eskimo way of life for several years and had an official Eskimo number in the government records, something that very few white men have. I have six sons and five daughters living who were all born and brought up in the north, and legally they are Eskimos.

Also, as it happens, for years and years the Bay required their employees to keep diaries at all their posts, and I kept my personal ones along with those, and also a lot of backup diaries with more details about a lot of things that happened.

So, maybe I'm not an expert, but I've had a hang of a lot of experience with the north and with Eskimos, so I figure I know at least a little bit about what I'm talking about, if not a lot more than most. More than those three-day "experts" anyhow!

Now it might help to have some explanations of some things you'll be running into in this book. For one thing, as you've already noticed, I use the old-fashioned word "Eskimo", or sometimes just "the people", instead of "Inuit", which is beginning to be used a lot nowadays and is the Eskimo word for "the people" — and I just do this because I figure everybody understands the word "Eskimo", and also because I'm used to using it for so long. For about the same reasons I don't use any metric terms for measurements or temperatures or that sort of thing. And, of course, when I talk about the south and southerners, I mean the southern part of Canada.

Up here, like everywhere, the rivers run down to the sea, but here they run *down north* to the sea, so generally old-timers like me say "down north". But most people think of north as up and south as down like on the maps, and a lot of newcomers up here these days speak of north as up, too, so I'm going along with what most people think, and when I say "up" that means north, and we won't any of us be confused.

There's another expression that we northerners use when we travel to the south or any place that's bigger than home, like in Spence we say we're going "out", or "outside", to Ottawa or Vancouver, or even just to Yellowknife or Cambridge Bay. Not "down" or "up" or "over to" — just "out". We say we're going "out" when we mean out of the settlement, even just out on the land to trap or hunt.

When I use the words "police" or "policeman" I always mean the Royal Canadian Mounted Police because they're the only police the people in the north have, or ever have had, which is not like the cities in the south where they have their own policemen besides the RCMP.

Where I say summer or spring, those seasons are later and shorter up here than in the south. For us summer always was the short time when the supply ships could get through the ice to northern posts in the early days, when the sea ice broke up enough, and you'll find out later that we couldn't always count on those ships because sometimes it didn't get warm enough to melt the ice. And there was always a little while on both sides of the summer when we couldn't travel anywhere because there was too much ice for boats in the rivers and lakes and the sea, and not enough ice to take a dog team across the inlets or bays or lakes or rivers. There's a whole lot more water like that in the north than most people think, more than there is land. So that's what I'm talking about when I say we had to wait till the "ice made" before we could travel, till it got cold enough for the water to freeze over so we could go somewhere by dogs, by dog team.

There are some things I'd better explain about Eskimo life. I sometimes talk about the people "being in bed" or "going to bed" or having "bed clothing", and then I'm using white man's terms, but I don't mean like white man's beds and sheets and things. I think a lot of people know by now that a snow house had a built-up place or ledge called a sleeping platform, and the people had skins like caribou or polar bear or whatever to put under and over them. In the summer, when the people lived in tents, the skins — "bed clothing" — were just spread on the ground. When I say "deerskins" for clothing or whatever, that means caribou skins.

Another thing, when I talk about the people being "married" in the olden days, they didn't have a formal wedding ceremony. They just agreed that they wanted to live with each other and that this woman would belong to this man, and they would have children with each other and be a family; it was as simple as that. Nowadays, of course, that's different. Even I can marry couples because I'm a Justice of the Peace — and I can tell you that the first time ever I did this, I was more scared than the groom!

I'm not going to bother to explain how to pronounce the Eskimo names you'll run into, because they sound pretty much like they look if you break them down into parts. But it would be nice to have my wife's name sound right, Nipisha, you'd say "NIP-ish-uh" — and my father-in-law, Kavavouk, you don't pronounce the "k" at the end, so the "vouk" sounds like "vow", it's "KAV-uh-vow".

Anyway in different parts of the north an Eskimo name is pronounced different. Eskimos from the western Arctic can hardly understand the people on Baffin Island. Lots of places where the French missionaries were, names are pronounced very different to the way they say them in areas where a Hudson's Bay trader maybe said everything with a Scottish accent. It's the same with spelling. I say the Eskimo names the way I learned them — the way the Eskimos told me — and I spell them the best way I can according to the way they sound. Others have done the same and can be just as right as I am.

Now, I guess there's one main thing I really want to get across right away, and that is that some people who've written books about the north are what they call anthropologists, or maybe sociologists; and there's been archeologists up here, and historians; also some that have lived in the north, even for a long time, have been mainly interested in the Eskimo languages, so they're probably language experts. But I didn't have any fancy education in any university, and I wasn't studying the land or the people as an outsider that's dropped in, or was living in the north for a while, or just looking in. All my life I've been *living* on the *inside* of what these other people have been looking at and writing about. And to tell you the truth — which is the whole idea of this book — the outsiders, or what I call outsiders, have written so much baloney that sometimes it's been hard for me to recognize in their books the land and the people that I know so well.

A wooden Christmas tree

My very first memory is when my family and I arrived in Port Burwell. I was only a little over one year old at the time, but I can distinctly remember what happened when we got off the ship at Burwell. The German missionary that came there on the ship with us was carrying a little spotty dog, and it jumped out of his arms. Then a pack of dogs from the settlement was running for his dog, and they just ate that little dog all up! That's the first thing that I can remember.

I don't know when my mother, Christiana, came to Canada, but I know she came from Ireland. My father, John, was Scottish and I'm not sure whether he was born on the Labrador or

17

whether he came over from Scotland, but I know that my grand-father came over in the 1800s with the Hudson's Bay Company. He joined the Company as a cooper, and my dad learned the trade from him. I was born April 17, 1910 at Island Harbour, a little place along the Labrador between Makkovik and Hope-dale, and in 1911, the year that we went to Burwell, my father joined the Moravian mission, not as a missionary but to do the trading part of the mission at their store.

The same ship that took us to Burwell used to come over from the old country every year to supply the Moravian mission stations along the Labrador. The ship's name was the *Harmony*, and she was a square-rigged three-master, but later they put a steam engine in her and used her for many years.

On the map, Port Burwell looks like it's on the north tip of the Labrador, but actually it's on a small island, Killinek Island, and it's part of the Northwest Territories. The way things turned out, some fifteen years later I went back there as a trader for the Hudson's Bay Company. The place is very rocky, very moun-tainous all around, and we were right up in a little harbour, a very deep harbour. The ships couldn't come all the way in because it was narrow and had dangerous tides and winds, so they used to anchor about a mile away, and when we climbed up the hill behind where we lived, we could see them out there.

At the time when we were there there were five or six Eskimo families, maybe a few more, but they weren't living right in the settlement, or what we'd call a settlement today. They lived about a mile away. The only whites there at that time were the Moravians, except for the Hudson's Bay Company that had a store about half a mile away and a man to run it for them.

There was a big crowd of us Lyalls. There were nineteen children in our family altogether, but I was the youngest and by the time that I can remember, most of them were out and away. I'm afraid I couldn't even name them all. The only ones living now are my two brothers — Henry in North West River, in southern Labrador, and Sam in Nain, which also is on the Labrador.

We shared a big double house with the missionary and his

family in Burwell; they lived on one side of it, and we lived on the other. They really built big houses at those Moravian posts.

There were three of us brothers at the time living at home — Henry, Sam, and myself. Two older brothers, Freddie and Abe, were sometimes home, sometimes out working. Upstairs there was what you'd call now a rumpus room, a great big kind of loft room, and three little bedrooms for us boys. The rest of the family had their bedrooms downstairs. There was a big pot-bellied coal stove in the living room, and pipes from it went up through the floor right to each bedroom. It used to be nice and warm, although in the mornings it got pretty cold sometimes, but never cold enough to see your breath.

My mum always had a lot of flowers, she kept them growing all the time — inside in the winter, and in the garden in the summer. She had a lot of rhubarb in her garden, and as a matter of fact, even today they say there's still a lot of rhubarb grows around there every summer, probably all from that patch of Mum's.

All of us kids always had chores to do. We used to always get up at six o'clock, and after we got dressed we had some chores to do even before breakfast time — we generally had breakfast at seven o'clock. We burned both wood and coal in the stoves, and us boys used to have to saw so much wood each day and bring it in before we could go out and play.

We couldn't play with the Eskimo kids of course, since they weren't that close to the mission, but Mr. Lenz, the missionary, had three children, two boys and a girl, and we used to play with these German kids. So at that time I learned quite a bit of German, I could talk in German quite easily, but now I don't think there's five words I could say in German.

My parents were very strict, especially compared to parents today, and I think this is a good thing for kids. We'd quite often get spanked or slapped, and if we back-lipped our parents we'd be punished for that. My dad always kept a strap and if we were really bad, we'd get that strap.

I remember well that one morning we were coming downstairs to go to breakfast, we were laughing and giggling and I farted, and I said to my brother, "Oh, I pooped," and we started to laugh even harder. Well! My dad and mum thought that what they heard was such a terrible thing that I got a real spanking, and I was sent right back to bed where I had to stay without even getting anything to eat until suppertime that night.

To begin with, Mum and Dad taught us the ABCs and how to count. But later a policeman, Sergeant J.E.F. (Jim) Wight, stayed at our house, and it was from him that I got my first real schooling — myself and Henry and Sam, and a sister, Margaret (she wasn't actually my sister, she was Mum's niece but Mum had adopted her). The sergeant didn't really have all that much to do, so he used to teach us from nine o'clock until noon every day in what we used to call "the schoolroom", that rumpus room upstairs. He started us off first at simple arithmetic and short words, but he was so good that when I went out to school at Makkovik, I went straight to grade four.

Sergeant Wight was a big fellow, at least six feet tall, but he looked even bigger to me at that time, of course, almost like a giant. He was very very good with us children. He was very softspoken, very pleasant, nothing ever seemed to upset him, I never knew him to lose his temper. He was one of the finest fellows I think I've ever met. He was my first hero, and years later when our paths crossed again I still thought he was the finest.

He very seldom wore his dress uniform, just like when a ship was coming, and we kids, when we'd see him dressed up in his red coat, used to kind of shy away from him — he looked so, well, I guess you could say, kingly. Besides teaching us our lessons, he used to talk to us about what the "outside" was like. After all, we'd never been outside and didn't know anything about it. He told us about horses and cows and movies and what Christmas was like in "white man's land", as they used to call the south in those times up there. And when we'd get a spanking or something like that, he'd sympathise with us, but also he'd tell us that it was wrong not respecting your parents.

Unfortunately, my father never did learn Eskimo except for a few odd words, like saying *atee* (come on, let's go) or *tuaveegit* (hurry up). If he really wanted to talk to the Eskimos about something he used to have to get Freddie, who learned Eskimo, to interpret for him. But my mother could speak very good Eskimo.

I'd often watch my father working, and would sometimes help to clean and keep the store tidy. We used to watch him when he was trading with the Eskimos, and this is where I began to learn a little bit about how to grade foxes, when I was seven or eight years old. Dad had very strict instructions on how to grade fur, and he was very good at it.

The Eskimos living close to the settlement were hunting just seals and foxes, and the mission had been built at Burwell to be near these people for trading. They used to live in what we called sod houses, actually houses built up with rocks and with a sod roof on. Sometimes they stayed there all year round. They were dependent on the Moravians for some of their basic food and supplies like flour, sugar, tea, tobacco, staple things. The store carried very little canned foods.

I used to get a chance to see the Eskimos quite a bit when they came in to trade. They didn't wear the same sort of clothing they wear these days; they used to make their own clothing, mostly out of seal skins. They were very friendly, and later I was fortunate enough to go back there with the HBC and deal with some of these same people.

Besides the work in the store, my dad used to go netting seals in the fall. My older brother and three Eskimos worked with my dad, and sometimes I got to go along. They used to set eleven seal nets and had to tend those nets every day. The mission didn't have motor boats in those early days, so they had this big boat they had to row out to the nets, and they'd leave about five in the morning and travel about two miles to the nets.

They got anywhere from 750 to 1500 seals a year, and the Eskimos were paid by my dad, a dollar a day for getting the seals. They'd bring the seals in and pull them to this big warehouse that we had, and some days they used to have to make two or three trips to get all the seals in from the nets.

They would skin out and dry as many as they could in September and October, and then the rest would be left to freeze. Gradually during the winter they'd haul the carcasses into the heated building and thaw them out, and the three Eskimos would skin the seals and dry the pelts. I used to watch them and when I was eight or nine I tried to skin some too, but I didn't make a very good job of it.

Once the skins got dried, any women that wanted to make sealskin boots, my dad would give them the skins; and when they brought the finished boots back to the store, he used to give them a dollar and five cents, at first. But I can remember that before I left there the boots went up to two dollars a pair. Of course that was in trade, never in cash.

We used to send out thousands of pairs of boots every year from Port Burwell. This is where Dad's coopering came in handy — he used to make big barrels, what they called puncheons, and they filled these puncheons with sealskin boots and sent them out to the old country and off to Newfoundland. Those big puncheons would hold 500 gallons of liquid.

After the seals had been skinned, the fat used to be frozen. When it got warm in the spring we would render most of that fat into oil, and then it was put into tierces, or oak barrels, about the same size as a 45-gallon gasoline drum. They used to send hundreds of these barrels of seal oil out, but they don't do that there any more.

Sharks used to get caught in the seal nets. They were very plentiful around Burwell. They had very big livers that looked like a codfish liver, a big white liver, and this made the best oil of all. We never ate the sharks. There were so many of them sometimes that they couldn't look after the seals and sharks both, so they would kill the sharks and throw them away.

Besides the big double mission house, there was only one building that had heat, the warehouse where they skinned the seals and Dad made barrels. It had an old coal stove that gave just enough heat to thaw the seals so that they could skin them, and they had ordinary coal oil lamps to see by during the skinning, and some hurricane lanterns.

The winter used to start about the middle of December when

things froze up, and it would generally break up there around the middle of June, and this is when the people would start fishing for cod. My dad had three cod traps that he put out, but the people themselves had what they called punts, like home-made dinghies, and they used to fish from them and bring the fish in. Then they'd gut them, split them, salt them and dry them, and sell them to my dad for $1.15 a kental, or quintal, which was an old-country 112-pound measure.

When the ice came in the winter, the people used to go trapping foxes, all colours — white ones, red ones. It wasn't real good country for this but usually good enough for everyone to get some foxes.

Besides the food I mentioned earlier, and the punts, the store used to have a little bit of clothing, like thick pants, and guns — shotguns, .22s. Mostly the clothing they'd have was this fleece-lined Stanfield underwear, really good stuff. And the people bought kettles and pans and things like that, and enamel mugs.

We didn't use money for transactions at all. There was no such thing as cash, it was all trade. The German missionaries had taught the Eskimos shillings, pence, and farthings as arithmetic, and they knew that in their heads.

For our family Christmas, we used to hang up our stockings and we used to get all sorts of presents — teddy bears and little sleds and a pair of new mitts, or something or other. Everything was home-made, we never had any bought toys. Because my dad was the trader in the store, we were very interested in "shopping" and one Christmas Dad made us a store with different little rooms in it, and we used to have that as our play store. We'd have candies and raisins and things like that to "sell."

Our stockings weren't hung up on a fireplace — we didn't have one — so we would generally hang them on the Christmas tree. Of course, at Port Burwell there weren't any trees, and in those days there were no artificial trees like you can buy now, so my dad made a Christmas tree himself, just out of wood, with wooden branches, and decorated it. Our Christmas stockings weren't anything special, just our own that Mum had knitted.

The big thing at Christmas was what the mission called a

"Love Feast" on Christmas Eve, and all the people that were near around would come in. There was a service at four o'clock, and then I can remember there were all these trays with mugs of tea, and sweet buns with a few raisins or currants in them, and after the service they'd feed the people that. This was a big thing for everybody to look forward to, for me too. They also had the same thing at Easter time.

During ordinary times, the Eskimos always used to come in to church every Sunday. The Moravian mission had a service at seven o'clock on Saturday nights, and three services on Sundays — the first one at nine in the morning, then one in the afternoon, and one again at seven o'clock in the evening. I was expected to go to every one of them. I thought that was one of my duties and this was something really sacred to my folks. They were very religious. My father became a Moravian. I don't think I ever missed a service all the time I was home.

The services generally lasted anywhere from an hour to an hour and a half, with Bible reading, and sermons of course, and it was very simple, very dignified. We wore what we called our "Sunday clothes", our very best clothes. Even as a small child I didn't find church long and dull, although we had to behave ourselves — we had to sit still, we couldn't speak, we couldn't move around.

There were two entrances to the church — one was for the women and the other was for the men. The men sat on one side, the women on the other, and any children that weren't carried would sit on benches up in front — the girls on one side and the boys on the other. The inside of the church had a real fancy sort of an altar, as I remember, where the minister used to preach from. There were no actual pews, just long benches with a back to them. On special occasions I think they'd have two candles, one on each end of the altar, but they didn't have any cross there.

Of course they used to baptise a lot of Eskimos, because there was no other religion except the Moravians in that whole northern area of the Labrador coast, from Burwell right down to Makkovik. But myself, I was baptised by Dr. Wilfred Grenfell, the famous missionary doctor, at a place called Turnavik, which is between Makkovik and Hopedale on the Labrador. This was in the summer before we went to Port Burwell. Dr. Grenfell was never as far north as Burwell.

The Eskimos that were there then — I must say this, which I'm afraid I couldn't say about a lot of Eskimos today — they acted, I think, more like real true Christians. They'd come into the settlement to listen and to learn. Besides the people near the mission, there were two or three camps, maybe four, nearly fifty miles away where they used to come in from.

But there was one family that never did turn to religion. They stayed as pagan as they always were. They were really friendly people, like when you would go to visit them, but they kept their own services, their shamanism. I didn't see any shamanistic things done then, though, but I did later.

A needless tragedy

My brother Freddie died in the fall of 1920, soon after the RCMP had opened a post at Port Burwell and sent up Sergeant Wight and Constable Ken Butler. There had been a lot of ships going into the Arctic which weren't paying tax to customs, so their main job was to make sure that no ship passed beyond Burwell without calling in for tax purposes. Until their post was built, Sergeant Wight stayed with us for a while, as I said before, and I think Constable Butler must have stayed with the Lenzes.

This Ken Butler later became a surgeon in Ottawa, and long after he was in Burwell, he wrote a small book about his experiences there and called it *Igloo Killinek**, which is the name the Eskimos gave to Port Burwell. One of the things he wrote about was how Freddie died, but that book is very confusing and a lot of it untrue.

For one thing, he said that my dad, besides being the mission's trader, was an interpreter, and hinted that he wasn't a

*Kenneth C. Butler, *Igloo Killinek*, Longmans Canada Ltd., (Toronto, 1963).

white and that my mother wasn't white either — that she "looked to be a full-blooded Eskimo". And he said that we lived in a separate "small" wooden house. I've already talked about these things that show he was wrong. He also got us brothers pretty mixed up, except for Freddie.

What happened was that my dad had got a motor for his boat, a little six-horsepower Mianus, and he used to send the boat along the coast of Killinek Island to bring back seal fat from an Eskimo camp about fourteen miles from Burwell.

Well, this time — it was on November 12 — Freddie and Abe and two Eskimos were going down to this camp to get a load of seal fat, and Ken Butler wanted to go along. A storm came up, the engine broke down, and they drifted into shore. In other words they were shipwrecked, but they all got safely to shore.

However, they weren't dressed for such cold weather or anything like the trouble they got in, because the winter weather hadn't really started yet. It was nice when they set out, and they didn't expect to be out very long. They didn't even have duffel coats on. Freddie and Abe were just wearing outside parkas, the cover of a parka, like the policeman had on too. But Butler says he was dressed in all kinds of warm clothing, that there'd already been a lot of stormy weather and the snow was three feet deep, and the day of the trip was "cold and sunless".

The thing is that when this accident happened they were only four miles from the camp where they'd gone to get the seal fat. So there was this storm getting worse, snowing and blowing, and my brothers and the Eskimos decided that they should walk back to that Eskimo camp, which would have taken them an hour, maybe a little longer, and get dried out. They knew that when their boat didn't come in, the people at Burwell would know that something was wrong and would send a boat out next morning to look for them.

But this young, inexperienced RCMP guy said that where they were was handy to Burwell and that he was going to walk there. But the others knew that to do that he would have to walk way up around this great big bay in all that storm, because that bay ran inland for five miles, and on each side there were just cliffs so there was no way anyone could get across that water.

As a matter of fact, Freddie and Abe and the Eskimos started walking back towards the camp, but they couldn't convince Butler to walk back with them. He started off on his own to try and walk back to Burwell. Now it was getting on to dark in the afternoon, so my brothers said, "You'll never make it." But he wouldn't listen to them. Finally Freddie said, "I'll follow him, because he'll never get there on his own."

It came on dark and Freddie was getting tired; he'd caught up with Butler who couldn't go any farther because he was so tired and cold. So Freddie dug out a hole in the snow and put Butler in there, right at the sea edge, handy to the sea, and told him not to move from there. Freddie told him there'd be a boat along the next day looking for him, and Freddie said, "I'll try and go on."

I don't know why Freddie went on. Probably he thought he could make it home and help the people who would come out to look for them. Or, if he got too tired, he would wait for the boat too.

So my brother tried to go on, and when the others were looking for him later, they saw where one time he'd slid down one of those cliffs around the bay and went right into the water.

Well, the next day they did find the policeman. He'd crawled out of the hole my brother had put him in; his hands and feet were frozen, and he couldn't talk. He was delirious. He couldn't tell them where the rest were or anything. He was just out of his mind.

But what Butler said in his book was that it was Freddie that wanted to walk around that bay, that Freddie thought the bay only ran in for two or three miles, that Freddie was all wrong and that he, Butler, knew all about everything. He made out like he was the one that knew all about the land and what they should do, when he'd only been around there two or three months. My brothers had lived there for years and probably knew the place as well as those Eskimos that were along that had lived there all their lives.

It was a week before they finally found Freddie. They thought afterwards that they'd heard him shooting signal shots, but in the storm it was hard to tell where the shots came from. The storm had covered up most of his tracks, so when they did find him, he wasn't where they'd expected him to be at all. When they found him he was just sitting right up on a rock with his rifle beside him, where he'd been shooting off the signals. He was frozen dead, just sitting right there.

We all felt that if that young policeman had listened to the local people, the people that knew about the land and what to do, Freddie needn't have died, and that there'd have been no hardships at all, except for them to lose their boat and the seal fat.

Kneeling on beans

My home schooling ended when I went out to school in Makkovik, about five or six hundred miles south. At that time Makkovik was the biggest settlement on the northern Labrador, with about a hundred to two hundred people, all whites. While it was really only a small village, for me it was like going from, say, Spence Bay to Edmonton today — there was a big difference!

I was just a kid when I left, and I felt really excited until the ship pulled out of the harbour. Then I realised I was leaving home, and it struck me really hard. However, I wasn't alone at least, because Sam and Henry and Margaret went out at the same time.

The sea trip from Burwell to Makkovik took around three weeks. We were on the *Harmony* again, and they were supplying the settlements with goods and picking up school kids, so we stopped at all the settlements along the coast and stayed over at most of them. The fastest that ship could do, as I found out later, was six miles per hour, with the engine. Sometimes, when we had a fair wind, they stopped the engine and put up the sails. The crew was around ten or twelve men. As I say, I missed my parents very much at first, all us kids were really heartbroken, but then we got used to it. The crew on the ship were really nice people, they were really good to us, even the captain. Unfortunately, we got really seasick on that ship!

Makkovik was down in the wooded country, there were a lot

of trees there on the coast. That was the first time I can remember seeing a tree—I didn't know what it was, at first! The place was mainly a fishing town, but they had a small sawmill and they used to make what we called "rough boards" for building houses and that sort of a thing.

The people there were what they called "liveyers", which came from the two words "lives" and "here". To be a liveyer, your parents had to have come from another country, from anywhere, like Sweden or Scotland or England, and settled on the Labrador to live. I guess I'm probably a liveyer, or was.

At the school they took Eskimo kids and the missionary kids and everyone; it was the only Moravian school on the Labrador and there were maybe twenty or thirty kids there. I'm not sure, but I think it had only been opened the year before we went out.

The school was part of the mission house and was a white building with a red roof, and it looked right out over the sea. There was two classrooms, a lower class and an upper class, and we slept in dormitories, one for the girls and one for the boys.

The teachers were terrible. Well, actually, the teachers themselves out of the classroom were pretty nice people, but if you got anything wrong at all they certainly did punish you. Like they used the strap a lot. It was very strict.

For instance, one time, I forget exactly what it was that I'd done — I think I was imitating one of the teachers that was bawling out one of the kids or lecturing some kid for doing this or that. I was behind the teacher and making a face and mocking her, and she turned around suddenly and caught me. We were just going in to class and she had a bag of dry beans there, and she put these beans on the floor — all together, you know — and put a clock on the floor, and she made me kneel on those beans, and I had to watch that clock for ten minutes without moving. I couldn't even look away from that clock. Watching that clock for ten solid minutes and kneeling on those hard beans was the worst punishment! I think that's the worst punishment I ever got besides the strap (which I think some kids should get in school today).

There were windows in the school, and it was lit by kerosene lamps. The desks were just long tables, and we wrote on slates — we didn't have pen or paper or pencil. We didn't have to wear any kind of school uniform, just the clothes we'd brought from home.

For games, mostly we used to play hide and seek, and we tried to learn soccer and cricket. We didn't get good at those games but we enjoyed playing.

The Eskimo kids in school in Makkovik were kids that had been brought in from other settlements. Maybe a third of the kids there were Eskimos, but I didn't notice any difference at all. I mean, they were just like the other kids in school. Years later in the north I would see places where Eskimo kids were separated from their families and taken off to school, and it caused a big gap between the way they learned to live at school and their home life, but in Makkovik it didn't cause that trouble because in that area a lot of the Eskimos, even the elderly people on the land, could speak English. As a matter of fact, in most of the places up as far as Nain, more of them talked English than Eskimo. They lived different to the Eskimos in the north, too — most had houses and weren't moving around so much. Those kids on the Labrador went back to their settlements, of course, but I think the schooling did them a lot of good.

We'd never hear from our parents during the year or get special holiday parcels or mail. There was no contact with them from when we left on the ship till we got back home again the next summer.

When summer came the ship would pick us up at the school on its way north, and we'd spend about a week at home with our parents while supplies were being unloaded. Then we'd go right back to school on the ship's return trip south. Of course, my brothers and sister were older than me and finished school before I did.

Christmas at the school wasn't very exciting since I couldn't get home and my family couldn't send any Christmas gifts. So the only thing was we got a little something different to eat, that's all. We got a few candies and a few nuts.

The food over-all was awful. We had porridge every morning — porridge and molasses — and hard tasteless biscuits called Newfoundland hardtack. But on Sundays we used to get bread and, if we were lucky, sometimes, not very often, say like on special occasions, we'd get either jam or marmalade. What we used to eat in the daytime was mostly soup, usually potato soup or something like that.

Sometimes, like on Sundays, we'd go down to the town in the afternoon and visit people that we knew, but we were never allowed to stay out to meals. We were instructed that when we were out visiting we weren't to eat between meals, but a lot of them used to give us stuff to eat, because they knew we were hungry. Of course we never told the school authorities about that!

When we walked into town from the school, there were no roads or streets or anything like that, just footpaths. In Makkovik all the houses were wooden, not like Port Burwell where houses were half stone or masonry.

There was only one store then, run by the Moravians. Their stuff, like for all the missions on the Labrador, was brought in by the *Harmony* from the old country and was tax free. There wasn't much difference between the Moravian mission store and the Hudson's Bay Company. They had just about the same things for sale, except in some of the Moravian stores, as far back as I can remember, you could get chocolates, which we never used to get in the northern Hudson's Bay stores. I never did know why.

I don't think Makkovik had a policeman or a nurse at that time, but in those days the missionaries all had some training in medicine so they could treat people that got sick.

At this Moravian mission school they really pushed their religion, like morning and evening prayers, church on Sundays, and all the rest of it. When I got out of bed in the morning, first thing, I'd get down on my knees and say my prayers. I really believed in what I was doing, too, at that time, which is quite contrary to what I think today.

Though it was a strict school, that was a fairly happy time for me. One thing still sticks in my mind, which lots of times I've

31

thought about, and thought that it must have been a terrible thing for me to do. When we first got there in early September, before the school was open for classes, the teacher used to take us out for walks, and she was always asking us all sorts of questions. I remember her asking when our birthdays were, and I told her what date my birthday was and I said, "Are you going to give me a holiday on that day?" She didn't say yes or anything, and I never thought of it again until my birthday came up in April and they declared that there was no school that day because of my birthday!

That never happened with the other kids, because I don't think any other kid ever had the nerve to ask such a thing.

Sizzle, smoke, and stink

While I was at Makkovik in school, my family moved south to Hebron, so when I finished school I went to my parents' home at their new place. In 1925 arrangements for me to go to high school at St. John's, Newfoundland, came about in sort of an odd way and led finally to me going with the Hudson's Bay Company.

A man named Herbert Hall, a free trader, came through Hebron. He was going to open up a trading post in the general area and was bringing his supplies up from St. John's. He wanted a young fellow to go with him as interpreter because he didn't speak any Eskimo. He was at our house one night and asked my dad if there was anyone he could get to go with him. I'd picked up a very little Eskimo, but it was more than anyone else around. I was willing to go, and my dad was willing to let me go.

However, just about this time the HBC ship happened to come to Hebron with Ralph Parsons, who was then the district manager of the Company's posts in the north. He heard about my plans, but of course the Hudson's Bay Company had been in the north for years and years and he wasn't going to let any rival get away with anything that easy. So he went to Dad and said,

"Look, tell you what I'll do. Ernie's just come back from school, and instead of you sending him off to work somewhere right away, I'll take him down to St. John's."

Actually, it wasn't St. John's. One of my sisters, we called her "Wealthy", was living at Clark's Beach nearby, and Parsons said, "I'll take Ernie down to Clark's Beach and put him to school there." (I just can't tell you how my sister came to have that nickname, or what her real name was.) Clark's Beach was a little outport of St. John's and at that time they only taught up to what they called primary four — it was different from now. So I went to school there for only two months before they figured I should go down to St. John's where they had a better school. So they took me down and put me in the Bishop Field College.

The Hudson's Bay Company said that they'd pay for some of it but Dad would also have to pay for some of it. So I went to the college and it cost $120 a month — Dad paid half and the HBC paid the other half.

St. John's was a really big town, a big city, as far as I was concerned. I'd never seen anything like it before of course. At that time I think it was about 25,000 population. The college was just about in the middle of the town and anyone going there that didn't live in St. John's, like me, lived in a place called Field Hall. It was a big dormitory, and I think there were 120 of us there. We ate there as well.

I think I learned a great deal. Like I took up geometry and algebra and that sort of thing. We had to learn both French and Latin, which I know I would have failed except that I had to leave to go with the HBC before I took my final exams. I didn't like French or Latin because I couldn't see why I should learn a language that I didn't think I'd ever have to use and never had any interest in.

I liked most everything else. Chemistry was the best, because I always liked exciting sorts of things, and I'd heard that it was kind of dangerous. I had one accident working with chemistry — I mixed some things they'd said not to, and everybody had to clear out of the building, because the stuff sizzled and made a lot of smoke and a hell of a stink. I did it just to see what would happen. I used to like experimenting with all sorts of things. If there was something new that I'd never seen before, I always had to try to do it, just to see if I could. When I found school dull, there was quite a few times that I tried to liven things up. I wasn't exactly your model student.

I made one good friend there, Bill Carson. His father was William Carson, an agent for the HBC in St. John's. We went to school there together, and we both left St. John's together to go up north. Like me, he joined the Bay too. He stayed in touch with me for a long time, but I haven't seen him for quite a while now. He retired from the HBC in 1976, so he was with the Company a very long time. The last word I had, he'd ended up back in St. John's as their district manager.

We got pulled out of school during the second year, in June of 1927, because we had to go to Montreal for a month for training and to get outfitted for the trip north.

Bill Carson and I never exactly talked that much about what our hopes would be, and why we wanted to join the Hudson's Bay Company, but I think that, like me, he was pretty excited about going north, to the unknown. For instance, I used to hear from my brother Abe of places in the north where the sun wouldn't come up in the winter. Well, this was something I couldn't believe! I mean I couldn't imagine it. And I wanted to go there just to see that this was so.

I guess you could say that already I wasn't a white that wanted to live south in white society. It seems like that.

I used to hear a good lot of crazy stories. In those days the whites, white people going north, thought of the Eskimos as savages. That wasn't the way I knew them, but I didn't get into any arguments about that sort of thing. As a matter of fact, I thought they probably knew all about the far-north Eskimos and their way of life.

My ideas were changing a lot from when I was a youngster living in Port Burwell, to when I was seventeen and about to go with the Company. All I knew was about the Eskimos right in Burwell and along the Labrador, and I thought that when you went up to the far north there'd be a lot of difference. The big

34

thing I had in my mind, what I was wondering, was would these people be wanting to be friendly or would you have to lock the door every time you'd go home so they couldn't get in. I really thought they would be savages and come and harm me — which of course was not true. But still I wasn't nervous about it. I liked the idea of an adventurous sort of life; I wanted to go see for myself what it was like to live in what I thought would be a true native way of living.

Until I lived with the Eskimos after I went with the HBC, I did always think that they would be dirty, greasy, hair all matted with grease, and this sort of thing.

It was in my mind that the Labrador Eskimos, like those at Burwell, were probably a much more civilised people than the people farther north. I thought I was going to a place where an Eskimo would meet you and probably stick a knife in you or want to fight with you or something. But that added to the excitement of the north, that attracted me to go north.

Of course I found it so much different! As a matter of fact, I found that the people, the farther north you went, were more friendly.

It seemed to me that maybe the Moravians tried to make it look like they felt the Eskimos were just as good as the whites. Yet when I was playing in that little yard in Port Burwell, the Eskimo kids weren't allowed into the yard when us white kids played. To be honest about it, I think that my own parents figured they were better than Eskimos, though they were always friendly and did what they could for them. And yet I sort of feel that they didn't like us to play with the Eskimo kids because they really probably thought we were superior.

And I think, looking back at it, that maybe there was a little bit of that in those early Moravian missionaries, that they felt they were helping the inferior person. For instance, if an Eskimo wanted to visit a missionary, the missionary wouldn't have taken that Eskimo into his sitting room like an equal and given him the best chair. He might take him into the sitting room, but he'd take a chair and put it down by the door for him.

I think that if the whites — including the missionaries and

my own parents — looked down on Eskimos as a lower people it was partly because they used to smell quite a bit, because they probably never had a bath from the day they were born. And they'd eat raw seal meat and different things.

But there certainly were differences between the Eskimos I came to live and work with when I went with the HBC and the ones I knew as a boy. The Eskimos along the Labrador used to build their own houses. They never lived in what you would call shacks — just one room with no partitions — they had really nice houses. At many of the settlements there'd be a sawmill and the Eskimos used to get wood right from the sawmill and build their own houses. A lot of them got really good at building. The Labrador Eskimo houses had kitchens, sitting rooms, and lots of them had dining rooms. You'd see pictures hanging on the walls. I remember a lot of houses where I visited. They always had a picture of King George V and the king before him, Edward VII, on the walls.

The Labrador Eskimos used to go out in the summertime, maybe go down the island fishing, but they never did live out in camps permanently like the Eskimos farther north. The Labrador Eskimos at the time of my youth were basically living in a fixed place, they weren't wandering around on the sea ice.

The whites had been in the Labrador there for a long time. The Moravian missions a while back celebrated their 300th year in Nain, so the Eskimos from the Labrador had been in contact with the whites for a lot longer time than most of the Eskimos in any other part of the Arctic.

Here Before Christ

My schooling at St. John's got cut short, as I say, so I could go to Montreal with a bunch of other apprentices to the Hudson's Bay Company before being shipped north. I signed a contract with the HBC for five years. The first year I was to get $20 a month and keep, the second year $25 a month, and on up to the fifth year, $40 a month and keep. I stayed in that category for quite a long time.

The ship that took me to Montreal from St. John's was the *Nascopie*, and she was to have a big part in my life in the north. She was a Hudson's Bay Company ship, in service since 1912, just an ordinary freighter and looked it. Later on they renovated her into a tourist ship; one of her big holds was made into cabins for carrying tourists, which gave her a total of fifty passengers including Bay personnel. When she started off she was a steamship using coal, and then in the last few years she was turned into a diesel and outfitted to be a sort of semi-icebreaker. In 1927 when I went on her to Montreal, each passenger was in a cabin maybe half the size of a small bedroom, with two bunks in it. Then there was what they called the saloon where we used to go and eat.

There was about nineteen of us new clerks on the ship, all eventually going different places in the north. All the HBC apprentices used to be made to do work on the ship, they made us earn our passage. As a matter of fact, when we got on the ship we had to sign on as crew—for a dollar for the whole trip — and work the whole time.

The trip to Montreal took three or four days and then after we got to Montreal we were split up and assigned to two ships, one going to one part of the north, around Baffin Island and other places, and the other going up along the Labrador headed for Hudson's Bay. That's when my school friend, Bill Carson, got separated from me; he was going to a different part of the north.

My ship was a brand new one, the *Bayrupert*, that had made her maiden voyage the year before for the HBC. She was much bigger than the *Nascopie*. She was a beautiful ship. On the top deck there was a great big suite that was called the commissioner's suite for the commissioner of the HBC. The captain's name was Captain T.F. Smellie, and there was a crew of around twenty to twenty-five, and there must have been about eight of us clerks on that one.

One thing comes to mind, as soon as we got off the dock, there was a place where a young French girl — we used to call her "Vanilla" — had a little stand that we used to go to every day and buy ice cream.

I was never really used to hot places; they put us in the Queens Hotel, and the first night in Montreal I couldn't sleep because it was so hot in the hotel. Since it was nice and cool aboard the *Bayrupert* I asked if I could sleep there, and they gave me permission, so I slept on the ship all the time we were in Montreal. I went from the port to my training centre by cab at first, but when I got to know my way I had to walk, because the Company didn't pay transportation and I didn't have that kind of money myself.

The training period was all spent in the Company's buildings, where some of us packed goods and some were put doing invoices. At one of the warehouses where they took the lot of us, they put out a whole lot of different sorts of fur that had already been graded ready for packing and shipping. There was fox, mink, marten, beaver, whatever you have, and they'd tell us how to grade these pelts. Then they'd make us all grade them ourselves and see who could come the nearest to the proper grading that had already been done. The HBC at that time had the best fur grader in the whole of Canada and, I think, of the old country as well. My early training from my dad helped me a lot. Grading fur was mostly what I was doing in Montreal, and packing what they called personal requisitions, which was what the traders in the settlements had ordered for themselves different from what would go into the post stores.

In our free time we used to stroll in Montreal. The city had busses as well as horses and carriages. Very narrow streets, with cobblestones, I think it was. Certainly different from the streets in Canada today. I only spoke French a little bit, not very much. As a young guy seventeen years old, I hadn't seen very much of cities or towns before, of course, but I didn't like it in Montreal. I was dying to get out of there. There were too many people, too many things going on, everybody was in such a rush. I still think the same today.

Anyhow, this training course lasted just while they were loading the ship. I was there a month altogether, and I certainly was looking forward to getting on to the north, although I didn't know where I would be going. The Company never knew for sure, never told the apprentices where they were going to send them when they boarded the ship. Since they didn't have any contact of any kind in those days with the various posts, except when the ship arrived at them once every year in the summer, they didn't know who might be sick somewhere and needed to be brought out and replaced, or who had resigned, or what the conditions might be, until the ship got there. So they really couldn't tell us.

When I went on that ship, my belongings went with me. Just the things I had with me, and it wasn't very much — I think I had a trunk about half full. I had a suitcase that my sister "Wealthy" gave me, and little things she gave me that she thought I should have. There was some clothing and a new pair of shoes that I paid about $2.90 for, and some little knicks and knacks.

The last night in Montreal they gave a dinner aboard the ship for all the clerks that were going up north, and two or three VIPs. They had the mayor and whatnot, and that's the first time I ever drank in my life, and I got bombed out of my mind. I remember that so well! It's a good thing I was sleeping on the ship, so I didn't have far to go to get to bed, but I certainly started the trip with a hangover!

We stopped off at Quebec City for one night, and some of us stayed at the Frontenac Hotel there. The first HBC port of call was Cartwright on the southern Labrador. They gave us work to do all the time we were on the ship, like going down into the holds, stowing cargo, anything they could find for us to do, or doing what we used to call "cost landing" for the stuff that was going to the different ports.

Cost landing means that when we'd get the invoices for the stuff that would be unloaded at a post, they would all be in wholesale cost, and we had to figure out the cost at landing, adding on all expenses, like the freight and whatever. And all the stuff that we got from the old country used to be marked in pounds, shillings, and pence, and we had to fix it up so it would come out in dollars and cents.

I forget how many days we stayed in Cartwright, but we had to unload all the cargo for there and for Rigolet, which was about fifty miles northwest in Groswater Bay, Hamilton Inlet. The freight for Rigolet was carried there by little ordinary coastal schooners.

At every port where we stopped, we had to work with the crew and hump cargo all the time. I think that's about the time that "Heavy Bloody Cargo" got tacked on to the HBC initials — I think that came from us young clerks that had to hump all that cargo. I also have heard that HBC stands for "Here Before Christ" and "Hungry Belly Company". As a matter of fact, later on it was written up in the HBC magazine, *The Beaver*, that a cheque for $100 dated June 26, 1932 was made out to "The Here Before Christ Co." and it was actually cashed!

On the last night at Cartwright the residents put on a little "do" for us, for anyone wanting to go ashore. They had a big school there where they had a dance, an old time square dance. I think there were four fiddlers, all from Cartwright, and that was the first time I think I met any young girls that really interested me. It wasn't the first time I'd square-danced, though, because I used to square-dance before I left home.

The shipwreck

After we left Cartwright and headed north, about the third day out and maybe 200 miles later, the *Bayrupert* hit a reef on the Farmyard Islands between Makkovik and Hopedale, about ten miles from the mainland.

It happened early in the morning on July 22, I remember it was five minutes to seven. I was in my bunk in the cabin, and not long before this I'd looked out; it was a warm, really calm, and beautiful day, bright and sunny, and I could recognise where we were because my family used to go fishing right near there. I'd just got back in my bunk and was going to sleep a little longer till the gong went for breakfast, and all of a sudden there was a scraping bump that just about threw me out of bed. I was kind of jolted right up and hit my head against the bunk above me.

On all these ships we used to have what we called exercises. When you weren't expecting it, they'd blow the siren and whatever you were doing, if you were in bed or not, you had to run up on the top deck and stand by the lifeboat you were assigned to. Now, it looked like maybe this was the time we'd been practising for!

I looked out the porthole, and I could see heads sticking out all along the side where the cabins were. They were all looking out to see what was going on. Some people were still in their nightclothes, and some men had one side of their face shaved and one side with soap still on it. But as it turned out, no one was hurt.

The passengers, remember, weren't tourists or anything like that. They were just people that were going north—us clerks, a few RCMP, and a few post managers that were going back up, some with their wives. And there was a few children.

Captain Smellie tried to reverse the ship and get off by going astern. Then he tried going ahead, and when that didn't work he sent all us men down into the hold. We had a lot of coal in 100-pound bags taking it up north, and he had all hands down, clerks and everybody, dumping that coal overboard to try and lighten the ship, but it didn't help. Then about four or five hours later a storm started to come up. The captain saw that he couldn't get the ship off the reef where it was grounded, and it was pounding on the rocks, so he got all the lifeboats lowered from the davits, and he ordered us all up on the top deck.

We were all given new instructions about what boats we should get into, either the lifeboats or the whale boats we were carrying. There were lots of boats. I think the ship carried six lifeboats and all of them had Kelvin engines, which were real good engines. And then besides them we had a lot of whale boats that were being taken north to sell.

We had enough time to get most of the stuff that was in our cabins. We took everything we could, like grub and tarps and everything like that, because we knew we would be a while on this island we were going to make for; it would be some days before any help would get to us. We did the usual thing — it was women and children in the first lifeboats put in the water, and one or two of the boats were filled up right away with provisions to carry ashore.

The captain was quite excited actually, yelling and giving orders. For instance, when they were getting into the lifeboats, his steward came out of his cabin with a typewriter, and the captain took the typewriter from the steward and just threw it overboard!

The way they fixed it, the lifeboats with the engines would tow the whale boats away from the ship to the land. I was in the very last whale boat, and the seas were so high that when my boat would go down in a trough below a wave, I couldn't see the boats ahead of me. I did feel really nervous, wondering that if the rope broke on my boat, you know, they probably wouldn't know it and I'd just go adrift. I was used to being in small sailing boats, but not in this kind of situation. It crossed my mind to wonder whether we'd make it to shore or not — I could only see the shoreline when I was on top of a wave. That made me specially nervous because with my kind of swimming, I'd have swum all right — right to the bottom! I can't swim at all.

It probably took us two or three hours to reach shore. The

island where we landed was quite flat, about four miles by six miles, with a kind of big hill in the middle of it, and there was a good harbour. Since I'd been on the Farmyards before, I knew there were good harbours. So did a Newfoundland mate we had aboard — he used to fish on the Labrador — and I think he was the one that chose the harbour that we went into.

Luckily there were quite a few fishing schooners there that had come up from Newfoundland. They had a few tents, not many, not enough for the eight of us clerks to get one. All we had to put up over us was a little tarpaulin. The weather, I can remember, was real bad the first two days, a lot of fog and a lot of rain. One night we had a big rain shower, and we had a regular river running right down the middle of our tent — this tarp over a few sticks.

There was a Captain Blackwood there that I knew, and we went down to visit him. He said some of us could sleep on his schooner, but Captain Smellie wouldn't let us do that after one night. We were given hell for leaving the camp site when he found out that we'd slept on the schooner.

So I was in trouble about that. But that wasn't the only trouble I got into on the Farmyard Islands.

The crew, along with the men that had been aboard, went out to the ship every day as many times as they could to try and salvage as much as possible of the cargo, and that included some livestock. In those days they used to take a pig up to every post, and this time they had some sheep and a couple cows too, and they managed to get them all off. What really did get me in trouble was that the captain was coming down along the beach, probably to give us hell about something, and he slipped in some cow dung and went ass over kettle. Myself and one of the second mates, we started to laugh like hell, so he made us stand there for half an hour without moving, because we'd laughed.

That Captain Smellie was very irritable, he was really nervous and excited and giving out orders. It seemed to us young fellows that anything that he could see we were doing wrong, or he thought we were doing wrong, he'd be right down our throats.

Some of us had to go around to different tents because we couldn't all eat in one tent, and when the cooks were cooking meals, we had to serve the passengers and ship's officers, and of course we had to wash the dishes. Anyhow, even on the land in a shipwreck, there was a difference between the officers and the regulars. The captain always had a table on the ship which was called the captain's table, which generally was the biggest table in the room, and he'd have certain people at his table. And that was the same there on land, although of course we had no tables or chairs.

As soon as they'd known that the *Bayrupert* was really stuck on the reef and we'd have to leave the ship, then of course they'd sent out an sos right away. There were five ships coming to the rescue, but the handiest to us was the *Kyle*, which was a mail boat nearby on the Labrador, and it was the first one to get to us. We were on this island for four or five days, and when the *Kyle* got to us, all the passengers and most of the crew left on it. We just left the cook, the chief steward, the engineer, and the captain there with the *Bayrupert*, and it just stayed where it ran aground.

Later the salvage crew came in to try to salvage the ship itself, but they had no luck, and it was left that the insurance company couldn't do anything with it. Then it was open for anybody to take what they could get off it.

As it happened, my dad was now in Okak Bay, not too far from there, about 250 miles. He was retired by then, and he had a boat. So two of my brothers and him took the boat down and went out every day to salvage stuff. They got a lot of things like sugar and flour that hadn't got wet, and bolts, rifles, all sorts of things.

You see, after my dad had moved to Hebron for the Moravian mission there, the Moravians pulled out and the HBC came in. So my dad worked for the HBC for a year. But he didn't like it, so he retired and got a bit of land of his own which was called Strawberry Island, and he exchanged that with the Newfoundland government for a bit of land up in what's called Okak Bay, and that was known as Lyall's Harbour from then on. It's still called Lyall's Harbour but I've looked and I've never seen it that way on a map. The nearest settled place nowadays is Hopedale, about 200 miles south.

A clerk is never idle

After the shipwreck the *Kyle* took us back to St. John's where I boarded the *Fort Garry*, which was also a Bay ship. At that time it was running up the Labrador and was loading up for its second trip when the *Kyle* got there.

The *Fort Garry* was a three-masted schooner with a diesel engine. I forget how many of us shipped out on it, probably four or five clerks that were going only to the southern part of the Labrador, and myself. I went up with the *Fort Garry* as far as Port Burwell where it met up with the *Nascopie*, which made the run out from Burwell to posts around Ungava Bay and then around and down into Hudson Bay.

My trip from St. John's to Burwell, stopping off along the way, must have taken a couple of weeks, because the *Fort Garry* was a small ship and there are some pretty stormy places along the Labrador even in summer. We saw some big seas and I was seasick, lying on my back most of the time when I could.

But we used to work hard when we were on the Labrador, we worked all the time, all the way up to Burwell. Sometimes we'd work all night long when the ship put in to some settlement, because there are big tides along there and when they were low during the day the ship couldn't get in close enough to unload. So as soon as the water started to rise in the harbour they'd get us out of bed at night to go to work.

Coming back to Burwell, it seemed quite different. When I was growing up there, when my dad was there, the HBC used to have a post at Fox Harbour, about a half a mile down from the Moravian mission, but by the time I came back they had shifted to the other end of Burwell to a place called Happy Valley. That is where you can still see some of the buildings today in Port Burwell. The population had increased quite a lot, too, and there were Eskimo people putting up little shacks all around the place. I came across a lot of the Eskimos I'd known from my early days.

We were two or three days unloading the *Fort Garry* in Burwell, and then the *Nascopie* came in. I left from there on the *Nascopie*. I was supposed to go on it to Cape Smith on the northeast side of Hudson Bay, but after we had left the Hudson's Bay Company post at Wolstenholme, which was the last call before Cape Smith, we couldn't get in to Smith for ice. So we turned back and they put me off at Wolstenholme and I had to wait for the winter's snow and ice until I could travel the 200 or so miles to Cape Smith by dog team.

Wolstenholme is located at the very northeast tip of Hudson Bay and was one of the windiest places I think I ever was in. It's like a valley right on the coast, with hills on each side, and there's quite an open bay, poorly sheltered. There were only a couple of buildings, just the Company buildings. The Bay post there was established in 1911, I think.

There were three clerks — myself and two senior clerks — and the post manager, Frank Melton, and his wife. We also had what they called a post servant that used to do all the chores. He was an Eskimo but he could speak English. He and I got on very well, and I used to visit him quite a lot. That's when I really started to learn to speak Eskimo. His name was Joe Gibbons. He had worked earlier for the police up north somewhere as a dog driver, guide, and interpreter, and everyone called him "corporal".

Seeing I was the junior clerk at Wolstenholme, I used to get up and get the fire going and put on the old coffee percolator. Everyone was supposed to get up at six o'clock, and then they had to work around at something until breakfast was ready at seven o'clock. By half past seven we'd be ready to start the regular day's work.

There were all sorts of things to do, like cleaning up the sheds and the stores, shifting goods around shelves. We were never idle, they were always finding some work for us to do. In Wolstenholme I didn't do much paper work, because I was new and there were two other clerks. We used to call one of them the "accountant" — that wasn't his title, but we called him that because that's mostly what he used to do.

Sometimes we had to work on Sundays; say if some Eskimos came in with furs, they might want to trade and get their supplies and leave right away again. And it was Company policy not to have the people just lounging around the post. They'd rather see them back out where they could trap.

Since I was meeting Eskimos lots of times, having to trade with them, I picked up a lot of Eskimo besides what I was learning from Joe Gibbons.

Being a junior clerk and being small, I had to do all the dirtier jobs, but I didn't resent this at all. I still find that all my work for the HBC gave me a really good training, which I'm afraid a lot of the young fellows don't realise today.

My size was sometimes a nuisance — I'm five feet five inches tall and weigh 135 pounds. I used to get pushed around some, but I couldn't do much about it when I first went in there. I just had to take what was given me, but I got so I was able to look after myself. I used to play tricks on people, like the time at Wolstenholme one of the fellows was giving me a hard time and I was getting kind of fed up with it, so one day while he was away seeing about his traps I took his bed all apart and put all his stuff up in the attic!

I used to go see the walrus hunting when I was at Wolstenholme. That would have been in late September. It was done just the same as they do it today. You have a couple of harpoons all ready with floats on them, and then you watch for a walrus swimming. When you spot the walrus, you only shoot to wound him because if your shot kills him, he'll sink right away. So you just wound him — when any animal is wounded in the water, it comes up very quickly — and finally you get near enough to harpoon it, and then you kill it. The harpoon has floats on it so that if the walrus should sink, you can find it by the floats.

The floats on those harpoons were made of sealskin, inflated. To make these, the Eskimos skin the seal from the head right down so the only opening in the skin would be where they slit around the mouth of the seal.

You could only carry out two or three walrus at a time. We'd tie them alongside the boat and cut them up while they were floating in the water, and fill up the boat with the pieces. You can cut up a walrus in about fifteen minutes if you know what you're doing. I only went out two or three times, because I couldn't get away from my work all that often.

I saw a strange thing at Wolstenholme. On the Labrador I used to see lots of lynx, something that was never known in Wolstenholme, but when I was there they were all over the place. When we put our fox traps out we were catching more lynx than fox. Lynx never go beyond the tree line, so we never did figure out why they came so far north that year.

With all that wind all the time, Wolstenholme was a very stormy place. They had an outhouse which was maybe twenty-five yards from the house, and we used to have a rope tied between the house and the outhouse. If it wasn't for that rope you could get lost just going to the outhouse. It used to blow so much snow that you literally couldn't see your hand in front of your face.

We had quite a few really bad storms. While I was there, as a matter of fact, the roof blew right off the store. A lot of stuff that was upstairs was blown away, like bolts of cotton, duffel cloth, pots and pans, things like that. We didn't even know that the roof had blown off because it happened during the night, and the next morning when we discovered this, of course, we had to go out and look for the stuff. We did pick up a few things.

At that same time we were putting up another building, a new warehouse, and we had just got the walls put up but nothing completed on the inside yet. Well, that was just blown down flat, most of the lumber we couldn't even find.

Later on, after I had moved to Cape Smith, I found out that when the Eskimos were coming in to trade in the spring and the snow had been thawing out, they found a lot of the stuff and brought it back to the post, but a lot of it was ruined, of course.

However, this really did show that the Eskimos were honest people, and of course they had the highest regard for the Hudson's Bay Company. This wasn't just true only in Wolstenholme. Most everywhere I went, the Company was like the king. If the Eskimos were in trouble or anything, they would always go to the Bay. I've known of places even where there would be RCMP but if the Eskimos would get into some kind of trouble, rather than going to the policeman, they'd go to the Bay. And the Bay was involved many times in helping people out that were starving or sick. I'll talk about this some more, later on.

Travelling by dogs

I had to wait at Wolstenholme for weather conditions to get right for travelling on to Cape Smith by dog team. It was late September 1927 when I arrived in Wolstenholme and it was January 2, 1928 before I finally was able to leave.

Now, since this trip was my first long one by dog team, and I made a lot of these over the years, maybe this is the place to explain all about this kind of travel.

For this trip we used a *kamotik* (sled) about twenty-two feet long, made with wooden sides and steel shoeing or runners. In the winter when it's really cold weather, we always put mud on the runners, and then we'd ice that layer of mud. It made it a lot easier going than trying to run on iron shoeing in the winter. The bars on the *kamotik* were generally tied with either quarter-inch rope or sealskin line. Nails or screws weren't used because that would make the sled too rigid — it has to have a little "give" to it.

The first thing you do is load up your sled and lash everything on. You have to be careful to put the things that you know you aren't going to use during the day on the bottom. Since you know that you'll be stopping during the day for a mug-up, your primus stove and your box of grub is always tied on the back of your sled separately so you won't have to unlash the whole sled for them.

A mug-up is where you stop for a break and have a cup of tea, and generally eat some bannock and maybe some frozen meat. It's like a lunch break today. The primus stove we used for heating water for tea, or for cooking things, and it's sort of like a lantern with a frame to hold a pot. We used kerosene for fuel, with methyl hydrate to start it, prime it.

The load for the sled depended on where you were going, what you were going to be doing — like hunting or trapping, or just carrying supplies — and how long you figured to be out. For instance, if you were just going out trapping, be away maybe a couple of weeks, you could travel pretty light. But you always had to carry all your dog food. We'd cut up frozen walrus meat or seal meat or whatever we had — fish sometimes — we'd get it all cut up and the pieces put in sacks. When we'd make a snow house in the night time, all we had to do was throw the dogs' feed out of the sacks. We'd take enough grub for ourselves to last two or three weeks on a trip that long, so we always had a little spare. We had to carry kerosene for the primus stoves too — for a trip like the one to Cape Smith, about ten gallons.

Later on we had to make some real long trips sometimes when the supply ship couldn't get in to a post because of the ice. Then we'd have to go by dog team to another post to get our year's supply of food and other things. When we did that, I think I could safely say that we were pulling at least 900 to 1,000 pounds.

The last thing you do is hitch up your dogs. The traces and harnesses will be all muddled up, so you lay them out on the snow and straighten them all out. The traces were made of seal-skin line and the harnesses were made of what we used to call harness webbing, or if you didn't have that, you'd make them out of sealskin. When you get your harness ready, then you call your dogs to harness them.

In the eastern Arctic, you use a fan hitch where there's a separate trace for each dog and the lead trace is the longest, about thirty-five feet, and the others are graduated out on both sides to the shortest traces, about ten feet long. That way, when everything goes all right, the dogs can all go along without interfering with each other. This kind of hitch is better in the eastern Arctic because you have a lot of rough ice there, which you don't get very much in the western Arctic. There they use the tandem hitch, where the dogs are paired up, one pair right behind another.

Another thing about using the fan hitch, in the spring when the cracks in the ice are opening, sometimes they're six to eight feet across, and when you've got the fan hitch, you can pull your sled up to the edge of the crack and get your dogs all across — sometimes they'll jump in the water — but with the tandem hitch, it's all one long line, and you couldn't get the dogs across cracks or over water as well as with a fan hitch.

Also, with a fan hitch when a dog has to stop to use a piece of ice or drop his load, the long trace gives him time to do his business and come on along. Where you have the tandem hitch, if a dog tries this, the rest of the dogs just drag him along.

The dogs were not savage like some people think, at least none of the ones I ever had or was around. You'd get the odd one, when you were harnessing him, he'd growl at you, maybe snap at you.

When you harness the dogs, mostly you start with your leader. Generally they lie somewhere near their harness, and as you harness them up and they're getting excited to go, you have to anchor your sled down so they won't run off from you. They're like people — they get bored just lying around, so they'd get really excited and want to get going.

When they're travelling with the fan hitch, the dogs often jump over each other's traces, going back and forth, and they get tangled up sometimes almost right back to the back dog on the shortest trace. When that happens you have to stop and clear the traces, unravel them. You have to take your gloves off most of the time for that because they'd be really knotted up, those traces, and that was very cold on the hands.

You had a long whip, maybe thirty or thirty-five feet long, and I had to learn to use this. The whip was usually made of braided sealskin lines. When you get used to them, they're not difficult to handle, in fact they're real easy to handle. Generally you hit the dogs around the buttocks, but a lot of the people go for the ears — I've seen an Eskimo cut a dog's ear right off with a whip. They were really accurate with those whips. Sometimes we had games with whips — we'd put a can out the distance away from you to equal the length of your whip, and then two fellows would use their whips on opposite sides of the can from each other and see who could keep the can away from the other fellow.

There's a lot of different ways to call instructions to the dogs, but the "mush" you hear about drivers using isn't one of them. I always used the Labrador calls. To go to the left you'd holler "Hairr*AH*! Hairr*AH*!" and to the right it would be "Owck! Owck!" In the western Arctic the calls are different. All of them are pretty near impossible to put in print. I can tell you I *never* heard anyone say "mush" though!

All the dogs I ever had were pure huskies, but they were never really real big dogs, except two that I got from Igloolik. It's known that the biggest dogs you can have up here come from Igloolik, or at least they did at the time I had mine — they'd stand about maybe three feet high. The lead dog wasn't necessarily bigger than the others. A lot of people liked to use a bitch for a leader, but I used to like to train a male dog for the simple reason that if you have a bitch for a leader, then of course she has pups and then you're without a leader for quite a while. The pure husky was the very best for pulling and travelling, and they could go a long time, two or three days or even up to a week, without being fed, if they had to, and still work hard.

Well then, to get on now with my trip to Cape Smith. We had two dog teams. One Eskimo, Kaloonik, was taking me and my gear, and the other team was Shavik and his wife hauling the grub and provisions for our trip. Our team had fourteen dogs and the man-and-wife team had ten or eleven. The dogs belonged to the Eskimos, but the Bay hired them to take me down to Smith.

I was anxious to get there as soon as possible, of course, but the one thing the post manager told me when I was getting ready to leave was, "Now don't you try to tell the Eskimos what to do, because they know. They stop and go when they want to, don't you interfere with them, because they're the ones that know the country, and they're the ones that know how to drive the dog team," and that sort of a thing.

The trip took us seventeen days altogether. The going was very hard because unfortunately we had deep snow most of the way. We used to travel for eight or nine hours a day — ten or eleven hours sometimes — it was all according to what the weather was like. If the weather was good sometimes we'd keep going for eleven or twelve hours at a time. We didn't have to cross any dangerous country on that trip. We did go over some land, not very much. At one place there was a long point or cape jutting out to the sea, and rather than go around it, we crossed the land. But going from Wolstenholme to Cape Smith there was no really great distance on land.

Generally, the weather was pretty good. I think there was twice that we had to lay up all day when it was too bad to travel because of blowing snow. When we knew there was a storm coming on and we wouldn't be able to go on, the first thing we did was to go out and build a wall right around the snow house that we'd built for the night, to keep the wind from blowing holes in the snow house.

Every night we built a snow house, though of course I could hardly be much help at that time. I learned to build them in later years, though not very good ones, but I couldn't build one now.

Generally we would start off about seven or eight o'clock, and at twelve o'clock we always stopped to have a mug-up. We'd build a shelter for the primus stove and have hardtack and tea and either frozen fish or frozen walrus — that trip we didn't take along any frozen seal meat. This was where I started to like frozen meats and ever since then I've liked most of them. It's rather strange but eating frozen meat really warms you up, and this is why I think most Eskimos in those days ate a lot of it.

On this trip the other sled didn't have as big a load as we did, and mostly they were half a mile or a mile ahead of us all the time. On the third day they were farther ahead than that because we could just see them in the distance, and it was just around ten o'clock that we saw them stop. We thought maybe they were stopping to clear the traces, or building a shelter for the primus. So I turned to Kaloonik and said, "My goodness, it's only ten o'clock — how come they're stopping at this time of day? We've only been on the trail two and a half hours or so." And he just said, "Maybe they're hungry or something."

When we caught up we could see they were cutting snow blocks, and I said, "How come you're having tea so early? And what are you building a shelter for?"

Shavik and his wife just kept right on, working fast, and Shavik said, "I'm not building a shelter, I'm building a snow house."

I said, "It's a nice day, it's good travelling on the snow. I'd rather move along. Why don't you go farther?"

He said, "Oh, my wife is going to have a baby."

Well, here we were alone in the middle of nowhere, and it was cold, at least 30 below, a really cold day, and I'd never seen a baby born before, so I was quite excited and a little worried. And of course I figured this meant we were going to be stuck there for three or four days, or more, maybe.

Shavik was all in a hurry to get the snow house finished, so Kaloonik and I made tea, and I'd say about ten minutes after they got the snow house up, their baby girl was born. By this time we'd made the mug-up, Kaloonik and I, so we all ate, and by half-past one that same day, the new mother was walking ahead of the dogs with the baby in her parka. Having a baby that way, in conditions like that, was not all that unusual for Eskimos, but you know, for me the experience was one of the highlights of all my years up here in the north.

A few days after that, we had a real bad day. We got into real deep snow and we were using snow shoes. I was walking ahead of the dogs most all day beating trail, and so was this woman with her new baby on her back, and the two Eskimo men. When we built the camp that night we were about halfway to Cape Smith. I'd thought my feet seemed extra cold when I was walking in snowshoes, but we made camp quite late at night and after eating, we turned in. A little later I woke up with a real bad pain in my toe. From being on the snowshoes so long, I'd frozen my big toe very badly.

Kaloonik said, "No wonder you froze your feet — look at your boots, you're wearing springtime boots." Mine were waterproof, made of *ujuk*, the thick hide from the bearded seal, but you don't usually wear them in the winter because they're not that warm. What you do wear in winter is moosehide, which is very soft and warm. But the rest of my clothes were all right. I was wearing a caribou parka, in fact I was wearing all caribou clothes. In those days you never used to get any cloth parkas in the store.

My toe got so bad and swollen that I couldn't even walk and that was the shape I was in when I finally arrived at Cape Smith where old Chesley Russell was the post manager.

Russell took a look at my toe, and it was getting worse all the time. Finally he said, "It looks like I'll have to cut it off. It looks like it's getting gangrene. Tomorrow morning I'll cut that toe off."

But the next morning when he looked at it, he says, "It's looking a little better." So finally it started to mend from there on, but it was quite a long while before I could walk on that foot.

Someone's at the door

Cape Smith is mostly south and a little west of Wolstenholme, and it's actually an island where the post is built. Chess Russell and myself were the only white residents there at first.

At this time I was earning $20 a month, and that's the only time I ever saved any money in my life. I had $240 a year, and through the Bay I sent five dollars of my pay to my mum every month, and at the end of that year I was $101 to the good. So I was a rich man. And that's the only time in my life I've ever been able to save money.

What I did spend mostly went for things like cigarettes, but one month all there was on my account was a pair of shoelaces that cost ten cents. There were other little odd things we needed, like say we got some washing done by an Eskimo woman or if she'd sew our boots or something like that, we used to pay fifty cents or so for doing that.

Now when I talk about "spending" or "paying" I don't mean actual cash money. What I spent personally was just put in the Company's books, sort of like a charge account today, to be deducted from my pay. And when I paid a woman for washing or sewing, I gave her something she wanted from the store worth that fifty cents or whatever, and that was also put against my account.

I never really handled money in the whole of my time in the settlements; all the time that I was with the Bay I never handled any money at all. We used to have tokens for the fur trading with the Eskimos, but I'll explain about those later.

Chess Russell had been in the north a long time. He must have been, I guess, close to ten years older than I was, so he'd have been in his late twenties at Cape Smith. He was a big man, a tough Newfoundlander, and I really liked him except he was a hard man to work for — as I say, the Company really trained their fur traders. But he was a good man to live with. Once the work was done, in the evening, we used to really relax and have fun.

All the post managers that I worked under right up until I left the Bay were like that, really official during working hours. I guess they had to be to keep the young fellows like me in line. During working hours we used to work and no fooling around sort of thing, but when your work was finished, they were really sociable people and most of them had a fine sense of humour.

In the evenings, to pass the time during the long nights, Chess and I mostly played cards, we used to play a lot of cribbage, of course. The first crib board that I had, later, was one made out of soapstone — a fellow in Lake Harbour made it for me.

There's a story that Chess Russell tells about when we were at Smith, and I guess he feels that it's his story, but actually it's my story no matter what he says. When we saw a dog team coming, or heard someone coming, we'd be so glad to see people that we'd run out as fast as we could to meet them. So this one night we were talking or playing cards or something and we heard the door open, the outside porch door, and of course when we heard that we knew we had visitors.

Well, I ran out to try to get ahead of Russell to open the inside door to the porch and see who's coming, and when I opened that door, there was an old polar bear looking at me! So I quick slammed the door shut, you can believe! Chess had a .303 rifle and I had a shotgun, and we got those and then we stood there trying to decide who was going to open the door, who was going to shoot first. I didn't want to open that door because I was afraid that bear was going to run inside, and Chess was the same way.

So finally I said, "Okay, I'll open the door." So I opened it, and as soon as I opened it the bear, instead of coming in like we figured, he got scared and he turned around and beat it out of there off the porch. Chess had his .303 ready and he let fly at the bear, and the old bear just rolled over a few times and let out a few growls, and then away he goes.

Well, Chess hit him, we knew he hit him, and we lit a lamp and followed his trail. We could see the blood and his foot marks, we could see he had been bleeding more all the time, but it was a blowing night and kind of drifting, and it was dark and cold and we were getting pretty far from the house. So Chess said, "Let's go home. We'll come back in the morning and we'll find him out here dead." And we agreed that whoever saw the bear or got to the bear first was going to own that bear, because bears were quite expensive at the time, they fetched about nine dollars a skin.

The next morning we started out, and it was a nice morning after blowing so hard in the night. We walked about half a mile and then we could see this hump with fur on it and the fur blowing in a little breeze.

Chess said, "There he is, there he is! He's dead!" I was actually ahead, but Chess started off to beat hell and he got up to that bear first and he kicked the bear, and that bloody bear jumped up! Chess got such a fright he dropped his gun and ran home as hard as he could go.

But the thing about this story, the way he tells it, it was me that kicked the bear and then I ran home. Anyhow, then I shot it and the bear just rared up, but it was wounded too bad to even try to do anything.

Funny thing is I don't know if I got the skin. To tell you the truth — I forget what happened. Of course I've always teased Chess about this. But he always tells this story like it happened to me, and I always tell it like it happened to him.

I've heard quite a few stories about polar bears invading people's homes, like once where the father was out hunting and the bear came to his snow house and got in there and killed the whole family. That happened in the winter just before I got to Lake Harbour where I went after Cape Smith. The father had gone hunting and left his family in the snow house, and they didn't have a gun. The polar bear came right in, and there was the mother and one small little kiddie and a bigger one, a 15-year-old girl, and the bear just killed them.

Polar bears do this because they're hungry, though, not because they're aggressive. I've seen a lot of polar bears in my time, and the Eskimos also say that a polar bear will never attack a man unless it's hungry or unless someone is aggravating him. It's people that aggravate a bear and unless that bear is very hungry or he is cornered or something, this is the only time that they'll attack a person.

When I was at Smith there were no Eskimos living near the post, but they would come in to trade periodically. They used to come in about once a month from their hunting camps and would be selling foxes and the odd polar bear skin. Trapping foxes was something that was taught to them by the Bay. In those days I think we were paying around $16 for a fox, and for a seal skin anywhere from forty cents to a dollar.

I only made one trip out to the Eskimos' camp, and that was when a new clerk came in March. I went down with him mostly just to see what the camp was like. It was about seventy-five miles from Smith and there were thirty-five or forty families, so that was quite a big camp. It was what they called a permanent camp, and they'd hunt out from there.

In those days they used to always have a boss at the camp, and like before they'd go hunting, they'd go to him at night or early in the morning and say, "Now, who's going where? Where's each one going?" So it wasn't just the Indians that had chiefs, because most every place that I've been in, except for later years, the Eskimos always had a camp boss.

The way that they used to decide who was boss was that it always was the best hunter — if he was an elderly man. They never used to have a young fellow, say twenty-five or thirty years old, as camp boss. Sometimes they'd even have a camp boss that was too old to do any hunting himself, but still they used to come to him and tell him what they were going to do, where they were going hunting, get his advice, that sort of thing.

Speaking of the elderly Eskimos, I guess everybody has heard stories about the old Eskimo custom of leaving old people out to die. And it is true that even in my time in the eastern Arctic, say like if they went inland caribou hunting or something, and a real old woman or a real old man got sick, they would leave them out to die.

White people felt this was bad, but I couldn't say if it was wrong. Sometimes I think it was the only thing they could do in those days. Lots of times the people used to go inland, and say they got no caribou, then probably they've had nothing to eat for quite a few days. They had to try to get to some place where they knew they could find food, they had to go some place where they could save the rest of the people. Generally the old or sick person would say, "Well, you go on and try to survive. I'm going to die anyway, so leave me."

About the stories of baby girls being put out on the ice in those days, well, it didn't happen when I was in the east as far as I ever knew, but when I went to Fort Ross, the people around there then were really pagans, and they used to do that sort of thing.

But in Smith, they didn't do these things. They weren't pagans, you couldn't call them pagans, because I think in my time there they had known Christianity for a long time back.

I was in Cape Smith from January 1928 till the following summertime. This time the *Nascopie* could get in okay, and I found out that I was to be transferred. It was generally company policy that you moved around a lot when you were young. Certainly they moved me around a lot. I figure the reason they moved you so much was so that you could get to know how different each place was from the other.

So when the *Nascopie* came in and it was time to leave this place that I'd just got to know, I was a little bit sad, but mostly I was quite excited, because it meant newer fields to go and see.

The arrival of the ship is something really special, because you'd only see the ship once a year, in the summer. Generally when the ship was coming, the Bay post people used to ask the Eskimos at the camps to come in to the post so there would be someone there to help unload the ship. So when we were expecting the ship in, there would be excitement building all the time, and we'd say to the people, "Okay, the first one that sees that ship, I'll give them a plug of tobacco," so you'd see them all the time running up and down to try to spot the smoke on the horizon.

Sometimes the water would be clear, and some places the bay or port would be full of ice, have ice floating in it. Of course when there was too much ice, like the summer before when I was trying to get in to Cape Smith, the ship couldn't get in at all. This time though there was no ice at all. So of course when the Eskimos could see the ship's smoke or see the ship with a spyglass, they'd yell and there was all kinds of excitement.

While the people were in at the post waiting for the ship to come, the company furnished the food for them and their dogs. When they were finished unloading they'd get their pay — in trade — and they'd go off back to their camps.

When the ship arrived the crew used to always ask the post employees on board, and then every mealtime we could eat on the ship if we wanted to. They'd give us things to eat that we hadn't been able to have for months — fruit and vegetables and steaks and eggs and things like that.

In Smith my bedroom was facing out at the water, and the

day we were expecting the ship I thought I heard some sort of noise out there at six o'clock in the morning, and I looked out the window and there I see the ship already anchored.

So I goes in to Chess and I says, "Chess, the ship's arrived." And he wouldn't believe me and he said, "Go on, go on back to bed." And I said, "Chess, it's out there and we'd better get dressed and get out to the ship."

So I kept at him, and I started dressing. We used to put on our best clothes, of course, to go out to the ship and see who was on it and this sort of thing. Finally, after about half an hour, Chess looked out and he says, "My God, Ernie, why didn't you tell me the ship was out there!" He'd thought I was pulling his leg, because we were always joking.

Usually if you were going to be moved, your replacement would come in on the ship, but mine didn't in this case because we already had this young fellow who had come up by dogs from Povungnituk, which is about 120 miles south of Cape Smith. He was the one I took to see the Eskimo camp.

When we'd get aboard the ship, the first person that would be on the gangplank to meet us would be the HBC district manager. He would be inspecting the various posts and taking out some personnel and putting new people in. At that time the district manager was a man named George Watson.

The first thing the district manager would do was take the post manager up and have a little talk with him. And then, say when I was leaving, he'd call me in and he'd either tell me I'd done a good job there, or I didn't do a good job, and that I'd done this or that that I shouldn't have done, or whatever. I had a pretty good report for Cape Smith, there weren't any criticisms, none at all. As a matter of fact, all the time I was with the Bay, I only had one run-in with a district manager and that was at Fort Ross, and I'll come to that farther along.

It's a strange mixed feeling to leave somebody like Chess Russell that I'd been close to for six or seven months — like losing something, I guess. But generally, I've always noticed, you'd very seldom more than shake hands with a fellow and then you'd wait till you got down to the boat and then you'd wave to him.

"Let's give him a shove"

My first trip to Baffin Island was in the summer of 1928 when I left Cape Smith to go to Lake Harbour. We had to call in at other Hudson's Bay Company posts before we got to Lake Harbour, going back up to Wolstenholme and then east across Hudson Strait, but at least this time I knew my destination before the ship left.

Lake Harbour was the first HBC post on Baffin — they went in in 1911 — and it is a really beautiful place. From the ship as you get near, you can see great big high land that looks like it's straight coast, but then you come in to a long narrow harbour, and there is a sort of cliff edge around you. Always the ship used to stop outside at a little island, Beacon Island, and there would be an Eskimo pilot out there waiting for the *Nascopie* to pilot it in to Lake Harbour, pilot all the ships that were coming in, and I think they still do that today.

Looking down the bay when I went in, I saw the HBC's post and the people's tents around it, and then about half a mile away the Anglican mission had built a mission house and a church.

The Eskimos came out in their little boats to see the ship. Everybody did, of course. The Company owned a good-sized motor boat when I was at Wolstenholme and Smith, and of course the post manager and clerks, always used to take that to get to the ship. When I went into Lake Harbour, the *Nascopie* brought their first big motor boat in there.

The manager I was going to work under there was a fellow by the name of Jimmy Thom. As a matter of fact he went in on the ship with us. He was a lively, jolly sort of fellow, a single man. At that time there were mostly single managers — not that the Company minded their managers being married, as a matter of fact I think they preferred their managers to be married.

Working at Lake Harbour was much different from the other two posts I'd been at, at least at first, because the year that I went in was a very poor year for hunting. There were a lot of people at the camps that were hungry, and this was where the HBC really helped the people and acted as sort of a welfare organisation. There weren't any government agencies to help in those days. And this is a thing that bugs me still: where people from outside were saying that the Company cheated the people, that they were making all sorts of money off the people. Well, this is *entirely wrong*.

The Company knew the people had nothing, and so one of my first jobs there was to take the big motor boat and put as much grub in it as that boat could hold — and it was a lot. Then I went around to the people and gave them ammunition and staple grub, and all this was paid for by the Company. They never expected it to be paid back. And they said to me, "Now ask the people where they'd like to go, where is a better hunting ground, and then help them to move where they want to go."

Now it was not only at Lake Harbour at that time that this happened, it was done at other times at other HBC posts too. It used to be done by the Company anywhere it was necessary, and they'd pay for the gas and everything. True, it helped the Bay by putting the people where they were going to get, say, foxes, seals, this sort of a thing, but the HBC would never ask the people to pay them back. I know they spent hundreds and hundreds of dollars doing this, which people outside don't realise.

One reason I was sent to this post, I guess, was because of this situation where they needed someone to talk to the people, and I was beginning to speak Eskimo pretty well. I didn't find it such a very hard language. I was very young, and I'd picked it up pretty quick. But it is a lot different from English, because for one thing the words are in a different order to English sentences.

Anyhow, you might say that I was going out on a sort of rescue operation as soon as the ship arrived, which was late summer, helping the people, and helping them to go to a new hunting ground. We'd take as many families aboard that motor boat on one trip as we could, with their dogs and everything, and it'd usually take a week to shift a whole camp by boat.

Of course they wanted to be at a place where they'd be getting seals to trade the skins, but also everybody needed to get enough seal or walrus or whale meat for themselves, and also for a whole lot of dog feed to keep the dogs during the winter.

63

They used to hunt the seals from the floe edge in the fall. How you do that is you just sit there on the edge of the ice right near the water, you wait there and watch until the seal pops up somewhere and then you shoot him and go out in the boat and bring him ashore. In this case, you don't have to shoot him to wound, like with the walrus. You kill him dead, because a seal is so fat at that time of year that it never sinks. Well, I shouldn't say never, because you might get one in, say, every fifty or sixty that would sink.

I mentioned that from the ship you could see the people's tents around the post. In the summer when they were out on the land they used tents in their camps too, generally maybe thirty or forty feet apart, sometimes only ten or twelve feet apart. Inside an Eskimo tent it was dim, and it was smelly — they're really smelly. It smelled mostly of seal oil which they'd be burning in their lamps, and of course the people themselves and their clothes smelled of this too — in the winter as well, when they lived in snow houses.

We'd notice this smell when they came in to trade. We used to have what we called an Eskimo kitchen, a special room where they'd come to in the house, and we'd make them a mug-up — make them tea and give them hardtack. Lots of times we'd cook up a batch of beans or give them tinned meat or something like that. And they wouldn't wash before they ate. But it wasn't really dirt that we noticed so much, it was just this seal smell more than anything else.

Well, I mean they always lived this way. We'd always get a post servant that was an Eskimo, that would live with his family in a little shack on the post, and sometimes when people from the camps were coming for overnight they'd sleep in his house, and the post servant would say he could smell the seals and that he used to be the same way himself.

But at the post we had to look at it differently from the white people that would say, "Oh, gee, I can't go near that fellow, he stinks." Well, in a way it was true because they were living in the cold, they were living in stuffy snow houses and tents, cutting up seals and fish, using seal fat for cooking, they had no bathrooms, and maybe if they fell in the drink, that was the only bath they'd ever get. And when you fall in the drink up here, I can tell you, you get out as fast as you can — you don't lay back for a nice soak! White people couldn't understand or wouldn't accept this different life of the people. Same as they couldn't understand the different customs that got the people in trouble with the white man's laws.

In Lake Harbour, before I went there, an Eskimo went berserk and shot up eight people, and the people in the camp were really scared of him. They couldn't go out and hunt or trap because they were afraid of what he'd do if they left their families — they thought this fellow was going to kill them all off. There was no RCMP there yet at that time so the people went to the Hudson's Bay post and said, "What will we do?" They were afraid to tackle this man on their own, they wanted a white man to go with them.

This guy had gone off by himself and built a little snow house, and of course they knew where he was, and they just decided they'd have to go and kill him, which they did. I mean, the whole bunch of them got together and just shot right into his snow house and killed him.

And my opinion of that thing is that it was the only thing they *could* do, it was the only solution. Either this fellow was going to kill a lot more people than he already had, or they were going to run out of food because they couldn't go out to trap or hunt, and a lot of kids would die and adults might die too. It was all for the good of the people, and it was according to their customs, and it was before they knew anything about the white man's law. This was well before the police came to Lake Harbour, and as far as I know the RCMP never did investigate that killing.

The RCMP, by the way, went into Lake Harbour the same year that I went in. And now here's a coincidence for you — Sergeant Wight was the policeman that came in, along with a Constable Dersch, to build the new post. The same policeman that lived with my family in Port Burwell and taught me my first schooling! Now we were together again in Lake Harbour. He went in on the ship with me, and meeting him like that, well it was like meeting your own mother!

He was the first one that I ever knew that had a camera. He had one of those cameras with a hood over it and on a tripod, and I remember when we were kids in Burwell, he took a lot of pictures of us, my mum and dad and all the family.

In 1976 I met his son in Fort Smith. When he found out who I was and that I used to know his father (who's dead now, of course), he said his father used to talk about me a lot, and he got out all those old pictures and things of his father's and showed them to me.

The RCMP hadn't much to do in Lake Harbour — there were days when there was very little for them to do in connection with the Eskimos, because they had very little crime there. During the year I was there, only one fellow was taken and put into a cell. They had to build a jail cell in the Bay warehouse for him.

It happened in the spring. This fellow got religion, he got religion so bad that he was threatening to kill people. Some of them came and told me that he was near their camp on a little island all by himself, and the people were afraid to go and see him. They were all afraid that he was going to come in to the camp, and they didn't know what he might do. They could see him with a spyglass doing all sorts of strange things. I went down to Sergeant Wight with my dog team and told him about all this, and we went into the camp to talk to the people. We wanted a couple of them to come with us to the island, but they wouldn't go. We could see this fellow's tent on this small little island. The island was so small it couldn't have been too much bigger than a good-sized house, and there was a lot of rough ice just around it.

That's the first time a policeman ever handed me a gun. Sergeant Wight said, "What we'll do is stop the dogs out here on the ice. We can't see this fellow but he might be waiting for us. You go around the other end of the island and we'll start up to the tent." And when he gave me the revolver he said, "Don't you use that thing unless he points a gun at you. Don't you use it."

Well, I was kind of scared, and very excited, because this

fellow was known as a dangerous person. We climbed up the rough ice and both of our heads came up looking around and we couldn't see a sign of this crazy fellow, just his tent, no movement. Then we got a little handier to it, and Sergeant Wight made motions to me that he could hear breathing in the tent, and then he made motions for us to both rush and jump the tent. So we rushed up and we jumped on the tent, and this guy never even tried to get up or stand up or anything.

We pulled the tent off him, and there he was just lying in bed. We asked him what was wrong, and he says, "Oh, I'm snow-blind, I've been snow-blind for a long time now, I can't get out or anything. I'm hungry." We made him a mug of tea before we went to take him to the sled, and Sergeant Wight said to me in English, "That old bugger, I'm sure he's not snow-blind, he's just making out he's snow-blind." We even had to dress him, put his boots on him and everything, and Sergeant Wight says to me again, "By jeez, he's just shamming," but it looked so real to me.

As we started taking him down to the sled, we each had one of his arms, and by now Sergeant Wight was sure from the way the fellow was walking that this all really was a sham.

Well, because this was in the spring, there was water in several sort of deep holes on the ice, and the sergeant said to me, but this time in Eskimo so this guy could understand, he said sort of out of the corner of his mouth, "That deep hole there that we just crossed coming here, that was just over our knees — just as we come to it, let's give him a shove." But when we came to this water, that guy just jerked right back away! So he *could* see all the time.

Anyway, we lashed him on the sled in case he'd try to run away or something, and we took him in, and that's the first and only fellow they ever took in at Lake Harbour while I was there.

The Eskimos' life in Lake Harbour was pretty much the same as anywhere else, basically. They were after seals and foxes and walrus. Walrus is good. It's hard to explain what walrus tastes like — it's something like seal meat, but the fat on a walrus isn't a fatty, greasy fat like on seal. When you're eating walrus meat, you want to eat some of the fat too because it's a stringy meat. The only meat that I couldn't eat, or didn't like — and don't like still — is whale meat. I could never take whale meat.

Of course when they caught the walrus they had the ivory and there they used to do all sorts of beautiful carvings. There was one man in Lake Harbour — the only fellow I think that has ever done it — he used to make a trap with a fox in it, and have a chain on it, and every link without a break in the links, perfect, made out of ivory.

Whether they used the whole walrus tusk and carved it, or made it into small pieces, was all according to what the Company had asked for. They'd tell the person what they wanted them to make, like dog sleds — a whole dog sled and all the equipment — polar bears, birds, most anything.

I don't just remember what sort of prices they would be paid generally. But I do remember there was this fellow that made a kayak carving; it had everything on it, all the equipment, a gun, a harpoon, everything the Eskimo used for hunting, and the Bay paid $80 for that, in 1928, the highest I can remember. That was quite a bit for that time.

But the carvings today are nothing like the ones they used to make in the old days. Today when they make a carving it doesn't take them that long to do it. But if you ordered a carving in the old days, you might have to wait a month or more for an Eskimo to finish even a small one.

People just like jelly

Lake Harbour was the first post I was at where the Anglican mission was there when I arrived, and there seemed to be quite a difference between their religion and the Moravians'. The Moravians had a simpler teaching, like love of God, but a fear of hellfire was more like what was taught by the Anglicans. This was a hard sort of thing for the Eskimos to understand — it had a bad effect on the people, impressing them with the fear of hell. I could be wrong but this is my personal feeling about it.

One thing especially that the Eskimos couldn't understand in those early days was that the Anglican and Catholic missionaries wouldn't ever work together about anything, or even speak to each other sometimes. It seemed like the Anglicans had a hatred for the Catholics and the Catholics had a hatred for the Anglicans.

The Eskimos never actually talked to me about this that I can remember, but I could see where they were wondering — a sort of "now what have we got to do?" kind of feeling. But we used to crack jokes, the rest of us whites, about those guys. It's hard to believe but later on when I was in Pond Inlet, if there was one missionary visiting us and he'd see the other coming, he'd go out the back door before the other would come in the front door. It was really as bad as that.

Sometimes the people went haywire due to religion. Right up to a few years ago religion was taught to them in such a way — if you do this or you do that, you're going to go to hell forever, and this sort of thing — that they'd get thinking about this so much they'd just get clear unbalanced.

There was one fellow in Pond Inlet — they were teaching him to be a lay minister — and when the missionaries left, this fellow and his wife both got crazy that way. He got all dressed up one time and he carried a little lantern around and a staff in his hand, and he was going around saying "I'm Jesus Christ." The guy was really nuts, and quite a few of them went that way.

It always used to be that the shamans and shamanism were looked down on by the missionaries, both Protestants and Catholics, as a bad thing; but the way I look at it myself is that this was the Eskimos' religion then, and I think it should have been respected and left. I think Christianity was pushed too hard.

The way it worked in the olden days was that, say there was some trouble, an Eskimo would go to the shaman and ask for help. Then the shaman's job was, I'd say, like a missionary's today, that if someone was disturbed or sick or had trouble, the shaman would go to his "god" for help. Different shamans had their own different helpers or gods, like a fish in the sea, maybe a whale, or a sculpin, or a polar bear — anything could be their helper. So the shaman would take the spirit of some creature and ask the creature to help him solve the problem.

All Eskimos respected, really respected, white people, and they wouldn't want to do anything that would offend a white man. But I know that, even today, a lot of people here in Spence, when they get into real trouble, don't go to a missionary; they still, some of them, go to the shaman.

There's a lot of missionaries, both Catholics and Anglicans, that I think have done a lot of good for the people, but again I think they've done a lot of harm. I feel that the people in their camps didn't need Christianity, they had their own beliefs that helped them.

I wouldn't be able to recognize the shaman when I first went into a community, but I'd get to know who it was. Talking with the people you'd learn, like when we first came here to Spence Bay, someone would say, "We're going to have a really big show," or "We're going to have a session with the god" to do something or other.

There were times that some of these witch doctors would get mad at someone for something, or think they should be punished, and they'd say, "Okay, you have an adopted son, you haven't got a real son of your own, and I'm going to see that he dies." Now when Eskimos adopted a boy, they used to think of him as their real son and would really treat him better actually than their own son, and it was something the boy would be really very proud of. So this shaman would say, "Okay, you've got this son and I'm going to see that your son dies." And then the family would think about this and worry about it, and they believed so much that a witch doctor could do these things, that something would really always happen. To me, this was so much on their mind, they believed in it so much, that it *would* happen.

For instance, one time soon after Spence was founded, a fellow out at his camp got shot through his leg and the post manager and myself had to look after him at the house. He thought he was going to die, so he asked an old lady to come down to the post house and give him help. He offered her three fox skins to help him. She did come down and, of course, we weren't right in the room they were in but we could hear things going on in there. In the end we did get him out to hospital on the plane, but of course the people all thought that it was through her witch-doctoring that he got better.

Mostly the Eskimos didn't talk much about anything they'd seen themselves. The way they'd put it was kind of second-hand. They used to say "I heard" or "my grandfather" or "my grandmother told me" that this thing or the other thing used to happen.

They used to tell us a lot of the old stories from way back, all sorts of different stories about different things. For instance, they'd say they used to see people that they couldn't contact properly. They were just like jelly, these people, they had no bones or joints. The Eskimos didn't know whether they were spirits or whether, the way they'd tell it, they thought people like this actually used to live at one time on the land.

Of course I have my own thoughts about the Eskimos and their shamans, but I do believe that they're sincere when they believe in shamans, and I respect them for it. There are quite a few stories I could tell, things I saw myself, but I'd rather not. There'd be so many people saying, "Well, there's a lot more bullshit written," so I'd rather not put that in this book. I also feel that I'd be letting the people down if I told some of these stories, because they trusted me. It was very special to them, and they knew I wouldn't laugh at them or make fun of them.

There was an interesting thing right here at Spence Bay a few years ago. The area administrator was telling this old fellow that was a shaman about the big news of the first man landing on the moon, and it didn't impress the old man at all, because, he said, "We've been sending people to the moon for years and years."

There was a woman used to be in Port Burwell, she was one of the oldest women there. Her name was Solominie Took-lavina, and this story goes back to when I was a kid in Burwell with my parents. They figured she was over a hundred years old, but she was quite active, she could still walk around at that time. She used to be a shaman and the word was around that she still was one, so one time when the ship came in, some of the sailors were bugging her to show them what she did as a shaman. She said, "Well, we don't do that these days, we're Christians now, we don't do those things."

But they kept on till finally she said, "Okay, if you want to see me do some shamans, you come to my house tonight when it's dark." She had a one-room sod house with coal oil lamps, not too far from the mission, and this old woman got some of her friends in there too, just to help put on this show.

So these three fellows went out there, and when they got in the house the friends blew out the lamps and made the place dark. Tooklavina told them she had to work herself into a trance, so she was mumbling away there in the dark, and finally she said, "Now my helper is going to come." She said, "My helper is sea weed, it's coming in on the water." Well, of course, since they were sailors they could recognize the sound of waves first, and then they were sure they could feel the waves carrying this kelp, sea weed, right back under them with this swishing noise.

So Tooklavina kept building that up, and they could hear all this kelp swishing, swishing, and finally they got so scared that they just took off and beat it! So they never did see the rest of the shaman act because they were too frightened.

Appendicitis holiday

In the summer of 1929 I'd had one year in Lake Harbour and was all set for my second year, and then just two days after the *Nascopie* pulled out I got this awful pain. Luckily the missionary had some medical knowledge and he came over to see me. I had a real high temperature, and I described the pain to him, which was so bad I could hardly stand it at times, and he said he thought I had appendicitis.

In those days before airplanes there was no way for any HBC employee, or any white, or anybody else in the north to get out when they fell seriously sick. There was no way out between the ship's arrival each summer with mail and provisions, and that's all there was to it. And of course there weren't any telephones or radios then to contact the outside for help — only some of the bigger ships had that sort of a thing. There just was no such a thing as medical help from the outside.

But I was in real luck this time because the *Beothic*, a sort of coast-guard ship, was just about to call in on her way to Greenland and when they got in, their ship's doctor saw me and said he was pretty sure it was appendicitis. So the *Beothic* sent a message by their radio to the *Nascopie* and described my condition, and the *Nascopie* turned back to pick me up and take me out to Newfoundland to St. John's hospital. It was a straight trip with no stops and took us about ten days.

When I was on the *Nascopie* I was up and around some but I suffered some awful pain, and when I got into St. John's — I clearly remember we got in there at four o'clock in the morning — Ralph Parsons happened to be in St. John's. This was the same Bay district manager that had arranged for me to go to school in St. John's. He came on the ship because they'd radioed ahead, and he says, "Good God, Ernie, I thought you'd be just about dead from what they said, so I brought the ambulance down!"

When I got in the hospital they examined me and said I had a ruptured appendix and they'd have to operate right away. So every way I looked at this, I figured I was lucky to be alive!

I was in a private cubicle with just my one bed in it, but the cubicle next to me had two patients and I used to lie there and hear all this racket going on on the other side of the divider like they were having a really good time. I wasn't supposed to move around much and all this sort of a thing, but I couldn't stand not knowing what was going on over there, so one day I climbed up on my bed and pulled myself up to look over the divider and see what they were doing. Well, I tore all the stitches out and had to go back so they could sew me up again. That wasn't exactly what I was supposed to be doing, so I got an awful ticking off for that!

73

I was disappointed to have to leave the north and my job for that year, but I knew that I would be going to get home for a visit with my parents after I left hospital, and that made me feel better about the whole thing. My parents were now in Okak Bay — I explained earlier about my dad's retirement there. He'd bought himself a little shop where he sold candies and tea and sugar, this sort of thing. There was no community there at all, but right where my dad had his place built is where the Eskimos from farther south used to go through when they went north inland for caribou hunting, and sometimes they'd camp at my dad's place overnight when they'd go through.

So in six weeks or less, when I was finished with the hospital, I could head up the Labrador for my family's place, which wasn't exactly a simple short little trip since it was over a thousand miles by boat and dog team. It was late in the fall by now, and I caught the last mail boat going up the coast. I went on that as far as Makkovik where I had to stay till after the new year, waiting for weather so I could go on by dog team.

It had only been four years since I left the school at Makkovik and two of the same teachers were still there, and one of them had taught me. Her name was Edna Perrett. As a matter of fact, the second night I was there the school put on a little "do" for me because I was one of their former students.

I must have stayed in Makkovik about two months waiting for the snow, so I just took it easy and visited people. I stayed with a couple that I called aunt and uncle, though they weren't actually any relation to my people.

Finally the snows came and I made the dog team trip to my parents' home by relays from Makkovik. First, I went to Island Harbour, where I was born. I had an uncle still living there, and I stayed with his family for a week and then his son took me up to Hopedale. From Hopedale I made the last lap, about 250 miles, with the mail team. The mailman wouldn't normally go to little places like my folks' that was outside a settlement, but he went twenty-five miles out of his way to take me home.

The weather for this travelling was pretty good except for

when we were crossing the Kiglapaits, which are well-known great big high mountains about fifty miles from Okak. They had a lot of deep snow there and we had kind of a hard time getting across them. Going down a mountain slope with a dog team is different from the things I described earlier about dogs and sleds, because you have to keep the sled from over-running the dogs — a heavily loaded sled could cripple or even kill the dogs. So for this we'd add what we called drags. They're made out of round pieces of walrus hide about eighteen inches in diameter and two inches thick, and you generally have two or three of them on the sled with you to put on the runners. Walrus hide is the toughest hide you can get. And then we'd have about six inches of chain linked into the walrus hides, so that would grip enough for the sled to slow down and the dogs to keep ahead of it.

Anyway, I got home eventually. My parents weren't expecting me, of course; they didn't have any way to know about my appendicitis, or for that matter that I wasn't still in the north.

They had their team of dogs outside, and when someone is coming in to a place, the dogs can hear a sled coming for miles and miles away, and they know there's something different around, so they all start barking. My folks' team set up a racket and my dad and mother knew that there was a sled coming, but they figured it might be my older brother who was living not far away in Nutak where he worked for the Bay. They were just getting ready to go to bed — it was about eleven o'clock — when the dogs started barking, so they waited up to see if there actually was a team coming. When they came out to meet us they recognised the driver, but they didn't recognise me in the dark at first. They were very excited, of course, and very glad to see me, and we stayed up and talked most of the night.

I stayed with my parents until the middle of May when the mail team was going back south. Incidentally, these mail teams were just a dog team operation and they used to take the mail to small communities along the Labrador about three times a year; I think it cost five cents a letter.

At Makkovik again I had to wait till the late part of June for the first mail boat, and then I went on that to Cartwright where I stayed and waited for the *Nascopie*, because she always called in at Cartwright on the way north from St. John's.

Just in case you haven't been keeping track here, altogether for that stay of some two and a half months with my parents, I spent nearly six months travelling, or waiting somewhere to travel, from the time I left St. John's till I could get back to where the *Nascopie* could pick me up to take me back to my job. So you can see why I didn't just sort of pop home for the weekend all the time like some young people do today!

Two icy dunkings

When I got on the *Nascopie* in the summer of 1930, I didn't know where I'd be going to end up — as usual — but it turned out to be Port Burwell where I'd lived as a kid, and where I'd had a short stop on the way to my first Hudson's Bay Company assignment.

Before the ship put in at Burwell, she went all around northern Quebec and down into Hudson's Bay and then back up to Baffin Island, which at that time was her usual run. They had this fairly young fellow that was the purser, and we knew that there was something wrong with him because he'd been acting sort of strange for quite a while, and we used to have to always be watching what he was doing during the voyage. Then one day when the ship was approaching Churchill, he went kind of nuts and caused quite a bit of excitement.

We'd been going through a lot of ice all that day and had just got to clear water at the mouth of the Churchill River — there's quite a current at the mouth of that river which is what kept the ice away — when one of the RCMPs that were aboard saw this fellow climb up on the rail of the deck. The policeman could tell that this guy was going to jump, so he made a grab for the guy and just got him by the coat, but the fellow wiggled out of his coat and jumped overboard anyway.

Luckily the captain, who was Captain Smellie of the *Bay-rupert* that was shipwrecked, got the ship turned around and got the lifeboat over, and they got this fellow back on board in twenty minutes. He was still alive, but he was pretty cold after being in that water for twenty minutes, I can tell you. Once he was back on board the ship's doctor took him in and put him to bed, and when we got in to Churchill they took him off the ship, so I don't know what happened to him after that.

For the rest of the trip, two of us clerks filled in for that guy — they called the other one the purser and they called me the assistant purser. So I had to stay on the ship as it went all around the posts till we came back to Burwell, the last port of call.

By the end of my year at Port Burwell I was acting as post manager and this involved me in some things that I hadn't had to do before. The Company had their own bookkeeping system which was a very good one, and actually it was fairly simple, but they wanted reports on everything that happened, so I had to keep a daily diary. Making out reports was bad, that always got me, but a daily diary was required all the time, at all the posts. I understand that isn't so now, which I think is maybe unfortunate, because all those reports and diaries really gave the Company a good overall picture of the settlements and areas where their posts were.

The hunting around Burwell was foxes and seals, and whales of course. They caught whales around there mostly by netting them. Some years there would be no whales there, but other years there would be plenty. We never had a net that was just for getting whales but we used to catch quite a few in the seal nets. You can't stretch these nets across a narrow passage of water in Burwell because you're right on the sea coast, so what you do is find places where you can anchor the net good. Setting a seal net is entirely different from setting a fish net, for instance, because you have to put it in as deep water as you can find near the shore, where with a fish net you have it just below the surface of the water. A seal net you'll have as far down as you can get it and it's anchored down by what we called kellies, which were made of wood and filled with rocks. Then the net would spread between the kellies on the bottom and the floats on the top that were made of cork.

Generally the whales would be dead unless you'd catch them right in near shore in shallow water where they could come up and breathe, come up and blow. Otherwise they'd drown because they wouldn't be able to breathe.

Then we'd tow a whale back to land and flense it, and use the fat for oil and eat the *muktuk*, of course, *muktuk* being the skin. You couldn't use it for clothing; some Eskimos used to use the under part of it, which was almost like a seal skin except it had no fur on it, to make white boots.

Some of the people at Burwell remembered me, and by now I was speaking Eskimo pretty fluently and I spent a lot of time with the people. I used to go out to the camps to see what they were doing, and we used to talk about how the hunting was and the trapping and all sorts of things, kind of like talking shop, I guess. The Eskimos always liked to talk about hunting — what they wanted to get the next time, or maybe about how they had a caribou hunt and they really got after the caribou that time.

Once I took a trip to George River which was the post next from us, about 150 miles, maybe 200 miles southwest down Ungava Bay, and spent a couple of days with the post manager and his wife. I didn't have my own dog team but the post servant had one. Actually the dogs belonged to him, but they were called the Company team and the Company kept and fed those dogs, bought all the dogs' food. So I could use that team when I needed to or wanted to, pretty much like it was my own.

One kind of funny thing happened at Burwell. When the RCMP was sending young recruits into the Arctic they would send them to Burwell at this time, sometimes half a dozen of them or so, and they would wait there until the ships came along to take them to their posts farther north.

The HBC sort of had to look out for these fellows while they were there, so one day I was taking several of them out in the Company motor boat to look for some seals. There was one young guy named Fraser who kept complaining about the way I handled the motor boat as we pushed through the ice pans. He was sitting up on the gunwale, and I got tired of his griping and finally I said, "Shut up or I'll knock you in the water." Well, he didn't shut up so I pushed him in! With all that ice floating around, he was about frozen before we picked him up, but at least he quit griping.

I never saw that fellow again until 1966 when he came up to Spence Bay on an inspection tour of RCMP posts. He had got to be very high up in the RCMP, and was known all over the north as "Wild Bill" Fraser. I didn't think he would remember me, and I wasn't too sure I wanted him to after that dunking, but he was very friendly and he wrote in my autograph book, "Ernie, remember Port Burwell! Bill Fraser, Superintendent."

The seals were Protestants

When the *Nascopie* came to Burwell in the summer of 1931 they brought in another fellow for that post. They told me that they thought I'd go to Pangnirtung or some other place, but I ended up going to Pond Inlet. That's quite a long way up on Baffin Island, well over a thousand miles from Port Burwell.

Pond is a beautiful place, really one of the best places I've ever been. It's got high hills all around, and it's built almost on the shore and sort of right under a big mountain with a big glacier on it. With the sun shining on it that glacier was all white when the snow was on it in the winter, and in the summer it was sort of bluish, just solid ice. Icebergs would break off it, and sometimes one would get stranded in the shallow straits north of Pond and the Eskimos would use it for a water supply all winter. They'd go out there and chip off big chunks of ice and bring it in on their sleds to melt for fresh water. There's no actual shelter like a bay at Pond Inlet at all.

The RCMP was there and the missions, both Anglican and Catholic, had been there since 1926. Replacements for those missionaries came in on the *Nascopie* at the same time as I did, and like in other places they wouldn't have anything to do with one another, even on the ship.

It was real good hunting in Pond. They'd get walrus and seals, narwhals, white whales, polar bears, and foxes. White foxes went from $16.50 to $23.50 that first year I was there. Hunting for the narwhal isn't the same as it is for regular whale. They never had to use nets to catch the narwhals because around Pond Inlet there were killer whales, and whenever killer whales came in, that used to drive the narwhals right into shallow water, into the shore and near the beach, and then of course the Eskimos could get them easy.

The narwhal tusk was valuable then to the people, they could get fifty cents a pound and some of the tusks weighed better than forty pounds. Of course, nowadays a really good tusk could bring around $500. They generally used to sell them whole — they ran about six to eight feet long — but a lot of them used to cut the tips off and make walking sticks out of them, which were very good sellers. The handle of the walking stick was made out of hardwood.

The narwhal is good to eat and it is quite a lot bigger than a white whale. Some of the narwhals got to be sixteen or seventeen feet long and would weigh sixteen or seventeen hundred pounds. The Belugas or white whales were more likely to run only eleven or twelve feet and weigh around a thousand pounds.

There was plenty of hunting up there and the HBC didn't have to help the people — I don't recall one person there ever getting a handout.

The Company had a policy of what we would call giving debt to the Eskimos in the fall when the trapping season was going to start. When they got ready to go out trapping we'd give them traps, and maybe a gun and some ammunition, and a lot of staple food, and put that on the books. They'd go off and in the spring they'd come back after trapping season and return the traps to the store till next year, and they'd have enough furs to pay off their debts, and nearly always extra over that.

We weren't dealing in pounds, shillings, and pence but in

dollars at this stage. But the Eskimos here didn't understand currency anyway, except the special coins that the Bay produced that we used for all our trading with the Eskimos. These aluminum coins were in different sizes and amounts from five cents up to a dollar — 5, 10, 25, and 50 cents were round, and a dollar was square — and they were just for transactions with the Bay. If a fox was worth ten dollars, we'd put ten of these aluminum dollars on the counter, so if a guy had ten foxes we'd put a hundred dollars down for him. Then he might want to buy some things, and if he bought something for, say, one dollar, we'd put that article on the counter and he would push back one of the one-dollar coins to us. They don't use these any more, but they were in use all the time I was with the Bay.

With the whales and narwhals and walrus they had quite a lot of ivory for carving up there, but they weren't doing anything like as much as they're doing today. Then they were doing it because the Bay encouraged it, but not as a regular job full time. The HBC has a museum in Winnipeg and they have all sorts of things there that show what life around their posts was like, and they have the early carvings that the Bay used to buy. They used to buy really good ones, they wouldn't buy anything but the best work — they'd get to know the good carvers and just ask them. But of course there was carving that was done before the arrival of the Bay. I've worked with archaeologists digging up old sites, and they've told me that they've found carvings from way, way, way back. I guess the Eskimos have always done them, especially small pieces, like for the kids to play with for dolls, and sort of lucky charms.

At Pond Inlet we had a coal mine where we dug out our own coal in the summertime. I was mining the coal myself with a crew of about six men. This coal mine looked different from others because it wasn't a shaft and you didn't go down in it in elevators. There was a seam of coal in a cliff right on the Salmon River, and the shelf of coal was a ledge about eight or ten feet wide and fifteen or twenty feet above the ground, and you could see the coal. We'd dig into that with pickaxes, and sometimes we had to do blasting. We used to work from the top if we had to do that, and after they'd lowered me down on a rope, I'd light the fuse on the dynamite and then we'd all get off the shelf.

We'd put the coal into sacks and roll it down the edge of the cliff. Then in the winter we'd haul it down to the settlement as soon as the ice made and we could use the dog teams. We also used to supply coal to Clyde River and Pangnirtung, well down to the south and east of us.

Right opposite the cliff, maybe about a couple hundred yards away, we had a cooking tent and the tent we lived in, and one day we were blasting and quite a big rock — I'd say it weighed about fifty pounds or so — went right through the cook tent and right through the stove.

I was cooking for the camp besides being the dynamite man and foreman. Cooking for these guys meant using mostly tinned food, and we'd make bannock or use hardtack biscuits. Of course we'd get quite a lot of fish there from the river, and some of the fellows would go over to their camp and bring up some seal meat or *muktuk*. They never got any caribou there.

Once we used the dynamite for something besides blasting out coal. We had a funny thing happen one night. I went out of the cook tent and down to the river to get some water in a bucket. The river was quite shallow and in places I saw some fish going up the river, so I took a stick of dynamite, though I knew this wasn't legal, and I threw it out in one of the pools. When the dynamite went off, all these fish came up and I was just throwing fish ashore like crazy when lo and behold an RCMP turns up! That night he walked up to the tent to see us and he had a sparkle in his eye while he was telling me it was illegal to use dynamite to get fish. But before he left, he said, "Let's try and see if there's any more fish in there," and of course when we did it again, we got a lot more fish.

At the post in Pond Inlet I was a clerk and interpreter for the Bay, and the post manager was Jimmy Smith. He was a Scotsman, from Aberdeen, and later he went back to Scotland and opened up a butcher shop. He was a very easy man to get along with. He was strict, of course, on the job, but off duty he was a really good fellow.

I played a lot of cribbage with Jimmy, and the policemen and us used to get together maybe two or three times a week and we'd play cards — poker and auction bridge, which was the big thing then. The missionaries played some with us too, though never at the same time, of course — they were very friendly to us even if they wouldn't speak to one another. Sometimes we played cards with the Eskimos when they came in, but the Bay had a strict rule against playing cards for money with the Eskimos, so it was just the whites that played cards for money. But I didn't play for money much, I'm not a gambler. I've got into two or three fairly big games, but I never do any serious gambling.

There were two Anglican missionaries in Pond then. One got to be famous for so much travelling around to Eskimo camps and visiting the people all the time. That was Jack Turner, and he made some of the longest dog sled trips that anyone's ever made up here. A few years later when I was at Fort Ross, he left Pond and went to Igloolik, Repulse Bay, Pelly Bay, Gjoa Haven, and back up to a place halfway between Igloolik and Arctic Bay where he had built a little mission — that was well over a thousand miles. He travelled alone a lot, but on long trips he'd have one fellow with him because he'd sometimes be gone for months at a time.

Jack Turner unfortunately got shot up in an accident some while after I left Pond — this was at that little mission that he'd built. He had this house built right near the sea, and he was a real good hunter and used to put up his own dog feed. This time he saw a seal coming in near the shore and he got his .22 to go down and have a shot at it. The girl that was working for him was bringing two buckets of water into the house — this was Kitsualik's wife, that's now at Gjoa Haven and is in the interpreter corps. As she was bringing the water in, he was going to open the door for her, and somehow his gun went off and he got shot through the roof of his mouth.

A lot of the Catholic priests were French, which was true of Father Girard at Pond. I don't know how long he'd been in the Arctic. There were twenty-four in his family, he had twenty-three brothers and sisters, and four of the brothers became priests. When I was at Pond he was already a fairly old man, and he didn't do any travelling, even to the camps that were close. As a matter of fact, in the three years I was there they had only one family, a family that came from Churchill; that was all the Catholics there were there, and I don't think they ever did get any converts.

The Catholics had the church as part of their living quarters, all in this one building, and the priest would ring the bell at six o'clock in the morning, and at noon, and again at six o'clock at night. This was a custom they had which the people in the springtime complained about because there used to be seals in the morning out on the ice, and they liked to walk out to get them, but every time the seals would hear these church bells they'd all go down in their holes and disappear. I guess maybe those seals were Protestants.

The Catholic churches were impressive inside, real impressive, they had their crosses and pictures of Christ and this sort of thing, and the services were held in Eskimo and Latin. At Christmas time I used to always go to the midnight Mass, most of us used to go to that.

Christmas was a really special time at any post. At the HBC it was the policy that at every Christmas when a lot of the people would come in, the Company always put on a holiday feast for them. We'd use one of the big warehouses — we'd clean that up — and then we'd make up a big feed in the house. Usually we used to give them a big stew — beans, rice, anything we could get our hands on — and after that a big pot of rice with molasses on it for dessert. We'd have this big feed and everybody'd be there from sixty or seventy miles away and be having a good time.

After they finished the meal we'd put on a big dance, square dancing, and we'd dance until early morning. The music came from accordians, because a lot of the Eskimo people — you wouldn't often see it now — were really good accordian players, and so quite a few of them would have accordians and they'd take turns playing for the dance. And the people, the Eskimos, would come and give you a little gift like maybe a pair of boots, or maybe a sealskin, something that they'd made themselves. Oh my God — Christmas time!

Father Girard was very strict about church, but he was a very nice person to get along with, and we liked to go to visit him a lot. He was a real good winemaker, he was always making wine. He made it out of just sugar and raisins and yeast, I think, and always had a good supply of it that he'd made himself, though I don't think he ever used to use his home-made wine for church.

Since he was too old to travel, he used to read a lot. Sometimes in the summer you'd see him walking back and forth by himself reading. He studied an awful lot. All the missionaries, the Catholics especially, used to do all sorts of things. They could knit, sew, bake, do all kinds of things around the house when it was snowing too hard to be outside. Father Girard never struck me as a lonely man. All Catholic priests I've known have been jolly and very very friendly.

Father Girard used to come down often and play bridge with us, either at the RCMP or the HBC, and one time I played a trick on him. His house had a wooden porch on it for protection from wind and drifting snow, and then outside that they built an ice porch with a regular door in it. They sawed blocks of ice about four feet long and a foot and a half wide and put those blocks together like they'd build a snow house, and used snow and slush to fill up the cracks and freeze the blocks fast together. Then they froze the door frame into this ice porch.

Well, one night it was blowing really hard and drifting when Father Girard came down to the house for cards, his long black cassock whipping in the wind and his fur cap on with flaps that turned down over his ears. After the game, while the others were having coffee, the RCMP and myself went up to Father Girard's house with a bucket of water and we sealed his ice-porch door all up with that. The water froze fast and it was about like cementing the door shut. And of course when Father Girard got back there he couldn't open the door. He had to come back to our place and we had to go up and chip open the door for him. He took it all in fun.

The Anglican house was about five hundred yards from the Catholic mission, and the Anglican mission had a real good team of dogs, about nineteen of them. In those days they never used to keep them tied up, so whenever anyone threw out the garbage, all the dogs would run to see what was in it that they might eat.

One day Father Girard was getting things ready for a new batch of wine and he threw out what was left in the bottom of his barrel, the dregs, and all the Anglican dogs went running over there. It was just a mush and they were eating this up, and we were watching. Then all the dogs got drunk and some of them couldn't even make it home, they were staggering and running around, and we like to died laughing watching them.

That's one time the missionaries got together to talk, even if the Anglican did most of the talking. He threatened to sue Father Girard and he went down to the RCMP and made an official complaint that the Catholic mission got the dogs drunk. The policeman thought it was funny too, he just laughed about it, he didn't do anything.

As far as I can remember, Father Girard just went on throwing his leftover wine outside, and the Anglican never did tie up his dogs.

There was another time when a policeman and I ganged up on Father Girard. He had a license to go trapping and he had a trapline out where he could walk to it, but he always used to wait until after noontime when he had to ring the church bell. One day when he was off to see his traps, it must have been in December because it was dark very early, myself and this RCMP fellow named Wishard got the idea that we'd go up to the church and tie this bell up. The tower was quite tall on that church — it's still there today — and we went up and tied the knocker up against the bell so that it couldn't ring.

Father Girard always carried a flashlight with him, and

around five minutes to six we could see his flashlight coming over the hill, going like anything. But of course when he got to the church and tried to ring the bell, he was just ringing away and it never made a sound.

Next morning he got up very early — we were watching for that — and he climbed up that tower with his flashlight to check that bell, and fixed it so it would ring again.

The way he's always told this story, he knew who had tied the bell up. He mentioned it quite a few times afterwards, and I think he was trying to get us to admit we'd done it, because I don't think he was quite sure, even if he figured he had a pretty good idea. But of course neither of us ever admitted it, until now.

He used to play little jokes on us too, but you know, it's kind of funny, for some reason or another I don't seem to be able to remember anything to tell you about what he did to us!

One of the RCMP put one over on the HBC manager one time at Pond Inlet. Whenever a ship was coming in to a settlement where there was a police detachment as well as a Bay post, the HBC people would always try to beat the RCMP aboard the ship. All the passengers, and the district manager of the Bay, and the RCMP inspector would be right at the gangplank to meet whoever was coming aboard.

Well, there was this RCMP corporal at Pond named McKay — we used to call him "Crazy Mac" — that was a real humorous sort of a fellow. So this time when the *Nascopie* came in, the police boat got ahead of us and got there first, and this RCMP introduced himself to everybody. Then he says, "Everybody here calls me Crazy Mac, but if you think *I'm* crazy, just wait till you see the Hudson's Bay post manager when *he* comes aboard!" Well, Jimmy Smith wasn't crazy of course, but he took it in fun and everybody got quite a kick out of Crazy Mac's joke.

Cooked egg-white with a nutty taste

In the summer of 1933, during the three years I was in Pond Inlet, I went out on the *Fort Garry* just to get dropped off at Pangnirtung for a month — it was for August — to relieve someone, I forget who, until the Company could get a regular replacement in there. Pangnirtung, to people who know the north, is one of the prettiest places of all because of the fjord there.

There were so many white whales there that I think it must have been their breeding ground, and while I was there we went on a whale hunt that was different from any other I'd been on yet, about thirty or forty miles up the fjord. Before this, at Burwell, I'd gone hunting Belugas, whites, with nets, and at Pond we'd get the narwhals when the bigger killer whales chased them into shallow water. At Pang and up the fjord the tides rise and fall as much as thirty to forty feet, and that was what made the whale hunt there different.

What used to happen is that the people would go up to this place in the fjord and they'd take up to as many as fifteen or sixteen whale boats, and some of them had motor boats. In each boat there would be six or seven people, sometimes a whole family would be in one boat. They would wait until a certain time of high tide, and then they'd start driving the whales, like herding them, right up towards the end of the fjord. When the whales would try to escape, the people in the boats would keep crisscrossing and making a noise so the whales wouldn't go out, they'd keep going on up the fjord. The whales were very nervous and they could be easily driven ahead that way. The people would finally drive them right up to the head of the fjord and then they'd shoot them. At a killing you might get 80 or 90, or even 100, at a time. I think they were there three nights non-stop but I didn't stay till they were finished.

After they'd kill the whales they'd drag them farther up on shore while the tide was out, and skin them. The women would be using *ulus* and the men would be using ordinary knives. And then they'd fill up the boats and take them into Pangnirtung to the big shed where they'd store the fat. They used the hides to make boots and suitcases to send out. They'd take as much of the *muktuk* home as they liked, and they'd eat it — it's real good. When people ask me what it tastes like, I always tell them it's like cooked egg-white but has a sort of nutty taste to it.

The blubber was made into oil just about like we used to do in Burwell when I was growing up. They also used the blubber in their lamps, but you couldn't just put a hunk of whale fat in a lamp and have it burn. You've got to get some grease out of it so, if it's frozen, you pound it with a hammer. As soon as a little bit of warmth is there, the fat melts into oil enough that you can light a wick.

The whale meat was used for the dogs, because everybody had a lot of dogs. The bones were the only thing they'd just throw away, they weren't used for anything. They weren't used for carving at that time like they are today.

There was never any time when I was frightened of the whales, when I thought they were going to attack or upset the boat. They'd never attack a boat. I've heard about whales having personalities and high intelligence, but it never struck me that way. As a matter of fact, I used to think whales were pretty stupid, because if they came in the harbour, and if you could get a whale in handy enough that you could throw rocks, even a small rock, at it or just over it, to make a splash, the whale would come right into shore. We often used to get one that way.

In Pangnirtung, besides the Bay post there was the RCMP and one mission, just the Anglican mission there. They seemed to be pretty active because they had a little ten-bed hospital that they'd built in 1928, and a full-time resident doctor. I don't know why Pangnirtung had a doctor and hospital when practically nowhere else I've been had one. They had a doctor there and one at Chesterfield Inlet, that's the only two that I can remember.

This was the first time I saw nurses in the north. They were sent up by the Anglican missions, and I think they were recruited mostly from the south. They were generally religious, very religious, but they were ready to nurse. They didn't only deal with just sort of minor stuff, but all sorts of situations.

That building in Pang isn't used as a hospital any more, but in those days they had operating facilities and everything. As a matter of fact, one summer they had a real sick woman there and their doctor was away somewhere, and a doctor off the *Nascopie* went in, and I went ashore with him and watched him do an operation. The commonest sort of thing they had to deal with was accidents with guns. Frostbite was really bad among the people, and appendicitis, that sort of a thing. In those days I never lived at a place where a doctor was stationed, but I know they used to travel around the camps a lot during the winter by dog team, and sometimes in the summertime they travelled around the camps by boat. The people didn't seem to be nervous about seeing a doctor, they would nearly always cooperate with him.

Later on when we had two-way radios in the posts we'd bring a sick person into the settlement, and we'd use the two-way radio to get instructions from one of the doctors. If there was some sickness we couldn't cope with, or the patient was getting worse, or we knew he was very bad, then the doctor would give us instructions about what to do.

Pangnirtung was a slightly bigger settlement of whites — it was generally whites that formed the settlements then because there were no Eskimos living right there, apart from the post servants for the Bay. But as I remember there were quite a few camped all year round at Pang.

I found the people there were very very pleasant and really friendly. They were always after me to go out and visit them because many years earlier, not too long after the First World War I guess, my brother Abe was there as a clerk for the Bay, and they knew that I was his brother and they wanted me to have tea with them or meals with them, and I really had a good time.

So it was a good month at Pang, and then I hopped the *Nascopie* which came around later than the *Fort Garry*, to get back to Pond Inlet.

Interlude at home

I went out for my first real holiday, the only holiday I ever took while I was with the Bay, when the ship came in the summer of 1934. Of course, I'd been out once before for a year when I had appendicitis and had to go to St. John's for an operation. That time I didn't have any choice, but I hadn't really wanted to go out and miss a year's work in the north then. So this was really the first time I had even wanted to think about going south to my family. For one thing both my parents were getting old, though they had always been in good health.

My parents were still living at Okak, and of course they didn't know I was coming, just as they didn't know I was coming after I'd had my appendix out. There was still no way at all of letting them know. And like before, I couldn't go all the way to their place on the *Nascopie* as it still didn't call in on the Labrador coast except at Cartwright. There I caught the last mail boat up to Makkovik and again I had to stay there until I could travel on by dogs after the new year. I finally got to my parents' place on February 14.

The time at home was very quiet though there was one scarey incident. My brother Henry was still working for the HBC in Nutak, and Mum and Dad sometimes used to go down there for a weekend, or two or three days, or maybe a week, because it was only twenty-five miles from their place. So this time they were down there, and I was going down with my brother's dogs to bring them back. About half way between the two places there was an Eskimo family living, just one family, a man and his wife and a girl about eighteen and a son about six years old.

Their camp was on the land near quite a big hill, and when I was arriving there was a storm starting to come up, and it began to drift and snow. These people gave me my dinner, and they said, "There's going to be a big storm," and they tried to persuade me to stay there with them overnight and wait until the storm went over, and go on to Nutak in the morning. But for some reason or other I decided I'd go on — it wasn't very far, and although I wasn't too familiar with that country, I figured I'd get near enough that my brother's dogs would know the way.

It's not true that dogs can always get you home if you're lost, but if you're handy, within five or six miles, then they will take you in if they've been used to going to that place. I did get lost for a while but we finally made it in, and when I arrived my parents weren't really expecting me because it was blowing really hard, drifting.

The next morning it was really a nice morning, though it was still blowing a bit. Dad and Mum and I were getting ready to go home, we had the dogs and everything all ready to go, when we saw this team coming. It was the man whose camp I'd stopped at the evening before, and he had his boy with him. We knew there must be something really wrong, because when I'd left there everything was all right, and that man very seldom came in to Nutak. He stopped his dogs way down on the shore and walked up, and told us that he'd lost his wife and his daughter in the storm the night before. He said that during the storm there was an avalanche from the mountain and it buried their house. When the avalanche struck, the boy and his father got out of the house somehow, but the house was buried quite deep and was all broken up, and the mother and daughter got killed in all this. And I might have got killed, too, if I'd stayed with them the way they wanted me to.

I've heard whites say that Eskimos just sort of take what happens and don't show much emotion, but you could certainly see that this was a real blow to this man, a big shock. Probably he would try and get married again soon to have a woman to sew his clothes and look after him and his boy and so on, but this was a real blow and this man wasn't young any more, he must have been forty or forty-five years old.

The rest of the year at my family's house was spent pretty quietly. I used to go out to cut wood with my dad and my brother and haul the wood in. My dad had a little sawmill there and I used to help him at that. And we used to go fishing by the house. Oh, we had plenty to do.

My parents used to say they wished I could have lived at

home, or at least closer to home, my mother especially. But my dad understood why I wanted to work in the north. He probably worried about me some, but Dad was the sort that had tried to train us to, you know, get up early in the morning and start work early, and he'd always keep us at work. He used to tell us, "Well, you've got to be prepared for when you go out on your own, be able to look after yourself," that sort of thing.

I know my mother worried about me an awful lot. We were very close. I used to write her a letter nearly every Sunday. These would build up over the year and then each summer when the ship came in, something like fifty letters would go out to her. Of course at the same time I'd get the letters she'd written, she was the one that used to write mostly, and I'd really look forward to getting letters from my mum and seeing what was going on at home. My dad wrote some, too, but my brothers very seldom wrote to me.

My mother wouldn't ask questions much — that was useless, because it would be so long before an answer could get back. She'd just tell the news about the family, mostly, and how she missed me, and all this sort of a thing. I was her favourite I think, because I was the youngest and so far away.

When the ship came in, I'd get maybe six or seven letters from mum and the family, and a few from friends. Letters to me, or to anybody at these posts, were addressed care of the HBC, Montreal, because the way we were moved around, sometimes only the Company would know where we were, so then the Company would forward our stuff to the posts where we were.

In those days we got what they called packet boxes off the ship, it wouldn't be mail bags. The Company had a certain type box they made up, and it wouldn't only have just letters, it would have parcels too, just small parcels, from the family. Mum generally every year sent me a pair of home-made pajamas, and she always did a lot of knitting so she used to send me half a dozen pair of socks each year, and some gloves, that she knit herself. The parcels were almost entirely clothes.

There wasn't any point me writing for anything of course, because I wouldn't have got it till maybe two years later — my letter would have gone out one summer and it would have been at least another year before the parcel could finally arrive.

People often think that, after I'd been up north for a long time, when these letters and things would come in I would miss home and wish I could be back with my parents. But to be honest, I never had that kind of feeling at all. I loved the north and I really enjoyed my work, and it never crossed my mind that I wanted to go back home to stay. Of course, there was many a time when I wished I could go back for a while, see my family for a little bit. Like times when I was feeling a little low or the weather was lousy. But I think that was just natural, and it would pass off, and I would know that it would pass.

Anyway, as you know now, there was just no way to make a quick trip or a short visit.

Well, my father and mother were in good health when I left home after this vacation, but that's the last time I ever saw my parents. My dad died in 1936, he was in his 80s. Mum was only three months short of her 100th birthday when she died in 1952.

An unsung hero

After my holiday, when I went back north I was sent to Port Burwell again for a year, and there was an interesting thing happened there. A government archeologist named Leechman came up in the summer, and afterwards he wrote a book*, which actually I could say is the only true story about the north that I've read that happened the way he wrote it.

This Leechman had quite a lot of stuff with him when he landed, and he was going out to the Button Islands just a few miles north of Burwell. He took an Eskimo with him by the name of One-Eyed-Bobby that had a small sailing boat, and Bobby went along so that if anything did happen while Leechman was out there, Bobby knew the place and could show him what to do and how to live out on the land.

*John Douglas Leechman, *Eskimo Summer*, Ryerson Press (Toronto, 1945).

But the Company was the only one that had a motor boat there at that time, so I had to go too and take Leechman and his stuff out to the islands, and then go and bring him back again so he'd be in time to catch the last ship out.

In his book, Leechman wrote about his experiences, and meeting up with One-Eyed-Bobby, and it was all really true.

Actually, this One-Eyed-Bobby was quite a character, and the way he got the name happened some years earlier when I was at the Moravian mission post in Burwell. They used to sell ammunition that the people could reload, and he was home one night and was going to reload some cartridges, putting a cap in the shell. It was a shotgun shell, and he was tapping with his pocket knife when it exploded and blew his eye out.

There's a story about One-Eyed-Bobby that I've never seen written in any book, not even in Leechman's, though maybe he didn't have any reason to know about it. Back in 1928 the Canadian government had decided that they were going to make what you call an ice survey, or ice inspection, to see how the ice travelled during the winter. They opened up three different sites — one at Port Burwell, one at Akpatok Island west of Burwell in Ungava Bay, and one on Nottingham Island, just north of Wolstenholme about fifty miles out in the Hudson Strait. And they sent up these old airplanes, they were Fairchilds, made of plywood — the first planes that ever came up here — that had about six in a crew.

Well, the plane at Port Burwell went missing, and Bobby was on that plane with them. They were flying on the way around the Hudson Strait, and when they were flying over Burwell it was getting kind of darkish, and Bobby tried to show them that Burwell was down there. But Bobby couldn't speak much English. Usually by using signs he could make himself understood, but these men in the plane weren't used to Bobby, and they didn't understand what he was trying to tell them.

They kept on flying till they ran out of gas, and they came down on the ice about a hundred miles south of Burwell. There was the pilot and engineer and some others, and a fellow by the name of Coghill that was in charge.

So they were walking and walking, and they didn't have any grub at all. Each night Bobby'd make a snow house for them on the ice, and once in a while he'd catch a seal right in the dead of winter through a seal hole. They even got a walrus. Bobby always used to carry his hunting equipment with him — his gun and his harpoon, snow probes to use at seal breathing holes, and his snow knife. He was wearing his deerskins that he always wore, and the other men had their own type of what they called arctic clothing which apparently was warm enough — at least they always kept warm okay. It was probably 30 or 35 below zero at least. They went through two or three real big storms, the kind that would have lasted more than a day.

They had the two planes from the other bases searching for them, but they couldn't find them and finally gave them up for dead. And then one night they all walked into Burwell after twenty-eight days.

What happened was that to begin with they were way out from land on the sea ice, but when they got on shore then Bobby knew where he was, and he knew where there was a camp up about sixty miles away. Some of the fellows wanted to give up, just wanted to lay there, but Bobby kept them going. Somehow he made them understand that they would get to a camp after a while if they would just keep going.

Finally, one day as they were walking along, they could see way off in the distance a black spot coming towards them. They knew it was a dog team, and they were so excited that they didn't wait for the team to come up to where they were, they just ran to meet that dog team. At that camp they got a good feed and a rest, and of course they felt really cheered up again. So the rest of the way to Burwell wasn't so hard.

That was quite an experience. And everyone knew that One-Eyed-Bobby had saved the lives of those fellows.

They wanted to go, Mr. Mowat

The Company transferred me to Arctic Bay after my year in Port Burwell. But before I get to that, there's a story I want to tell that started back just before I left Pond Inlet, about how the Hudson's Bay Company moved some of the people to where they were setting up a new post farther north — Dundas Harbour. This is about why the Bay did that, and how they did it.

One of the reasons I want to tell about Dundas Harbour is because Farley Mowat — he is pretty famous in Canada and has written a lot of stuff about the north — wrote a few years ago about this move to Dundas in a story that was part of a book he called *The Snow Walker**.

Now I know that some of Mr. Mowat's stories are the made-up kind, what's called fiction, but when he wrote about the people going to Dundas and what happened afterwards, he used names of real people — including my own — and dates, and made it look like it was real official and he knew all about what happened. So if that is supposed to be true the way he wrote it, then he got a lot of it wrong as far as I'm concerned, and I was in on this personally.

What actually happened was this. Along in the winter of 1934, my last year at Pond Inlet, we got a message over the radio from the Company (the same message went to the posts at Pangnirtung and Cape Dorset) that we should ask the people if any of them wanted to go to Dundas Harbour, because the Company was going to open a new post there.

Dundas was just north of the northern end of Baffin Island. If you can picture an area like the shape of an upside down fan below Dundas, there was Pond Inlet to the southeast about 150 miles, Port Leopold to the southwest about 180 miles, and between Leopold and Pond was Arctic Bay, about 125 miles south of Dundas. This whole area was very good hunting, but at that time the best was the northern area right around Dundas, so the HBC asked permission from the government to open a post at

*Farley Mowat, "Dark Odyssey of Soosie", *The Snow Walker*, McClelland and Stewart (Toronto, 1975).

Dundas Harbour and take some of the people north with them. The point of the new post wasn't that the other posts weren't perfectly okay — they went along operating like always with the people that stayed. But in those days the important thing was fur trading; the people liked to go where they thought was the best place to get the fur, where there was good hunting so they wouldn't be hard up and could make a living for themselves.

As a matter of fact the HBC had opened posts at both Arctic Bay and Port Leopold back in 1926. Some of the people had been up there then, and they always had a wish to go back as it was such a good hunting ground. Some of the people from Pond Inlet used to go up, even as far as Dundas, by dog team in the old days and go bear and walrus hunting, and they knew it was good hunting there. But the Company had to close those posts at Arctic Bay and Port Leopold in 1927 because the government had decided that those areas should become a game preserve just for the Eskimos to use, and off limits to any traders or other outsiders.

So anyhow, now the government gave its permission for a new post at Dundas Harbour. Chess Russell was the manager at Dorset by then, and he told the people there that the Bay was going to open the new post, and that three families from Cape Dorset could go up there. The post manager at Pangnirtung was to see about getting three families from there, and the manager at Pond Inlet was to do the same thing. At Pond this was done through me, since I was the clerk and interpreter there. All the people from these three posts that decided to go to Dundas really wanted to go because they knew about the good hunting.

But Farley Mowat made it out that the people didn't want to go to Dundas at all, that they had to be sold on this idea, and that the families from Dorset only went finally because they were in bad times and hungry at Dorset. This just wasn't true at all. Mr. Mowat was also wrong about how many families went up — he said six from Dorset, two from Pang and four from

Pond — so because of this he named some people that didn't go to Dundas at all, including the Soosie of his story.

Kakak, Aneelik, and Esolootak were the three men whose families went to Dundas from Pangnirtung. The three from Pond Inlet were Kootshik, Koogaseegeetoo, and Kayakooshook. The three from Cape Dorset were Kavavouk, Takolik, and Inuk.

These families and their dogs and sleds and everything were all taken up on the *Nascopie* in the summer of 1934 when Dundas Harbour was opened as a Hudson's Bay Company post. Now this was happening at the same time as I left Pond Inlet to go south for that holiday with my parents, and I was in Burwell during the second year of the Dundas post.

In August of 1936 I boarded the *Nascopie* at Burwell with instructions to go to Dundas for closing that post because bad weather and bad ice conditions had made it too hard to supply, and then to go right on to Arctic Bay to help re-establish the post there.

At Dundas we talked to the people and told them why the Company was going to close that place. We said the post at Arctic Bay was going to be opened again, and that if anyone wanted to go there the Company was willing to let them do this; and if anyone wanted to go back to Cape Dorset or Pangnirtung or Pond Inlet, they could do that and the Company would take them on the *Nascopie* as it went back.

The ones that chose to go to Arctic Bay were the three families from Dorset, and two of the families from Pond. The Pangnirtung people and the one Pond family that wanted to go home were taken on back on the *Nascopie*.

Well, in Farley Mowat's story he says that when the *Nascopie* left Dundas it was headed somewhere else than Arctic Bay to build a new post and then got into rough ice conditions and had to backtrack to Arctic Bay where a "hurried decision" was made to offload the supplies and the people. Baloney, as you can see.

And then he says that the Pangnirtung people wouldn't even

go ashore at Arctic Bay because they were afraid that the Company was going to make them stay there, and that the Company only agreed to take them home because they saw they'd have to use force to get those people off the ship. All very untrue.

He also says that the Pond Inlet people later harnessed up their dogs and "slipped away" and went back to Pond. Well, those two families that stayed in Arctic Bay were still there in 1974 when I made a trip up there. I saw those people still there myself, and I'm pretty sure they're still there now.

So Mr. Mowat made a big thing, a big tragedy about the HBC getting the people to go up to Dundas Harbour and then to Arctic Bay (and later to Fort Ross and Spence Bay), trying to show that it was right against the people, that the people didn't want to go, that everything was terrible in Dundas, and that they all wanted to go back home but the Company wouldn't take them back.

And all this just plain wasn't true. Takolik, and Inuk's widow Mary, and my wife, who is Kavavouk's daughter, and Kavavouk's other four children, all live in Spence Bay now, and they were involved — they were from Cape Dorset. Anybody could find out from them that they went to Dundas of their own free will, that the hunting was good there, and that they never wanted the Company to take them back to Dorset.

Mr. Mowat also got his facts wrong about me, although maybe I shouldn't complain since he makes me out to be kind of a hero, looking after this bunch of deserted Eskimos that nobody else cared about and wandering around with them from here to there through "desperately hard" conditions for years after we left Arctic Bay. But we were far from wandering around — especially to some places he named where we never even were. I was a Hudson's Bay Company clerk assigned to Arctic Bay, and later to Fort Ross and Port Leopold, and eventually to Spence Bay, though for several years I worked only part time for the Bay and did make my living as an Eskimo, trapping and hunting. But there weren't any "desperately hard" conditions. And it was Kavavouk and Takolik and the other people that looked after *me* and taught *me*, not the other way round.

Another thing, he wrote that I have Eskimo blood in my veins. Well, that's baloney of course, though I'd be proud if I did.

But I'm getting ahead of my story here.

I went to Arctic Bay with some of the Dundas Harbour people, and it's a pretty place, I think it's one of the prettiest places I've been. You're in a harbour, a narrow harbour, and there's cliffs all around, just like in Pond Inlet — it's a really beautiful place.

As I said, a post had been established there before. Now, ten years later, we had to build new buildings since only the staff house of the original buildings was still there. We lived in it until we got our own building up, which we started right away.

The crew on the *Nascopie*, or as many of the crew as could be spared, worked at this construction as they always did at a new post. They put up the shell of the building for us, and also the flooring and walls and the rafters on the warehouse, before the ship left. The crew stayed working maybe four days, and the Eskimos all helped out too.

Now, you've already met some of these people, these families from Cape Dorset, and they were with me as we later went to Fort Ross and then on to the founding of Spence Bay. But let's get them straight again, since Arctic Bay is where the romance began that eventually made them my family.

The three Dorset families were headed by Kavavouk, who became my father-in-law, and Takolik who is my wife's step-brother, and Inuk, who was Kavavouk's nephew. Kavavouk had five kids — Nipisha was the oldest and she became my wife, and then came Ootookee, Napashee, Kooyook, and Tucktoo. These people all live in Spence now except Inuk, who died of flu in 1939 in Fort Ross, and Kavavouk, who died here in Spence on November 10, 1968 at the age of 82 (not in a 1943 flu epidemic in Fort Ross as Farley Mowat wrote).

Kavavouk had been the leader of the Eskimos at Cape Dorset and had been with the Company as a post servant for many years, and he was in that same position when he came to Arctic Bay and later at Ross and Spence. Nipisha was then what we called a house maid, she was working in the staff house at the post, and like most romances I guess, I just fell in love with her.

It began mostly, I think, just as we were finishing the last building. I fell off a ladder and hit my arm on a rock and was laid up for a good two weeks. My arm wasn't broken, but it was very badly bruised and swollen and I couldn't use it at all. My bedroom was upstairs, and Nipisha used to come up there to bring me my meals and look after me while I was laid up.

I think that's where it first started. Later we used to go out rabbit hunting and ptarmigan hunting together, or just walking, and then when the snows came I found she could drive a dog sled. I guess you might say that was our courtship period. Now that maybe won't sound very romantic to some, but I'm not writing a love story — I'd be too embarrassed to even try. Nipisha was a fine girl, and after nearly forty-two years together I think she's a fine woman, so I guess you'll just have to be satisfied with that.

Problems with a tourist

Around 1933 I think it was, anyhow in the early thirties, the government started promoting tourist trips to the Arctic — that was the beginning of tourism in the north which is a big business now with the government of the Northwest Territories. As I mentioned earlier, the *Nascopie* had been refitted to carry tourists and could take around fifty passengers altogether. Of course this included the HBC personnel, missionaries, RCMP, government people, Eskimos — whoever they used to bring in or take out or move between posts, that sort of thing.

The government always had an official party on board with people they had invited to make the tour of the north, and for many years a Major David McKeand was always in charge of that. The tourists and reporters on these trips called him "the great white father" of the Eskimos. The Eskimos had a name for

him too that he was very proud of, but what he didn't know —
he didn't speak Eskimo — was what his Eskimo name meant.
The funny thing about it, probably a lot of the people know as
well as I do, was that what the Eskimos called him all through
the north, *Keeseemayouk*, actually means "crosseyes", because
his eyes were crossed.

On this particular trip in 1936, when we were all coming in
from Dundas Harbour to Arctic Bay, the *Nascopie* also had this
bunch of tourists aboard. One of them was an American named
Adams, and he wound up causing us some problems and worries
in the middle of all our unloading and building new buildings
and trying to get settled in.

Looking at my little diary dated Arctic Bay, September 10,
1936, what I have in there is: "Clear and calm. Everyone at
unloading. The government party with Major McKeand left for
a run in the post motor boat with Adams. Adams lost, walked
home, but spent most of the night looking for him." And then it
says, "Look up page one in backup diary." And this is what I
wrote there:

> September 10, 1936. Today the government party with
> Major McKeand left for a run in the post motor boat. They
> were supposed to be back by tea time. As they had not
> turned up by 8 o'clock, Jim Cantley [HBC district manager for
> that part of the north] told me I'd better take the ship's boat
> and go look for them. We travelled about ten miles up along
> the fjord when we met the motor boat coming back with the
> Major and party.
>
> There were seven in the party, and they told us that they
> had lost Mr. Adams. They'd been searching for him for five
> hours and could not find him. They thought that he'd fallen
> over a cliff, as he had climbed up on one, and they'd never
> seen him after.
>
> Alan Snow and Dr. Keeling [the ship's doctor] was in the
> boat with me, so we decided to go and search along the bot-
> tom of the cliffs for him, as we thought that he might have
> got his legs broken. The party we met in the boat looked a

pretty frightened bunch so we gave them all a wee drink of whiskey, and we went on up to where they said they had last seen Mr. Adams.

We got up there and looked around for him until we got tired and it was too dark for us to look for him any longer. So we gave it up, until we could get a search party out. We started on home. We could see the lights of the ship and we were just saying what a feed we would have when we got there, when we met the post motor boat coming back with Chesley Russell in charge of the search party. With him were Corporal Martin, Constable Taylor and Dr. Orford [the doctor going to Pangnirtung] with all the huskies they could put together.

When we met the boat on the way up they wanted me to go along with them, so I transferred to the boat with this bunch. We landed up at the bottom of the bay where we thought would be the best place to start the search. We put up a tent as we were not going to start looking for him until daylight. We had been there about two hours, we were just getting the search party ready to leave, as it was getting daylight, when we heard a motor boat coming and they brought the news that Adams had walked in, pretty hungry and exhausted.

What a relief! He had walked about 30 miles in 18 hours. We put all our gear aboard both motor boats and arrived back at the ship about half-past five. After getting a good feed in the Officers' mess, we all turned in and slept till dinnertime.

After that episode, the fjord where Mr. Adams got lost was called Adams Sound in Arctic Bay. I just forget, in all the excitement, why he climbed the cliff in the first place. I guess, like a tourist, just to climb it, or maybe to take pictures from way up on the top. That cliff, by the way, was about a thousand feet high.

A bit of history

After a year in Arctic Bay there was another change of location for me, and as things turned out it also gave me a close-up view of some history being made, and a chance a bit later on to make a little history of my own. It also was the end of me being transferred around every little while, because I stayed in the same area for the next twelve years.

The Hudson's Bay Company decided that they were going to establish another post some 180 miles southwest of Arctic Bay at Fort Ross where there was very good hunting. Again they asked the people whoever wanted to go could go, and if they didn't want to go they didn't have to. The only ones to come at that time were the ones originally from Cape Dorset: Kavavouk, Takolik, and Inuk with their families.

As it happened, we couldn't build the Ross post exactly where the Company had planned. They originally had picked Thom Bay which was farther south on the east side of Boothia Peninsula, but when the *Nascopie* got to Thom Bay the place was full of ice and we couldn't get in, so the post got built at Fort Ross, right on the southeast end of Somerset Island. Somerset is separated from the northmost tip of the North American continent, which is Boothia Peninsula, by about a quarter of a mile or so of water which is called the Bellot Strait. This Bellot Strait is the famous passage the early explorers of the Arctic had been looking for, the Northwest Passage, but they missed it because they always thought that Somerset Island was part of the mainland.

Way back in the early 1800s when Captain John Ross was searching for the passage he came down there with an Eskimo interpreter from the Labrador who tried to tell Ross that this place was the strait, but Ross didn't understand him and he turned back. So no British explorers actually went through it.

The first Canadian ship ever to go through this part of the Passage was the *Aklavik*, the HBC supply ship for the western Arctic, and that was in September 1937 just after we arrived in the *Nascopie* at the east end of Bellot Strait. So I was there actually at Fort Ross the first time one of our ships got through the Northwest Passage.

We got there on the *Nascopie* on September 2. Captain Smellie was still in charge. When we dropped anchor at the east end at eleven o'clock in the morning we could already see the *Aklavik* and in fifteen minutes the *Aklavik* came through the strait from the west to meet us. At that time Scotty Gall was in charge of the *Aklavik*, and he had with him a fellow named Patsy Klengenburg who later on ran that ship for the Bay.

The two ships exchanged some of their cargo — furs from the west and some trade goods from the east, and this was the first east-west trade through the Northwest Passage.

As a matter of fact, that first day at Ross was a real busy one. The manager for this new post was Lorenz Learmonth and later that same day he came in from Gjoa Haven in a 16-foot canoe with an outboard motor. Actually there were two canoes, because he had with him an apprentice named Sturrock and two Eskimo families. They'd come about 300 miles with some portaging.

Learmonth had been in the north a long time. I guess he knew more about the north than anyone else. He was one of the best. He was very quiet spoken and very very interesting, you'd never be bored while he was around, he had so many tales to tell. He worked at just about all the Hudson's Bay Company posts, right from Cartwright on the Labrador in the east to Aklavik in the west.

He was very interested in Sir John Franklin, the explorer that had disappeared in the Arctic in the 1850s trying to find the Northwest Passage. Franklin's crews had left their ships and were trying to get to the Back River, hauling their boats over the ice, and they were dying of starvation along the way. Learmonth, while he was based at Gjoa Haven, and Paddy Gibson, another HBC man who was at Gjoa at different times, found quite a bit of stuff that was left from the Franklin expedition, boats that they left along the way, and instruments. I think he found a sextant and quite a bit of silverware, stuff like that. Gibson and Learmonth also found a lot of skeletons of the men that died.

Franklin died on that trip, and people even today are still trying to find his grave where the crew buried him, and the two ships he had, the *Erebus* and the *Terror*, that probably got crushed in the ice.

When Learmonth got in, he told us that there was a camp about twenty-four miles from Fort Ross, and so while the ship was there with some of the government officials, we went and brought some of these Eskimos from that camp that wanted to come in to see the ship. They'd never seen a ship like the *Nascopie* before.

Farley Mowat in his book had some things wrong about this stuff here at Fort Ross, too. He had Mr. Learmonth's name spelled wrong as Lorenzo Learmont, and he had him coming in to Ross on the *Aklavik* and said he was "on hand to greet the *Nascopie*", and he had the *Nascopie* getting in to the west end of the strait, the other end from where we actually were.

The Fort Ross site was a nice place to build a post, and there was drinking water there. When you go into the little bay, you're surrounded by very high hills, they're 1200 feet high there, and we built right on the edge of the northeast end of Bellot Strait.

As soon as the ship got there everybody had to get to work. There was never much time between when the ship would come and the first cold weather, and we wanted to get the buildings up as soon as possible.

I was chosen to be the cook. They set up two tents on the shore, one for us to sleep in and one for me to cook in. I did a lot of cooking in my day. I wasn't an exceptionally good cook, it just fell to me because I was the junior. I was good at making macaroni and cheese and that's what I used to feed them most. That was my favourite dish — for cooking, not necessarily for eating — because it was easy and everybody seemed to enjoy it. My favourite meal for eating, these days, is sweet and sour spare ribs.

The ship stayed there for six days I think, and the crew used to come ashore at six o'clock every morning to help us put up the shells of our living quarters and the store and the big warehouse.

The store was about 34 by 40 feet and the post house a little bigger. The house had three bedrooms in it, for the manager and myself and the other clerk.

There used to be eight or ten guys off the ship helping, probably more than that because the clerks or managers that were going farther north or going out were all ashore pitching in too. And the Eskimos that came with us helped, and some would be helping unload the ship, taking cargo ashore, and it all had to be carried up off the beach. Finally the ship took off one morning around four o'clock and I was glad to see it leave, to tell you the truth. I think we were always glad to get rid of the ship so that we could relax a little bit for a change.

The hunting around Fort Ross was really good. You could get everything there — narwhals, white whales, walrus, caribou, all sorts of seals. And trapping was really good. As a matter of fact it was so good that Patsy Klengenburg decided to winter in the area. He used to have a trading post between Coppermine and Cambridge Bay, but he also used to do trapping in the winter, and so he decided to stay around Fort Ross because it was such good hunting ground.

So after the *Aklavik* took a load of supplies on down to the post at Gjoa Haven he went back up to the Pasley Bay area, about 135 miles south of Fort Ross, and made a camp at Three Rivers where he stayed for two winters with his family and another family that helped on the ship. Not too long after that second winter he and his adopted son were loading the ship for the trip to Gjoa; no one knows just what happened but the *Aklavik* caught fire and blew up, and Patsy was killed.

I had a team of dogs at Fort Ross and the Dorset people had dogs too, and after we built the house we had to try to put up enough dog feed for the winter before the sea ice froze over. We got a few whales that fall, and some seal meat and a couple of walrus.

Right after we first opened the post, the Company sent me up to Cresswell Bay to teach the Netsiliks there to hunt seals on the floe ice. I went up with Takolik, Kavavouk, Anaija, and Peealak to teach these Netsiliks, because they'd never hunted seals that way. They'd always depended on getting seals from their breathing holes in the ice, and sometimes it is hard to do this because the seals can die and sink down under the ice where you can't get them after you've hit them. But at the floe edge you could get twenty or thirty seals a day any time you went out. The Netsiliks soon got used to this new way, they learned very quickly.

Farley Mowat said the Dorsets thought the Netsiliks didn't like strangers around, and that the Netsiliks were "inhospitable" and that the Dorsets "disliked and distrusted" the Netsiliks. But that wasn't true, there weren't any such feelings and they all got along perfectly okay, then and later on as well.

In the late fall, once the ice made and we had everything under cover, we could travel around the area by dogs. We went down about halfway to Thom Bay to about three different camps the people had around there and spread the word about the Fort Ross post starting up. Thom Bay is a fairly long way from Ross, maybe 150-160 miles, and it would take three or four days to get there.

Travelling like this was old stuff to me by now. In the evenings after we'd made camp and had some supper, sometimes we used to play cards, or sit around and talk, but by the time you had your snow house up and got in and had a feed, you'd be pretty tired anyway and we'd generally go to bed pretty early.

Sometimes we used to play cat's cradle — that's basically working a long joined string into patterns with your hands and telling a story along with it. Somebody would make a caribou, like the caribou was running, and other things like polar bears and dogs. It would often be a real story like about a hunt, but I think sometimes the people used to make up things too.

When we'd pull into a camp for overnight, everybody would run out and greet us. They'd come out and shake hands and then they'd pitch in and help us to make our own camp. Sometimes some of the people, if they had a big snow house, would invite us to stay with them. When you'd do that they'd give you the best that they had, they'd make you comfortable and they'd dry your clothing out for you — we always used to wear deerskin clothing. Even when we made our own camp, they'd come over and they'd say like they had two lamps going, and take our stuff over and hang it above their seal oil lamps to dry out.

Probably I should explain about these lamps because they didn't only use them for light. They could be pretty big, some as long as a couple of feet or so, and they were made out of stone in a long narrow sort of half-moon shape, hollowed out with a shallow place for the oil or fat. The people would fix racks over them to hang pots from for cooking, or to put their clothing on to dry out after they'd been out in the snow or weather.

The people at these camps wouldn't have to ask what the new post store at Ross was carrying, what kind of goods, since they were all the same in those days. At that time the Bay just carried the basic things — guns and ammunition, tobacco, tea, sugar, oil. I don't remember that they carried any tinned goods at all at that time. Rolled oats, of course, and lard and flour — just the basic things. Of course the people never depended on these things. As long as Eskimos could hunt and had some sugar and tea and tobacco, they were satisfied.

In the old days after ships started coming into that part of the world, there were a lot of shipwrecks and the Eskimos would get pieces of iron and copper and stuff like that off those wrecks and make their harpoons, and when the Bay came it used to stock metal they could use for that.

So the stage the people were at then, they used the white man's goods, but if that wasn't around handy, like at a post store, they could still live by their old ways, as long as there was game around and they could get enough to feed themselves and their dogs.

All but the guts and feathers

When we'd got the post house finished at Fort Ross, Nipisha moved in with me, so we were now living common-law. That's when my marriage really began. We were formally married several years later.

There was no hassle with the Bay about me being married to an Eskimo lady, and they put us in the records as married at that time. But the Company was very strict about their employees and their relations with Eskimo women, and I'd known that their policy wasn't in favour of this kind of thing. But I thought this was my own business, so I just waited to see if anything would happen.

Nipisha had plenty to do to keep her busy while I was out visiting camps and doing other things for the Bay. She was still the house maid and she used to do the cleaning in the post house, washing up, and keeping the house clean, so she was an employee of the Bay too.

In 1938 we had our first child, Bella, born on February 14. I called her that after my brother's wife who used to treat me really good when I was a kid. We also gave her an Eskimo name, Ningyooga, after my wife's grandmother.

People are always asking me what it was like for a woman having a baby up in this part of the world then when there was no medical help. They usually know that Eskimos have done this this way for centuries, but somehow I guess they think me being white would make it seem worse or something.

Actually it was very simple. I was never excited about it. Well, I was excited about having my own first child, sure, but by now I thought birth was a very natural thing, and I never had any nervous feelings or anything like that. My wife was up the next day, and within a day or two she was back to normal, which is enough to make you think some of the fuss down south about this isn't necessary at all.

To carry the baby around, or "packing" it as we say in the north, she'd carry it in the hood of her parka, and at first, when the kid's real little, it's naked. This is the way it was done all through the Arctic as far as I know, from the Labrador right to Alaska they did the same thing.

The baby sits in the back and the parka's built so that if the baby wants to show its face out, it can, and so that the baby's not cramped up, his legs always fit around the body of the person that's carrying him. The parka hood can be pulled up to

111

protect both the mother and the kid from the weather, and it's made so that the baby can be swung around to the mother's breasts without having to take him out of the parka.

For diapers we used flannelette that the Bay sold. I don't think that was what the Bay carried it for, but that's what it got used for a lot of the time. Eskimo women living out on the land didn't have this, of course. They used to use moss instead; they had nothing else.

At Ross I had a lot of freedom to go out hunting and trapping. Mr. Learmonth, the manager, liked to do that sort of thing himself. Once we had our work done and the books up to date, and there was no great rush for trading, he and I used to take turns going out hunting. As long as we had everything up to date, one of us and the other clerk could manage the post easily.

Sometimes I'd go out to the floe edge for seal, and other times I'd be trapping foxes or fishing. We'd hunt most anything, we had to get a lot of food for our dogs. Kavavouk would go with me sometimes, but not always, because he was our post servant and he had his work that he had to do.

A Hudson's Bay Company employee was expected to look after his own dogs if he had his own. Not all did, but since I'd bought a dog team of my own now, of course I had to look after them. At that time I would have paid $10 for a bitch and $15 for a male, and I'd have anywhere from twelve to eighteen dogs. Eighteen is a lot of dogs and it took a lot of hunting and fishing to keep them fed.

Of course the only time we'd use eighteen dogs was when we were going on long trips, like if we were going away for a week or so. On short trips, with little or no load, eight or ten dogs, twelve at the most, was enough.

On some posts the Bay owned its own team. They bought the dog feed, but the post servant used to have to look after that Company team, feeding them and seeing that they had proper harness and traces in good repair all the time, and the Bay paid for this.

Anything that I was able to catch hunting or trapping was mine personally, not Bay property. I'd trade it just like the people did, so I had a chance to make some extra dollars. In fact, I made more by trapping than I did with wages most years. I would say that in those days I probably had more freedom to do that sort of thing than a Bay employee would nowadays, and that was a good thing with my family getting started.

In the spring of the first year at Ross, while we could still travel by dogs, I took Kavavouk and Inuk and Anaija and we went up to Port Leopold where the Company had had a post ten or eleven years earlier. It was about 120 miles north of Fort Ross. When they'd closed it down, a lot of things were left there and they wanted me to go up and take an inventory. There were things like coal and coal oil and other stuff, they weren't sure what, and they were getting ready to re-open Leopold as a little outpost, just a seasonal operation for trapping foxes.

On the way up we had good going, lots of grub and everything. While we were there, we were stormed out for a couple of days and got kind of short on grub, but we still figured that actually we had plenty to get back.

Well, because of storms on the way back, we couldn't go along the shore, we had to go out on the sea ice. Around Cresswell Bay there's cliffs anywhere from about 100 to 1400 feet high all along that coast, and we couldn't get across there on the land because of all the new snow, so we had to swing farther out on the ice. Unfortunately, another storm came up from the southeast right in our faces, and we drifted farther out on the ice.

If it had been good weather, we could have hunted and got some fresh meat, but it was too stormy for us to do that, so we were getting very short on grub.

It took us seven days before we got back onto the land again, that's seven days after we got out of grub. We'd gone that long without anything to eat. We had no tea either, but we could melt ice on our primus stove and boil water just for drinking.

Finally we got on shore. It was around the middle of May and the gulls were just coming north and hovering around those big cliffs, I'd say there were probably about a thousand of them maybe 1200 feet up. We had a lot of ammunition and so we thought that by firing at these we'd probably be able to hit one. I kept firing away and finally I hit a gull, just hit one feather in his wing. This gull started to fall, but he looked like he might almost be able to fly away again, so we all started to run to where he was coming down, and as soon as he hit the ground, we just pounced on him!

Well, that was the first thing we'd had to eat for all this long time, and I don't know why we even bothered to cook it, but anyway we skinned it and cooked it, and we ate everything of that gull except the guts and the feathers. Then we felt a little better.

Now that we'd got on shore, we put our two teams together because the snow was really deep and soft, and two of us had to walk ahead of the dogs all the time to keep them going. That's very hard work, especially when you haven't had much to eat, and it was that way until we got about ten or fifteen miles from home. Then we got onto some ground where the snow wasn't so deep and it was easier going.

We were pretty near home then, but Kavavouk and Inuk and Anaija figured that I needed something to eat more than they did. They said they could stand being hungry better than I could, so they picked the ten best dogs from both teams and hitched them to a bear skin we had, tied the hitch to the bear's nose, and told me to go on ahead. They figured I'd probably get in an hour or so ahead of them. I put my sleeping bag in a box on the old bear skin and jumped in, and this was a lot lighter for the dogs to pull than a sled, so we practically flew the rest of the way with me hanging on for dear life. Most of the ten dogs I had belonged to my father-in-law and they took me straight to Kavavouk's camp, right up to the tent door, and I could smell the beautiful smell of cooking coming out of the tent.

I just left those dogs standing there in their harness and went into the tent. My mother-in-law was making something like what you'd call doughnuts, and she had a whole plateful of them by her side on a little table.

I didn't say anything, I don't think I even looked at her, I just started eating those things, and when I did finally look up at her

she was just bug-eyed watching me. I probably ate a dozen without stopping.

Of course she was wondering what had happened to us,
where the others were, and why I looked so really thin. But I
didn't tell her a word about it until my belly was full of those
goodies.

Moscow Molly

At the beginning of our second year at Fort Ross, when the *Nascopie* came in Paddy Gibson was on it. He was supposed to take
Learmonth's place as post manager, but they talked it over and
decided that Learmonth was going to stay in Ross and that Gibson should go to Gjoa Haven to take charge there. And that's
when I had my chance that I spoke of earlier to make a little bit
of history myself.

Gibson stayed at Ross till after the *Nascopie* left and things
settled down a bit and I could get away. Then Inuk and I took
Gibson and his gear and supplies down to Gjoa in the HBC Peterhead boat called the *Seal*, which had been brought to Fort Ross
on the deck of the *Nascopie*. It was a 45-foot motor schooner
that carried about twelve tons (Farley Mowat called it a "little"
motor boat).

With this trip, we were the second Canadian craft to go
through the Bellot Strait part of the Northwest Passage, because
we had to go from Fort Ross west through the strait, down the
east side of Prince of Wales and King William Islands to get to
Gjoa, and then of course back through the strait to Ross again.

Paddy Gibson moved around quite a bit because he used to
go and inspect HBC posts in that area. On one of his inspection
trips a few years later, the plane he was on crashed and he was
burned up in the crash. There's a memorial cairn for Paddy in
Gjoa Haven now.

When the *Nascopie* came in, besides Paddy Gibson and the
usual supplies and stuff, some more people from Cape Dorset

were aboard. They'd heard about the good hunting at Ross. This was actually sort of a family reunion because one of the newcomers was Kavavouk's elder brother, Okitook, and he brought his wife and all his family; and there was Kavavouk's nephew, Napacheekadluk. And then there was another fellow, Sanganee, that came over with his family, his daughters Soosie and Akina, and his son, Kitsualik.

Farley Mowat's story had a whole lot of this wrong. He said Napacheekadluk was Kavavouk's youngest son and that he and Soosie went to Dundas Harbour with the very first Cape Dorset people that went there. And he said Soosie was a sister to my wife, Nipisha, and of course they're not related at all. Also he named Soosie's brother, Kitsualik, as her father! He also said later on that Kitsualik committed suicide in 1942, but he's still alive today in Spence Bay. Well, he got a lot more wrong that I'll mention as I go along.

After we got back from taking Paddy Gibson to Gjoa, I could go up to Port Leopold to get that outpost started again. I took some people, mostly the Dorset families, to get set up for them for catching fox. It was real good trapping country up around Leopold.

We moved up there by boat, and Nipisha and Bella went up with me. Kavavouk had a big Peterhead boat with a 36-horsepower engine, a 48-foot decked-in schooner with sails, and it could carry about nine tons of supplies. It was this boat, Kavavouk's boat, not the HBC *Seal*, as Farley Mowat said, that took us to Leopold. The second summer we had two of these boats — one of the other Dorset fellows got enough money from his trapping to buy another Peterhead. Both of these had been ordered from the HBC and brought in by the *Nascopie*, and they couldn't very well have afforded those boats if we were having "a desperately hard time of it" in Leopold and Ross as Farley Mowat wrote in his book.

After the ice made in the winter, we'd go back to Ross by dog team for more supplies for ourselves and for trading. In the spring of 1940 we left and moved back to Fort Ross so I could help get ready for the ship's arrival, and the rest of the people came along later by boats.

We didn't have to build anything new to live in at Port Leopold because the house the Company built when they were there originally was still okay. It had a kitchen, sitting room, and three bedrooms, and then there was a big area upstairs that was partitioned off and we used it for storage. The house also had a front and back porch.

I was expected to keep records and rather small diaries as usual, of course. The Company was very very strict on that. That's where I say you got a real good training with the HBC. I know I did.

I spent my time trapping mostly, and when the people wanted to trade, I'd come in and trade. We never came in contact with any white people up there. One time we saw an airplane passing over, heading north — probably to the Arctic islands somewhere.

I was in Port Leopold when war broke out in Europe. Up there I couldn't find out news of the war, how it was going, because I didn't have a radio, but they did have one at the post in Ross so I could sort of check up on the war on my trips down. They had both a transmitter and a receiver, but at first it was all in Morse code still.

When I was away at Leopold, I was always wondering what was going on. I can remember during the First World War, after three or four of my brothers had joined up, I know it seemed to me that my mum and dad were always wondering what they would hear from my brothers in the next mail.

At Fort Ross later on we used to get real good radio, wireless as they sometimes called it in those days. We always made sure that we listened three or four times a day, especially as the war went on, to keep up with the news.

Sometimes what we listened to came from Montreal, but the best station we could get was the BBC in London. Also during the war we could pick up Russia, and we used to always listen to "Moscow Molly". She used to broadcast in English, propaganda stuff.

This whole war thing was very confusing to the Eskimos. They'd ask about what we heard on the radio, and we'd tell them about how the whites were fighting and killing one another in other countries. But mostly they weren't really particularly interested in it because it didn't affect them as long as the war didn't come where we were. There was one thing they couldn't understand though. They'd say, "Well, how is it that when an Eskimo kills another man it is wrong, he's got to suffer for it, he's got to go to jail?" and "How is it that the white man can kill hundreds of people every day and get away with it?"

E5-1, an Eskimo

In the fall of 1940, after thirteen years with the Hudson's Bay Company, I quit after the new manager Bill Heslop came in to Fort Ross and took over from Lorenz Learmonth.

It wasn't because of either Heslop or Learmonth, though. What happened was that when the *Nascopie* came in, the Company wanted me to go back to Arctic Bay to work there. Well, I didn't mind going back to Arctic Bay; I'd liked it when I was there before, and I said I'd go as long as my wife and our child could go with me. But the district manager, Jim Anderson, and I couldn't see eye to eye about this. He said, "Well, why don't you go on to Arctic Bay and then come back and get them again another year."

I guess he didn't think I was serious about my marriage, but I wouldn't go alone, I wouldn't go without Nipisha. We were about to have our second kid and I thought it was my duty to stick by my wife, so I said I'd resign. But there was this new manager, and a new clerk, Allan Thorburn, and Heslop asked me if I'd stay on until they had all the stuff stored away and marked and everything, and this I agreed to.

Now, I'm not going to add any more details about leaving the Company, because it would involve too many people, and I'm not doing this book to criticise other people for what I think they did wrong years and years ago. That doesn't do any good now, and anyway everything came out all right in time.

But what I was going to do was something I had to think about pretty carefully, because I knew that if I wanted to stay in the north I was going to have to live entirely as an Eskimo. I knew it wouldn't be hard for me really, because I loved the north and I could handle myself pretty well — I had the language and the skills, and I'd be with Kavavouk and other members of Nipisha's family and other Eskimo friends. So this is what I'd made up my mind to do.

When I told the Bay that I was going to resign, they asked me what I was going to do, and I told them I was going to stay in near Fort Ross and trap. But they said, "There's no white man allowed to make a living by trapping in this region."

Major McKeand was on the *Nascopie*. He was a government man and I knew him, so I went and talked to him and told him the circumstances, and he said, "As long as you live as an Eskimo — do as Eskimos do, trap as Eskimos do, and consider yourself as an Eskimo — you can stay and trap and hunt in the Northwest Territories." This is how my status became Eskimo. I was officially on the books as an Eskimo.

When the government began giving Eskimos numbered discs in 1941, I was given the Eskimo number of E5-1, which was the first Eskimo number given in the eastern Arctic. Eskimos were given numbers because they generally only had one name and a lot of Eskimos had the same ones, and sometimes they even changed their name to something different. All this was very confusing in the records that people were trying to keep, like the RCMP, missionaries, doctors, even the Bay in some places. So the government decided to give them numbers, which I think was a very good thing.

Each settlement area had its own number — Fort Ross and Pond Inlet, for instance, started with E5, and so each person in that district had their own number with E5 in front of it, and there was no confusion at all. You could always tell where they came from by that number.

But later on the government changed all that. They started a program which they called "Project Surname" and everybody was given a second name, and I think this has caused a lot of confusion. I guess whoever suggested getting rid of the numbers said why should Eskimos be known by numbers — it's only people in jails that have numbers. But as I tried to explain, whites all have numbers — social insurance numbers, medical numbers and so forth. By getting this name-of-the-father sort of thing, we're getting all mixed up again, I think, and I favour the number system.

Anyway, name or number, I became E5-1, an Eskimo, and as far as I know, I'm the only white like this in the Arctic. If there's others like me I've never met them.

I didn't leave the post officially till October 4, and by then Kavavouk and Takolik and their families were out at our camp about six miles out of Fort Ross. We'd already moved most of our gear out by boat, and I'd bought some lumber off the HBC and had built a one-room shack about 12 by 16 feet. On the inside of the walls we'd tacked newspapers and magazines, covered the walls with them for warmth. Heating was just the seal oil lamp, and cooking was on a primus stove. We had a couple of sleeping benches and I'd bought mattresses from the Bay, and we had sheets, with deerskins for covers.

On the last trip from the post, I took my own sled and a team of fourteen dogs, and we brought the last of our cooking gear and grub and clothing. Anything we didn't want to take, we packed in a trunk and stored it on the post. Bella was dressed all in deerskins and sitting on the load on the sled, lashed on so she wouldn't fall off. Nipisha was carrying the new baby on her back. This was Johnny, and he was born October 1, just three days before we left the post.

Johnny was my second child and he was adopted by Kavavouk, his grandfather, because their kids were grown and they wanted a little kid again to look after. This was something Eskimos often did. Years later, after his grandparents died, Johnny came back to our family. My third child, Bill, was born exactly one year later, on October 1, 1941.

Our main camp was at Brentford Bay, but in the next few years we were sometimes gone from it for a while because we'd move around temporarily to be nearer to something, like the seal hunting on Brown's Island, but we were never far from the Fort Ross post.

I thought probably I was through with the Bay and with whites, but it didn't work out that way. For one thing, the Hudson's Bay Company asked me to come back to the post in spring-times on a part-time basis when they started to clean up the post and paint and this sort of a thing. I was paid a casual wage, not taken on as a full-time employee, but I did live on the post at these times. Also here and there, as you'll see, I was working along with the RCMP as interpreter in some of their investigations. In fact, I sort of had to fit my own trapping and hunting in around these other jobs.

The story of Josie

One of the first things I got involved in after we left the post at Fort Ross had to do with the Cresswell Bay people on Somerset Island, about half-way up between Ross and Port Leopold. There was a whole lot of people camped in several places up that way, hunting and trapping, Netsiliks and Dorsets.

One day this man Josie from up there came in to my camp, and he said to us, "I've lost all my family except one kid."

So we got the story out of him. He told us that he'd built his snow house, a big double snow house, at the bottom of quite a big hill, almost like a cliff, and there was himself and his wife and his mother and five kids living there. One night a big storm came up, a really bad storm. The way Josie put it was that the snow was coming over the top of that hill so fast it was like a river, just like water flowing, and he said this river of snow was flowing into his snow house and over the snow house like an avalanche.

He and one of his kids, a boy, managed to get out, but according to the way he told the story, there was so much snow that he couldn't get the rest of the family out.

121

His brother Jamesie, and Jamesie's son Jonnie, and their families were camped on the ice about half a mile away, so Josie and his boy walked down there in the storm. The next morning it had cleared up quite a bit, he said, so they went back to try to get the rest of the family out of the buried snow house. He said they dug all day and couldn't even find the snow house, so then they gave up.

When Josie told us about this, Kavavouk said, "I bet those people must have lived a long time after you gave up looking for them."

Well, this was in February of 1941 when Josie told us about the storm, and the big storm had happened about a month before. It would have taken Josie about two days to get to our camp from Cresswell Bay, so we couldn't do anything to help, because we figured those people certainly wouldn't be living by then.

Josie had just his clothes left, the winter clothing that he had been wearing, and he had most of his dogs. Some of his dogs were okay he said, because he always kept them outside, but some of them might have been inside, he thought. He had his rifle because he had left it outside, he told us.

All this was reported over to the RCMP in Pond Inlet by radio from the Ross post. When the police made their patrol in April, Constable Jack Doyle, who was head of the Pond Inlet detachment, got in contact with me for interpreting, and we went up looking for the snow house and the people that had died in it.

We found where the snow had come over the cliff and we dug down, twenty-five feet straight down. When we could pick up little bits of chips and things, we knew we were near the snow house, so we started to tunnel in. We were using shovels because the snow was packed really hard.

We finally struck one of the snow houses and got in there, and of course it was really dark down under the snow, but we could tell that the snow house was almost intact, it was only caved in a bit. We could crawl around enough to see that there was no one in that part of the snow house, but we could see dog droppings, the whole place was covered with them, so we knew that at least one dog must have been living a long time. There was seal meat and fat and stuff like that in the porch where he could eat it.

We could see where the people trapped in there had been digging a tunnel, but we couldn't follow it through because the snow they'd dug out and piled up behind them was packed so hard and so frozen. So we gave up and said, "Well, we'll have to wait till the snow melts some and then see what we can do."

Doyle went back with me to Fort Ross and stayed at the post. By then I'd started helping with the spring work and we were living there too. In August we took a boat up to Cresswell and got ashore where Josie's camp had been. There was still some snow and ice but we started to look around. About half a mile from where the snow house had been, the sun had made a little hole through some ice, and when we looked in this hole we could see a naked body. So we chopped through about a foot and a half of ice, and there was the old lady, the grandmother, lying in her bed.

What we finally figured out was that instead of coming out away from the cliff with their tunneling, they'd followed along the base of the cliff. We could follow this long tunnel they had dug through the snow along the bottom of the hill, like it would go about maybe fifty feet each time; there were six different places where we could see that they stopped when they'd got tired or couldn't dig any more. You could see where they'd stayed, they'd taken grub with them, and fat, and they'd been using their *kudliks*, their seal oil lamps.

Besides the grandmother, we found her two older grandchildren, one was twelve and the other was fourteen, and they were laying on top of the bed too without a stitch of clothing or anything on, so they would have died in their sleep.

Josie's wife was sitting up with one kid in her arms, a kid about three or four years old, and she had one in her hood that was probably around one year old. The mother must have died before the kid in the hood, because you could see where the kid had chewed on her face and her nose, probably from hunger. Probably they all died of exposure and starvation. They must have been a long time alive, because Josie said that when he left them, one boy had a brand new pair of boots, and when we found them there was a hole worn right through the heel of one of his boots.

We had Josie with us part of the time, we made him help. He was behaving okay until we found the bodies, and then he started to run towards the boat. I asked him what he was doing, and he said he was going down and shoot himself. I got him to come back, but after that he was really depressed for a while, and we had to watch him pretty close.

The policeman, Doyle, arrested Josie for criminal negligence and took him in to Fort Ross to be ready when the *Nascopie* would come in and they could hold a trial.

When the ship came in September they had an inquest, which was conducted by Inspector Martin in the ship's great big dining room. They couldn't hold a trial too, because there wasn't time, the pack ice was drifting in and the ship had to get out or take a chance of getting stuck there for the winter.

So they released Josie and they said for me to look out for him and see that he came to the ship the next year, to see that he'd be there for the trial. I said, "Does that mean I have to keep him in the camp here with me?" and they said no, that he could go where he liked but for me to see that he was there next ship time.

We were pretty sure he wouldn't run away. And he'd got over his depressed feelings, it looked like, because he'd even already taken another wife. Her name was Soosie, and she was with him down at Fort Ross when his hearing was held.

Two or three days after the ship went out, Josie and Soosie left for Cresswell Bay by boat. The first night out of Ross they camped on shore, and Josie must have got depressed again or something because he drank down a whole bottle of Sloan's Linament and just killed himself right there. And that was the end of that.

This is another part of the Soosie story that Farley Mowat told where things are wrong, especially the ending of it, which

I've just told the way it really happened. The way Mr. Mowat tells the ending is that after the hearing, Josie was by himself in Fort Ross. Then he left alone to walk the seventy miles to Cresswell Bay where Soosie was waiting for him; that when he got to within a mile of her tent Josie saw the light shining out of the tent, stopped, and put his rifle in his mouth and pulled the trigger. Well, that's a lot of baloney, as you can see. I was at the hearing. And I was the one that went to see his body at their camp by the water, and I was the one that notified the RCMP about Josie's death so they would know they wouldn't be having the trial and that the case was closed.

Mr. Mowat wrote that the two women in Josie's snow house were his mother and his aunt, instead of his mother and his wife. He also wrote that even before the snow house trouble, Josie and Soosie were planning to be married — well, Josie was already married, at least he was till his wife died in that snow house. Also he made Josie out to be very helpful during the investigation, which he certainly wasn't. I was doing the interpreting so I was there all the time, and any "help" he gave was because the policeman, Jack Doyle, made him.

Mr. Mowat made the whole thing look like Josie wasn't really guilty of anything, only that he was a victim of white laws that he didn't understand. But I think that when Josie was charged for negligence, that was the least the law could do. We all suspected that he'd left his family to die when he shouldn't have. Everyone thought there was no need for them to die; if he'd really worked at it, either during the storm or afterwards, we felt he could have rescued them. And when I say "we all suspected" and "everyone thought" I don't just mean the policeman and myself, or the white men at the post — I mean his own people too. They didn't like Josie, they didn't trust him, he had a bad reputation with them.

A lot of people don't believe it's fair to judge Eskimos by the white system of laws that were made for a different way of life. This is the reason that for a long time, and not too long ago either, Eskimos were given the benefit of the doubt. Very few

Eskimos were found guilty of murder, for instance, they were let off or given reduced sentences because whites thought that they didn't know better because they were Eskimos.

But in this particular case, I did feel it was justified to judge the Eskimo Josie by the white man's laws. I think myself that breaking the law is something you shouldn't do, and if it's punishable, you should be punished. I don't think that the law was made just for the white people.

Anyway, Josie'd been in contact with white people all his life, and his people had too. He came from Cape Dorset, and the HBC had been there since 1913, and even in those days they had the police and the law. Josie didn't need any special leniency. He couldn't help knowing he should have tried hard to save his family, harder than he did. He acted guilty. Running away when he found the bodies, I think, showed that he was aware that he'd done something wrong.

I'd been in the north for many years by then, and I knew these people; they did know better, they knew the law, what was wrong and what was right, as well as I do.

The St. Roch makes it

In 1941 the historic ship, the *St. Roch*, was trying to get through the Northwest Passage from the west, and she was supposed to meet the *Nascopie* coming from the east. They were going to meet at Fort Ross, but before the *St. Roch* could even get very close to Ross she got held up in ice and was driven in on land on the west coast of Boothia Peninsula. Luckily there was a good harbour where they went in, because she had to winter there.

The *St. Roch* was an RCMP ship and was called the floating detachment. She used to come from Vancouver every summer and bring the RCMP freight for the western Arctic, supplies they needed at their posts. She'd always winter at some settlement along the coast, and they carried a two-year supply of provisions in case they'd get stuck in somewhere like happened this time. The *Nascopie* you know well by now, and on this particular trip she'd picked up nine dogs from Greenland which were supposed to be transferred to the *St. Roch* when the two ships met at Fort Ross.

But as I say, the *St. Roch* didn't make that meeting. Skipper Larsen figured that where they got driven in was at Cape Christian on the west coast of Boothia. Larsen sent word by radio to the Ross post that after the *Nascopie* got in he wanted the dogs sent over at the first opportunity when the ice made in the fall. It needed to be four or five inches thick to travel on by dog team. Though this was after I had quit the Bay and was living at my camp, the dogs were turned over to me to look after until I could get them over to the *St. Roch*.

Well, Skipper Larsen (probably I should call him Sergeant Larsen since he was a sergeant at the time) told us he was at Cape Christian, so when the ice made some time in the beginning of November, I asked a fellow that lives here in Spence now, Anaija, and his brother Pelak, if they'd take the dogs down to the *St. Roch*. I told them that they'd be paid by the RCMP at the ship, and they were only too willing to do this. I showed them on the map where Cape Christian was, and in the meantime I told Sergeant Larsen over the radio that they would be leaving with the dogs, and that they figured it would take about three days to get there. But in about ten days they came back and said there was no ship at Cape Christian. And of course Larsen was getting kind of anxious when these men didn't turn up at the ship.

When Anaija and Pelak got back, we got on the radio and asked Larsen was he sure he was at Cape Christian, and he described what the place looked like. He said there was quite a big bay there and he said there was two arms to it and that the *St. Roch* was in the north arm.

I'd been trapping down around that way, and I said it sounded more like Pasley Bay to me. So I asked Larsen, "Have you been into the southern arm of this place you're at?" And he said, "No."

"Well," I said, "if you go up on the hill and look down on the southern arm, see if you can see a little shack there. If you see a shack there, this is Pasley Bay."

I guess Larsen was a bit embarrassed, but probably the mistake was due to his compass being out. It turned out that it was off about a degree and a half — about ninety miles. The north magnetic pole is only about 300 miles from there so it probably affected his magnetic compass.

Not long after that Larsen came over to Fort Ross with an Eskimo that he had working on the ship with him, Equallak from Gjoa Haven. They picked up the dogs that the *Nascopie* had brought, and went back to the ship. Now that's another story in a book that got things all wrong. In a book called *Plowing the Arctic** they had me practically saving Skipper Larsen's life on that deal.

What actually happened was that Skipper Larsen radioed the post that he was coming over from Pasley Bay to my camp to get the dogs I was keeping for him. But of course he didn't know the way, so the post manager sent a note down to my camp asking me to come to the post when I could and take Larsen back with me.

Now generally if I was home at the camp on a Saturday — I used to be away a lot, trapping — but if I was there on a Saturday, I'd always visit the post and stay in there until about midnight or one o'clock. We'd be playing cards or something. We'd often go in to the post other times too, and because of all this going back and forth there was a hard-beaten path for the six miles between the post and my camp. So when I'd leave Fort Ross to go home, I never had to watch where the dogs were going, the dogs would just gallop down that path.

That's the way it was on this trip with Sergeant Larsen. We did start out late at night, I think it was about half past one, and it was quite stormy, that much is true; but there was no sweat, my team took us right home in about twenty-five minutes.

But according to this book, Larsen also had a team and the storm was so bad that his dogs gave him trouble and wanted to stop, and he couldn't see anything and was sure we were lost and had gone past my camp. The book said that I was his guide and

*G.J. Tranter, *Plowing the Arctic*, Longmans, Green & Co. (Toronto, 1945).

128

that I'd stop our teams now and then and put up my head to "sniff and listen, and sniff and listen", to try to figure out where we were so we could keep travelling. But it said Larsen wanted to stop and make camp and wait out the storm, that he was worried that "it would be easy to lose one's way, travelling in wild circles before one became exhausted and froze where one stood." But the book said, "The guide had his nose on the alert now and he was following it with swift, sure steps." And then finally I was supposed to have called out, "The coast! The coast! We've found the coast! It is not far now." Oh boy!

So you can see for yourself what a lot of b.s. some people put out, how they make such a big thing out of nothing at all!

While the *St. Roch* was wintered in, they were doing patrols from the ship to Gjoa Haven, Pelly Bay, even to Cresswell Bay and the Prince of Wales Island where there were some camps. There wasn't any crime in that area at that time for them to investigate; what Larsen was actually doing on those patrols was taking the census.

There was only one incident I can remember that Larsen had to investigate, and that was about two hunters that had got a hole knocked in their boat by a walrus, and the hunters got killed. They didn't drown, but they perished in the icy water before another boat could get to them.

We got to know the *St. Roch* people during the winter, and there was one sad thing happened. One of the fellows, his name was Chartrand, had a heart attack — it was on February 13 — and he died. This happened one day when Takolik and I were going over to visit the ship, and we were able to help bury him, and also to help build part of a cairn that's up to his memory today there in Pasley Bay. That cairn is fourteen feet high and it's marked with a bronze or copper plate saying who he was and how he died and this sort of a thing.

In August 1942 the *St. Roch* finally left Pasley Bay. They had an awful hard time, but they finally arrived in Fort Ross at night after coming through a lot of ice. It was what we'd call growlers — big, big chunky ice, the leftover winter's ice, some of it six or seven feet higher than the ship. It was a great feeling, seeing the ship make it through. Of course the post manager was on hand, and we were invited aboard for supper. The crew had a thing written out that they were the second boat ever to go through the Northwest Passage. But actually the second boat through was in 1938, as I already mentioned, when myself and Inuk had taken Paddy Gibson through the strait down to Gjoa in the *Seal* and we returned that way also. The first, as I've said, was the Hudson's Bay ship, the *Aklavik*, in 1937.

Anyway they had this record thing about the *St. Roch* to put in the cairn at Fort Ross. The cairn is right up from the old post house and it's got all sorts of names and records in it. It was put up by McClintock when he was there looking for the remains of the Franklin expedition, and when we first arrived at Ross on the *Nascopie* in 1937 we were told to go ashore and get this old record out of the cairn if possible. Unfortunately a couple of the RCMP boys got ashore before any of us HBC fellows did, and they went up to where the cairn was. It had been broken down by bears, but they did find the record outside of it. So that's once the RCMP got it over the HBC. Since then there's been I guess fifty or sixty records put in there by different people. It's almost like reading a history when you go there. You can dig in and pick out a can or a jar of almost any sort — cigarette cans, pickle jars — they have all sorts of records in them.

The *St. Roch* was a fairly good-sized ship, 104 feet long, made of wood. They had a dining room, and of course bunks down in the forecastle for the crew to sleep. The skipper had a room on the upper deck, and the wireless operator also had a room on the deck. The dining room was nicely furnished, and in their sleeping quarters they had pictures on the walls, like their girlfriends or some magazine pin-ups, in there above their beds. That ship is now in Vancouver in the Maritime Museum.

We all talked up a storm at supper on the *St. Roch* that night, though I don't remember just what we talked about. I guess generally when a bunch of guys get together they talk about females, but we didn't at that occasion because Barbara Heslop was there, the post manager's wife. Since their ship had been wintered in, the men were anxious to get back "outside" and they talked a lot about what they'd do when they got out and this sort of thing.

They stayed in Ross a couple days because all the water around there was full of ice like the strait. Some of the crew could come ashore, but they always had to have three or four fellows on board all the time as lookouts.

Finally a lead opened up. Skipper Larsen didn't figure he could get through, but Kavavouk and myself knew how deep the water was and we knew they could get through. We piloted him through between Brown's Island and what we called Possession Point, which was around on the north side from the inlet into Bellot Strait, and that's how the *St. Roch* finally got away.

Now just after this the *Nascopie* tried to get in to Fort Ross. We could see her out there in the ice for about three days, but the ice had already closed up too much, and no leads opened up, so she had to turn back. She was only eight or ten miles out, but there was almost solid ice, pack ice, between her and the shore, so we had figured that she wouldn't be able to get in; and of course they couldn't any of them from the ship come across the ice and talk to us either — with pack ice there's little bits of water too wide to get over by jumping across.

But nobody felt too bad about the ship, because there was a fair amount of supplies left over from the year before. We were most disappointed really about not getting the mail. But working up there we had to learn pretty quick to accept whatever happens. Even Mrs. Heslop took things as calm as anything. The ship couldn't get in the next summer either, but by then it was different. The supplies were really low, with just a small amount of flour and tea left. Still, the Heslops shared everything they had with us.

Ernie Lyall in 1951 when he was a clerk for the Hudson's
Bay Company at Spence Bay. (E. Lyall collection)

Major McKeand presenting Father Girard with a medal for long service in the north, Pond Inlet, 1935. (Jack Doyle)

Lake Harbour on Baffin Island in 1918, ten years before
Ernie Lyall arrived here to work at HBC post. (Hudson's Bay
Company)

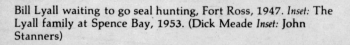

Bill Lyall waiting to go seal hunting, Fort Ross, 1947. *Inset:* The Lyall family at Spence Bay, 1953. (Dick Meade *Inset:* John Stanners)

INFORMAATION FORWARDED TO ROSS FROM PANGK
RE CASE OF PITSULAKS WIFE AT SIKERNIK.

Nearly hopeless stop Midwife insert hand into
womb grasp one or both feet pull them and
body down while assistant helps turn baby by
manipulatiom abdomen stop Baby is delivered
with back to mother's front stop Head now delivered
by resting baby on ~~in ~ forearm inserting finger~~
in mouth to keep head bent on chest, right hand
pulling steadily on legs , assistant keepimg steady
pressure on womb both hands   stop   With head
at outlet bend body towards mothers abdomen
so that chin face forehead delivered stop
Very difficult but only chance save womans life
Hope you understand stop   Probably infection
stop   Best of luck would like to hear result

                    Dr T J Orford
                    Pangnirtung

Telegram from Dr. T. Orford at Pangnirtung, with instructions
to EWL on delivering a baby, 1951. (E. Lyall collection)

Kavavouk, EWL's father-in-law, Spence Bay, 1955. (Ernie Lyall).

Soosie, Kavavouk, Napacheekadluk, and Keegotak, Spence Bay, 1963. (Bill Pringle)

Inside the HBC store at Spence Bay, 1962. *Left to right:* Napachee, Barbara Lyall, Kathy Lyall, EWL, and Ralph Knight. (George Hunter, Hudson's Bay Company)

Commissioner Stuart Hodgson
and EWL at Spence Bay, 1976.
(Ed Ogle)

Equalla, Aqqaq, and Takolik having a mug-up at EWL's house
after trading, Spence Bay, 1963. (Ernie Lyall)

Ernie Lyall as Justice of the Peace administering the RCMP oath of allegiance to his son, Charlie, while Corporal K. Hunter looks on, 1973. (courtesy Superintendent H. Fagin)

"Kawgk! Kawgk! Kawgk!"

When the *Nascopie* couldn't get in to Fort Ross that summer of 1942 she landed all the freight, mail, and HBC mess — winter's food for the post employees — at Arctic Bay, so we knew we'd have to go over there by dog team to haul some stuff back. There were still no supply planes just yet. While it was maybe only 180 miles between Ross and Arctic Bay on a map, it was close to a 300-mile trip travelling that stretch by dogs. In the next few years we made that trip several times, what with the ship not getting into Ross the next year also, and later after that post had to be closed, having to go to Arctic Bay for our trading and supplies, and one thing or another.

Travelling conditions didn't change much from year to year, it was always a hard trip. We couldn't get away while the water was still open and the ice was floating around. It takes a long time till freeze-up there because Prince Regent Inlet, which we had to cross to get to Baffin Island and Arctic Bay, is moving ice all the time. You can't cross until a certain time of the year, generally around March, and even then you are still crossing on moving ice and there's only certain times you can make it across.

Up in Prince Regent, when the tide is going out, the ice goes off from the shore, so far off you can't even see it. In twelve hours the ice comes back in on the coast with the tide; then as soon as it gets in, you have to get on it right away, even though it is moving. Once you're out on that ice, a great big ice pan like a mile wide and ten or twelve miles long, you start moving across it. Even crossing a big pan like that you might come to long leads of open water, and then you have to travel either north or south to see if you can find a place to cross. If you can't, you have to stay there for a day and a night or so until the water freezes over.

If you've got a small crack of open water that the dogs can jump, well then the sled can cross that. Sometimes though, if it was a little wider than we figured, we'd have the dogs half falling into the water and then they'd just swim to the edge. Generally most of them climb out, but some can't and then you have to go over and pull them out. But we would never drive dogs into the water unless we knew that the sled could bridge the crack. This builds a sort of trust between you and the dogs — the dogs will trust you that they can do this thing, and you know that the dogs will get where they're going.

Sometimes we'd find the ice thin enough to give way as we were travelling across. Ice like this is sort of rubbery, it ripples, and if you actually come to a complete stop, the sled can go through the ice; but as long as the sled is going fast enough, it won't go down. Sometimes we had to fool the dogs a little bit to get them moving fast enough over this kind of ice. Our dogs were trained as bear dogs, and we'd give this certain call that meant bears, and they'd get so excited they'd just take off.

Of course we expected to hunt along the way on these trips. When you see a bear before the dogs get on the track, you give the bear call, which is like a crow sound, "Kawgk! Kawgk! Kawgk!" We'd go on like that, and then we'd do it easier, "Kawgk," just once and softer, and the dogs would look around, and then we'd make it louder, "Kawgk! Kawgk!" and point the way we wanted them to go. Then they'd really take off like hell — whether we were just trying to get across the thinner ice, or really going after a bear.

If we were really going after a bear, we might just see the tracks and we'd use the bear call to get the dogs going along till they could pick up the scent. As soon as we'd sight the bear, we'd let a couple of dogs loose that had been trained for bringing bears to bay. I had a good bear dog, a bitch, and she could stop two or three bears at the same time. She'd be barking all the time, and if the bears started to run, she'd go up and nip at their hind legs — that's where she'd generally bite a bear.

Sometimes when we were running races, we used to use this bear call to get the dogs all excited and make them run faster. But we had to be careful not to use it too much when there really wasn't a bear around, because the dogs would get suspicious and wouldn't respond to it.

On these trips to Arctic Bay, when we got bears we used the meat for dog feed, and then sold the skins at the post. I think we sold them for about $5 each, because we didn't flense them or anything — we couldn't when we were travelling like that. But one time I took five bear skins to the HBC for trading, and they were really clean and good, scraped clean and white, and I got $9 each for three of them and $12 each for the other two. Of course nowadays, if you walk in as a customer to buy one, you'll pay between $400 and $800 for just an ordinary one, and not too long ago they were selling for $2000 for a big one in real good condition with the backing and trimmings on it.

One time Takolik and myself made one of those trips from Fort Ross to Arctic Bay, we had one sled and nineteen dogs. The post manager at Arctic Bay then was Jimmy Bell, and the clerk was Ken Hunt who'd been with us earlier at Fort Ross. When we got in, the first thing Jimmy did was hand me a glass of scotch, but he says, "For God's sake, Ernie, go and have a bath!" We stayed there about a week that time I guess, so we had a really good pow-wow with them. Then we stocked up with grub mostly, and mail of course, and anything we could haul, like tea, sugar, flour — stuff like that. I figure we must have been carrying back over a ton of stuff. The sled was twenty-two feet long, and it was loaded very high.

The trips back to Ross were tricky when we had a heavy load on, and getting in shore was real rough on us. Sometimes there was so much ice we had to take the stuff off the sled and portage it, relay it, come back and get the rest later.

Once you get to shore and travel over the land along the shore ice, it's smoother. Once you've crossed that 75-mile stretch across Prince Regent Inlet you can hug the land the whole way, and it's fairly easy going except for crossing the bay right into Fort Ross. It's the sea ice that's really rough going sometimes.

By the way, these trips were nothing like Farley Mowat made them out to be. They were tricky because of the special ice conditions that I've described, and they were hard going as I've said, but we never ever got lost, or "staggered in" to Arctic Bay in bad condition, or were ever starving — either us or our dogs — like he said. There was plenty of good hunting on the way.

So we had to bury him again

Two years in a row the *Nascopie* couldn't get in to Fort Ross, and the second year, in the summer of 1943, it couldn't even get near enough for us to see it. The Hudson's Bay Company had to deal with this situation, and they were sending messages back and forth on the radio between Fort Ross and Winnipeg to Bill Heslop, the manager at Ross. Well, they decided on an airdrop, and that was something new for us.

It was November, as I remember, when the ice got thick enough so they could make a drop, and they sent in a load of stuff on a C-46, which is the American style of a DC3. This was enough stuff, they figured, to last the HBC staff at the post a month or so, and also enough to share some out with all the people, until the ice got thick enough that they could land a plane on it.

It was really very exciting, seeing the parachutes opening up. Besides the regular grub and stuff, there were special goodies — some cigarettes and chocolate bars, even some liquor, everything they could think of. And some mail, too. They really thought of everything. Nothing got down where we couldn't find it or couldn't get to it, and nothing got smashed at all. We carried everything back to the post about half a mile away.

Some time before Christmas we told them the ice was thick enough — they wanted it to be forty-eight inches — to land a plane on. They told us they were going to send a plane over first to drop a parachutist, his name was Stanwell Fletcher, and he would pick a landing place and fix it up and get it marked okay for a plane to land on a few days later. Later on Fletcher had a nearby lake named after him.

They decided to drop Fletcher at Hazard Inlet, which is about half a mile along the bay from the post, and they told us to get all the people we could and have them scattered around the area so they could help Fletcher in case he got into trouble when he landed. We were all ready, and the plane came down to 3000 feet, and when we saw Fletcher come off the plane he looked just like a little matchstick figure.

We had the people spread out in pairs all over the place. Napacheekadluk and myself were together, and Fletcher landed not too far from us, so I said, "Run like hell," because it looked to me like the parachute was caught up around him. Napacheekadluk was running ahead of me, I couldn't keep up with him, when all of a sudden he stopped and began running the opposite way. I kept on running and as I got up to Fletcher he was pulling out his flare gun — he was to shoot off a red one if he was hurt, and if he was okay he'd shoot off a green one. For some reason or other, he shot off a red one and, of course, the plane thought he was in trouble. While he was fumbling around trying to find the green one, the plane started to come lower — that old plane was just coming right down over top of us, almost touching the ground. But finally he found the green one and shot it off.

The day afterwards I said to Napacheekadluk, "When you were getting up to the parachutist there, why the hang did you run away so suddenly, run back?"

"Well," he said, "I saw him pulling out his gun and I thought he was a German and was going to shoot me!"

At this time the Eskimos were still a little bit scared, they had this thing about the Germans and the war, and they thought that maybe the Germans were going to come and kill the people, and all that sort of thing.

It was quite an event for the people, seeing a person parachute down, and for me too. It was the first one I'd seen.

Fletcher found a place about ten miles from the post on the lake which was pretty smooth and could be used for a runway, and we got it marked out. We made humps of snow with coal sacks draped over them so they looked black, and this was the first time ever that we had to fix up for a plane to land.

This plane that was coming was a U.S. Air Force plane and when it landed it was going to pick up the Heslops, the post manager and his wife, and the clerk, Darcy Munro, and take them out. They were closing up the post because it couldn't operate with no provisions after the ship couldn't get in for two years in a row.

About four days after Fletcher was dropped, they brought the plane down, which was a real event. There weren't too many of the people around at that time, but the ones that were didn't know what to make of it all. This was the first plane they'd ever seen on the ground and up close.

It was getting dark when the plane was coming in, so we had a Gibson Girl to help it land. A Gibson Girl is a beacon that sends out a signal and there's a 500-foot aerial on it, a wire aerial with a balloon attached to it, and you have to be cranking, cranking this thing all the time for it to send out the signal. You can also talk to a plane with it if you use Morse code, but you can't talk and send out the beacon signals at the same time. I didn't use it to talk to the plane this time because it was getting late and it was blowing really hard, so we were in a real big hurry.

We had to load the post staff's gear on the plane and then get the staff and the parachutist aboard. We didn't even have time to speak to the pilot or any of the fellows on the plane. But just as the plane turned around for takeoff, the pilot opened his window in front and threw out a few cartons of cigarettes.

Farley Mowat, after he wrote about the Bay post people being flown out like it was a big dramatic rescue of "marooned" whites, said someone asked me years later why I hadn't "taken the opportunity to escape in the plane" too, and that I said, "Don't know why I stuck it out there. Things didn't look too good at all, you know. Nothing left at the post and nothing to get from the country. Sure was hard to see that plane take off and head south, but my wife and kids, it was their people here, and I guess you'd say they'd sort of become my people too."

Baloney! I never would have said any such thing to anybody! There wasn't anything to "escape" from — this was the place where I'd *chosen* to hunt and trap and live with my wife and family, and these people certainly *were* my people. Also there were some supplies left at the post but we didn't really *need* them because there certainly was plenty on the land to keep us going. And it certainly wasn't "hard" for me to see that plane head south — I never wanted to leave the north, and still don't.

Anyway, the Fort Ross post was closed temporarily, and after all that flap I could get back to more like normal, trapping and hunting, supporting my family which was getting bigger, because my fourth child, Barbara, was born on December 28, 1943.

The *Nascopie* not getting in affected more than just the way things worked for the HBC post, it also changed the way an RCMP case got worked out.

In 1942 I'd been helping in a murder investigation at Thom Bay. At that time there was a whole lot of people at Thom, probably twenty families. In the latter part of June that year, some of the people came in to Fort Ross from Thom and they told us that a woman shot her husband there.

The *St. Roch* was still frozen in at Pasley Bay and so we reported this to Sergeant Larsen. He would have come over to investigate, but it was too late in the year to come over by dog team and too early to get there by boat, so it had to be turned over to the RCMP at Pond Inlet. They couldn't come then either because of travel conditions, so the next year they came over on patrol in the spring with two dog teams, and they left this police-man Louis DeLisle at Ross to investigate this case. I was on the case with DeLisle to interview the witnesses, I was translating.

What happened, the way the people told it to us, was that a fellow named Ekooteelook had been shot by his wife, Mik-tayout. She had earlier fallen in love with another man and was promised to him, but the camp boss made her marry Ekootee-look instead. She kept wanting to be with the man she loved, and even tried to run away one time, but the camp boss and another fellow went after her and caught her on the sea ice and brought her back. So after less than a year of living with Ekooteelook she just shot him one morning when he was sleep-ing, took a .22 and shot him right through the head. I don't want to give the name of the other man, the one she wanted to be with, because he's still alive.

We knew that after interviewing the witnesses we had to get the body back to Fort Ross, so before we left Ross we'd made a coffin, made it a little bit big to make sure that it would be big enough. In those days the people were pretty superstitious about disturbing a dead body, and no one wanted to show us where Ekooteelook's body was at the beginning, but finally Elijah and his brother and two other fellows showed us where it was, right on top of a big hill under some rocks. So we had to dig it up, and finally we got the body to Ross and we reburied it there.

A few days before the ship was supposed to come in, we got a message from the *Nascopie* to dig the body up, open up the coffin, and have everything ready for the ship's doctor to do his autopsy. Well, the people were already collecting there to meet the ship and we had to try to do all this without them seeing us. We decided to do it late at night by lantern light, and we got the body down into one of our sheds, and it was pretty high by this time. And then, of course, it turned out there was so much ice the ship couldn't get in after all, so we had to bury it again.

The next year, 1944, when the ship was coming, they told us to do the same thing, to get the body out and have it all ready for the doctor. And this time when we opened it up, it was sure rank, but the ship got in this time anyway, and the doctor had an autopsy and they held an inquest right there on the ship.

We had gone and picked up the woman, Miktayout, from Thom Bay, and with the prisoner there, and the witnesses, they had a trial on the ship. Sub-Inspector Peacock charged her with murder, but she was convicted of manslaughter and was sentenced to one year and sent to Pangnirtung. She never did go back to Thom Bay — she was married at Pang and then she died a few years after that of tuberculosis.

Tea leaves on your eyes

In 1945, on September 8, Nipisha and I got married officially. This came about on the ship when it came in to Fort Ross that summer. Major McKeand, the fellow that used to come up representing the government, was on the *Nascopie*. I went to him, I knew he was a judge and he was an old friend of ours by this time, and I said, "Do you marry people?" and he says,

"Yes," and I says, "What about marrying us?" and he said, "Sure."

Of course there was always some photographers on the ship and they wanted to get pictures and all this sort of a thing, but we didn't want this, so we just had a private civil marriage in the saloon of the *Nascopie*, with two witnesses there, that was all. The HBC district manager, J.W. Anderson, was one witness, and Dr. Dennis Jordan was the other. He was the ship's doctor, employed by the Hudson's Bay Company.

After the ceremony we went ashore, and Dr. Jordan and Mr. Anderson said what about putting on a little "do" for us, so that night they did, with wine and a good dinner. There was a lot of people present, including the tourists off the ship, I'd say twenty-five or thirty people. I guess the tourists had heard a little bit about me living as an Eskimo, and they bugged me with a whole bunch of questions, but I didn't want to get involved in all that and I told them that I had my own life to live and that was it.

The newspapermen — there always were some that came up with the *Nascopie* to write about the north — were really mad at me because they wanted to take pictures of the wedding and the dinner, but I especially asked that there be no pictures taken. Dr. Jordan, though, had been coming up for quite a few years and he was a good friend of ours. All these years, I think it was six altogether, he'd been taking a series of movies, and he asked if we'd let him take some, just a few pictures, and we let him do this.

At this same time I was asked about being rehired by the HBC, I think it was Mr. Anderson asked me. He was the one that I'd had the argument with in 1940 when I wouldn't transfer to Arctic Bay without Nipisha. John Stanners was the post manager who'd come in with the *Nascopie* the year before to reopen the Ross post, and he asked me before the ship came this time, "Do you want to go back with the Bay?" I said I would if I got the chance, though it would mean I wouldn't be so free, of course. I'd been used to the freedom of the Eskimo way of living, going where I wanted to and being my own boss. They sent a message to the Bay in Winnipeg that John said I'd be a good one to work for the Company, seeing as I knew all the people around Ross and spoke the language and whatnot. The Bay records don't show that I was hired then — not until 1949 when they started the post at Spence Bay — but since I was getting payment from them during this time, I guess it doesn't matter how they listed me. They did get our marriage in the records, though.

On December 3 that year my fifth kid, Pat, was born. That was pretty hectic because Nipisha and I had moved into our house at the post again after the ship left, but the rest of her family was still out at our camp. The night that Nipisha was going to have the baby, it was really blowing and storming, so I got John Stanners to come down to my house, and I harnessed up the dogs to go out and get Nipisha's mother.

My first child, Bella — by this time she was nearly seven — always used to go with me when I'd go with the dog team, so I took her, and in the storm we got lost. I didn't know where the hang I was, and it was about three or four hours before I got to camp, which as you know by now, was only six miles from the post.

This time it wasn't like when Skipper Larsen and I made that trip, because by now "home" for the dogs was the post, and also there wasn't that much of a path to the camp, so the dogs weren't any help to me. Finally I had to go by the wind for my directions; if you can see the snow on the ground, there's ridges where the prevailing wind generally blows.

Well, I was getting really worried because all of Nipisha's kids were born very quickly. When we finally found the camp it must have been about four o'clock in the morning and I got them out of bed and got Nipisha's mother. Going back was faster, and I guess Nipisha probably held back till her mother got there, and then it wasn't a very long labour, and so Pat was safely born that night. Betty, my sixth kid, was also born at Fort Ross, on November 17, 1947.

In the spring of 1948 John Stanners was still at Ross, and we got a message saying that the *Nascopie* wouldn't be coming in again that summer, but this time it was because she had sunk off

Cape Dorset — I heard that she ran on an uncharted reef. Well, John had expected to go out on holidays when the ship came in, and also the HBC were thinking now that they'd close Ross because the rough ice conditions had been making it so hard to get the supply ship in. They wanted to build another post somewhere between Ross and Pelly Bay. John got a message saying that no planes would be coming to Fort Ross with supplies, but that the company plane would be going to Gjoa Haven on an inspection trip — they had a Beaver, I think it was — and that he was to close the post and meet the plane on April 1 in Gjoa.

That winter Stephen Alookee had frozen his feet pretty badly. We'd had him in the staff house there looking after him, but he was getting worse all the time with gangrene and we couldn't control it. We decided to take him with us to Gjoa and we made a box to haul him in on a sled with us so he could be evacuated out to hospital on that same plane.

So myself, Takolik, Napachee, Johnny Tucktoo, and John Stanners loaded up. We were taking three teams because we had Alookee and John's gear and, since this was a long trip, around 250 miles, we had twenty-five bags of dog feed and our own grub and stuff for the trip. We encountered a lot of bears going down, but we only shot five. They weren't any danger to us, we shot them to be sure we'd have dog feed on the way back.

None of us had ever gone down to Gjoa before by dog team, but there were a lot of Netsiliks around Fort Ross and they knew the way, so we asked them, "Well, how do you go to Gjoa?" and they said to just go straight across Boothia south, but they said, "You won't be able to see Gjoa Haven from Boothia." They told us we could see across to nearby King William Island, and they said, "The first thing you'll see is a big high land, like cliffs, but don't head for that because that's the north end of King William and Gjoa Haven is south, the post is on the south end of the island."

So we left on March 19 and when we did see those cliffs it was hard for us not to go towards them because it looked like it really ought to be the right place, but we kept on going anyway, the way we'd been told to. Once we had some trouble with snow-blindness though we were all wearing regular goggles, white-man kind. The remedy we used to use was to put wet tea leaves in a cloth and hold that on your eyes for a while — the only thing we ever found that was any good at all. Once when we made camp we thought we were going to have to backtrack, that we'd gone the wrong way, but I went up on a hill, and down below I could see the sea ice and this little bay, and so instead of having to backtrack, we were okay and in a couple of days we got into Gjoa.

It was April 2 when we got there, and we thought the HBC plane would be waiting for us, but they'd got held up, they'd been stormed out at Cambridge, and they got to Gjoa the next day and we got Stanners and Stephen Alookee aboard all right. After that the rest of us went back to Fort Ross. We got back on April 19, two days after my birthday which I'd forgot all about till after I got home.

We were intending to come right back down south that spring and help with the new post the HBC was establishing in Spence Bay, but unfortunately just before we were ready to leave, one of the fellows got shot in the foot and of course he couldn't make a trip like that, and then I got involved in some other things, so it wasn't until the next spring that we moved down to the new post.

"I don't want to die in white man's country"

Some time after we got back to Fort Ross, to our camp, after that trip to Gjoa Haven, we heard that there was some sort of sickness going around with the Cresswell Bay people. At that time there was nothing we could do about it as it was the in-between season when we couldn't travel, so we couldn't go up there and see. As a matter of fact, we didn't think then that it was very bad.

Late one day in August, this was in 1948, we heard a plane come in, and from our camp we could see that it had landed near the post. Then we heard it take off again, and of course we were all wondering what this was about and whether the plane had left someone at the post.

We'd had a storm the day before and our motorboats were all pulled up on shore, so we had to wait for the tide to rise before we could go and check. When we got there we could see there was a light in the house at the post, and we were really excited. Lo and behold it was Mr. Learmonth, who had been the first post manager at Ross. The float plane that brought him, a Canso, was the Bay's plane but this time he was going around doing archaeology work.

The first thing he asked us was if we'd have a cup of tea. Well, with the post closed we didn't have much grub left, a little tea and no sugar and a little bit of flour, and this was the first time we had sugar in our tea for several months.

Mr. Learmonth said he didn't bring any food in because they'd told him there was enough stuff left in the store, which was true, so we were really glad when the next day he took us in to the store and gave us all the grub we needed. There was flour and sugar and lard and baking powder and things like that which we certainly could have used because we'd been getting used to what we called "white man's grub". I didn't have a key to get in for anything because when John Stanners closed the post and left, we all figured we would be leaving for the new post at Spence right away.

By the way, any time I say "grub" what I mean is this kind of "white man's grub" — not just food in general. There was always food on the land from hunting or fishing, though of course sometimes you had to move around to find it.

Mr. Learmonth told us why he had come in, and it turned out what he wanted to do was to go up to Cresswell Bay before it got too late in the fall. He wanted to see a lot of old stone houses up there because later he was going to try to construct one like they used to have.

He asked me if I would take him up there, and so we went by motorboat, Mr. Learmonth, myself, Takolik, and Kavavouk, in early September. There was no floating ice at all, so it was straight going, though kind of rough weather and blowing some.

The boat was just an open motorboat, a small one with an eight horsepower Acadia engine, and it just took us one day to get there.

Where we were going at Cresswell wasn't where the peoples' camp was, they were across about ten miles to the west of us. But when they discovered we were over there, these two people walked to where we were. They told us that the people at camp were real sick and that they had no grub, but they had enough seal meat and caribou and bear meat to keep them going. We went over to see what the situation was and stayed there overnight. It was the same camp where they are now, right up on Union River which is a big fish river that flows out of Stanwell Fletcher Lake.

There was seventeen people there, six or seven families, in tents. They'd run out of kerosene but they were doing their cooking with seal oil lamps. They had a lot of dogs left yet, and enough feed to keep the dogs alive.

At this time only one person had died. We had no idea at all what was wrong with the people — they told us that there was a lot of people that were getting sick right from early summer, probably around June or July. So we left them all the grub that we had and the medicine we had — Mr. Learmonth had brought along the Company medical kit with us — and we left to go back to Fort Ross for more supplies.

But sometimes it freezes up early in the season there, and by the time we got back to Ross the ice was making and we couldn't get back to Cresswell by boat. Because there's places where the ice is always moving in Prince Regent Inlet like I said, it was quite late before the ice made as far as the Cresswell Bay area, so we had to wait until November before we could get back there by dogs. When we got back up there this time we found they were in a terrible state and nine out of the seventeen people had died.

With the Fort Ross post closed we had no radio so we had no way to get word out quickly about this trouble after we got back from Cresswell. Finally, Mr. Learmonth decided that he'd try to get to Arctic Bay where they had a radio and he could send out a message to get help. It took him an awful long time to get up there because of the ice situation in Prince Regent, I think it took him just about a month. But before he left, just in case he had trouble getting to Arctic Bay, he had me write a letter to Cambridge Bay for them to radio out from there. Of course, the only way my letter could get to Cambridge was for it to be taken from one camp to another by different dog teams from those places. It went from Fort Ross all down through the camps to Gjoa Haven, and from there they sent it on along through the camps to Cambridge, where they got my letter at the end of January. That was from about the end of November that I wrote it — about two months — not much worse than the mail service is nowadays!

Here is some more that Farley Mowat got wrong. He said Mr. Learmonth (or "Learmont" as he spelled it) had sent out that "message of distress" to Gjoa Haven, that it was Takolik that took it, that he took two months to get it to Gjoa, and that his dogs had died of starvation and he'd been found wandering around half-conscious. More baloney!

Finally, on February 7 around mid-day we heard a plane coming over. We could see it circling over the post, and then it came down the coast and spotted our camp and they dropped all sorts of things to us by parachute.

John Stanners was in Cam Bay and he had packed up a lot of stuff for the people and a lot of things personally for me — candies and everything you could think of. It was just like Christmas, maybe better than any Christmas, because by this time we were running really short of grub because we'd taken so much to the Cresswell camp.

Along with this stuff they parachuted down, I noticed a little parachute with a small package attached. It was about eighteen inches by six inches and I thought it was a camera, but I didn't have time to pay any attention to it just then. The sun wasn't back yet, and there was only a while during the middle of the day when there was some light, like you get just before the sun comes up. It was getting dark again fast and we had to collect all the stuff and get it in the house.

When I looked at this small thing that I'd thought was a

camera, it turned out to be a walkie-talkie, something I'd never seen or used before. All it said on it was, "Pull out antenna, press top to talk, release to listen."

Well, fortunately, they also had dropped a letter with this and there were some more instructions about how to use it. In the letter they said they'd be back the next morning at eleven o'clock to talk to me over the walkie-talkie. There was also a diagram of how to build an air strip on the sea ice, which I had to do that night because they wanted to land on it next day when they came back.

I still have that sheet with the instructions and diagram — I kept it as a souvenir. This is exactly what it looked like and what it said:

WALKIE TALKIE

WE ARE TRYING TO MAKE RADIO CONTACT WITH YOU — PLEASE FOLLOW INSTRUCTIONS ATTACHED ON HOW TO USE. IF WE CANNOT MAKE RADIO CONTACT WITH YOU WE WILL DROP YOU SOME SIGNALLING PANELS TOGETHER WITH SOME QUESTIONS WHICH WE ASK YOU TO ANSWER

NOTE: KEEP THIS WALKIE TALKIE IN A WARM PLACE WHEN NOT IN USE.

IF CONDITIONS ARE SATISFACTORY FOR LANDING MARK OUT A 3500 FOOT STRIP, 150 FEET WIDE, INTO WIND AND FREE AS POSSIBLE FROM OBSTRUCTIONS ON APPROACH. SURFACE MUST BE FREE OF ANY SHARP OBSTRUCTIONS SUCH AS RAISED ICE. A SLIGHTLY ROLLING SURFACE IS SAFE. LAY OUT AS INDICATED

It was all typewritten in capital letters just like that, and then underneath was the diagram that showed the measurements, the direction of the wind, and the approach direction for the plane. And I marked on that sheet that it would take 1150 strides to measure off the length and 50 strides for the width of that strip.

It happened to be a bright moonlight night, which helped a lot, and we worked all night to mark the runway the way they wanted it. What we marked it out with was a lot of coal bags, like we'd used that other time for this sort of a thing. And also that year quite a few of our dogs died — we figured they had distemper — and their bodies were frozen stiff with their legs right out. There were six of them and they were black, so we stuck three of these on each side of the strip. They made really good markers, and the crews thought this was really something, so they took some pictures of that and later on they sent me some of them.

Next morning the airplane, it was a DC3, came back and landed with some more supplies for us, and the pilot asked me about the people and their sickness. I told him they were up at Cresswell Bay, and he says to me, "Could I land up there?" and I says, "I don't know for sure." He said he'd go up and take a look and see what it looked like from the plane, and that when he came back he would check with me by walkie-talkie because it would be getting too dark to land again.

In an hour and a half or so he was back again and he called me on the walkie-talkie and I answered — it was a strange feeling to me, using the walkie-talkie. He said that it didn't look too good up there, that it was a lot better at Ross, where we had the runway marked out. He asked me if it was possible to bring the sickest people down to Fort Ross (actually to Levesque Harbour which is where this landing strip was, about six miles southwest of Ross). I told him that there'd be no sweat there; we could go and get them. He asked how long it would take. I was just going to say I thought we'd be back in three days' time, when I thought to myself, "Well, if it should be stormy or anything, we might be held up," so I told him five days.

Takolik and I, just the two of us, left that night and arrived some time into the next night at Cresswell. Of course, we didn't know how many really would be sick, but we found that there was only one fellow, David Kaymayook, that was then really sick.

We went to his snow house, which had some extra porches on it for a windbreak and to keep it warmer. We went through two porches and when we came to the third to go into the house, we saw a severed foot, just lying on the snow in the porch. What had happened was that Kaymayook's feet were really rotten and gangrene-y, and his mother had just cut off the one foot the day before. She had cut it at the ankle with her *ulu*.

Kaymayook — I think he was sixteen years old at the time — was really really sick and really depressed. I felt pretty sure he wouldn't die, but I was terribly worried when I took his temperature and it was way below normal. I knew that if the temperature was too far below what it should be, it was getting to a dangerous point. He was taking a little food, not very much, just liquids; he couldn't stomach any solids at all.

Anyway, I told him what we'd come up for, to get him to take him to Fort Ross, and a plane then would take him out to Edmonton to hospital, and he says, "No, leave me alone," he says, "there's no one can do anything for me now." And he says, "I don't want to go, just leave me alone." I said, "Look, we can take you out and get you fixed up, they can give you new artificial feet." But he kept saying "No," and "I just want to stay here because I'm going to die," and "Leave me alone to die in peace, I don't want to go and die in white man's country!"

We kept talking to him and his mother decided he should go. She helped convince him, and finally it worked, and his mother said she'd come along with us down as far as Fort Ross anyway.

Takolik and I had made this trip straight through without stopping and we were pretty tired, so we had a little bit of a rest, about two hours' sleep I think, and then we made a box to put Kaymayook and his mother in on the sled so we could cover them up. We also had a couple of parachutes which we made like a tent over the *kamotik* to keep them warm.

Of course we were slower going home, we knew we couldn't make it in one day like when we went up. We knew it would be too hard on Kaymayook, and of course Takolik and I were tired and so were the dogs.

It was getting on in the day and just as we were talking about making camp, a big storm came up. We could see it coming up very quickly ahead; we could see these dark clouds right ahead of us and the land was gradually disappearing, and we knew there was a really big blow coming up. So we stopped, but by this time the storm had hit and we couldn't even make a snow house, because as we cut the blocks, they'd just blow to pieces. But Takolik and I had good deerskin clothes on and we weren't cold, and we knew we wouldn't get cold, so we just lay down, one on each side of the sled. We had to stop there for quite a while, but the following night we got off again.

It was still blowing quite hard, and drifting — sometimes we couldn't see our lead dog at all — when we got in to Ross at five o'clock in the morning on the day the airplane was supposed to come. It did seem to be getting a little better, but we figured that there was still enough storm that there'd be no plane that day.

After we had something to eat, we built a little snow house for Kaymayook and his mother near the air strip so it would be easier to get him aboard the plane, and then we went to bed. I guess it was half past six or maybe seven o'clock before we got to bed, and we were hoping to sleep most of the day.

Lo and behold, at eleven o'clock the plane landed right on schedule. The pilots came up to the camp and brought us a bunch more goodies — tea, tobacco, cigarettes, a lot of other things. The whole crew came up and had coffee at my place, and then we got Kaymayook on board and sent him to Edmonton.

Later in February they decided to send two more DC3s with a load of grub and clothing and whatnot for the people at Fort Ross and any of the people that were around the camps that needed anything, and this was all done by the government. The government paid for the whole thing, the Eskimos didn't have to pay anything for it at all.

So these two DC3s were coming in, one behind the other, the second about ten or fifteen minutes behind the first. I was talking to the pilot of the first plane on the walkie-talkie as he was coming in. He never said anything to show he thought he might crash, or was worried or having trouble or anything, but as the plane started to drop, it slanted to one side and dragged a wing along the ice, and then of course it had no control. It lost both engines and it came to a stop, and I could see what I thought was black smoke coming out, and I thought it was on fire. I was only about a hundred feet away on the side of the runway, so I ran over and I was going to break in the window with the walkie-talkie because I could hear someone at the door and he couldn't get it open. But by this time the hatch came open on the top of the plane and the crew all came pouring out.

When I'd got up to the plane I could see all this red stuff on the ground and I thought it was blood, I thought someone was really badly hurt in the plane. For a little bit the pilot was really concerned too, because he thought the same thing, but then he realised this was hydraulic fluid and he told me the pipe had burst.

Only one fellow was hurt, which was really lucky because it could have been a lot worse. This one fellow, the navigator, had been standing up looking out the window, and he got thrown down and broke his wrist. That was the only real injury, and there were nine men on board that plane.

The sea ice that they were landing on was fifty-six inches thick — I know because I had to measure since they wanted it to be at least forty-eight inches thick to be safe — and the plane crash didn't even crack the ice.

Then I had to talk to the second plane and I told them that the first plane had crashed, and when the pilot was close enough he said he could see it. But he was able to land all right, and that was lucky because they could take the crew of the first one back out with them.

The wrecked plane was left there until spring when four teams went out and pulled the plane on to the shore. They used the plane then as a shed for storing stuff in. I think it took four teams to pull the airplane, anyway twenty-five or thirty dogs.

After all this Cresswell Bay sickness over that winter of 1948-9 I got letters from all over Canada from different professors and people asking me about this thing. But I'm no doctor, and I had all I could do to handle what was on my own plate around this time. There was another RCMP investigation of a murder that I had to help with, and an X-ray team project that I worked with, and I had to get ready for a big move to Spence Bay, and besides I got sick myself with the flu, and I'll talk about all of this pretty soon. So I didn't have the time or medical knowledge to puzzle around about the sickness, even though I wondered a lot about it of course. All I know is what I saw and what some of the people told me.

It's hard for people to believe, and I wouldn't believe it myself if someone told me, but I saw Kaymayook's father, his legs were right off at the hip, right off from his body, and he was still alive. He laid for two days like that before he died. His legs weren't cut off, they just rotted off, rotted off at the groin. Doctors say that such a thing can't happen, and I would never have believed it, and probably no one will believe me, but that's the truth.

They didn't all die this sort of death, with their legs falling off, but they did die with no feelings in their legs. I don't know what it was, but they couldn't move, they lost all feelings in their legs, their legs went dead.

But some of the people — Jonnie, for instance, that lives here in Spence Bay now, and Pauloosie, his brother — visited Cresswell that summer, and they ate some walrus there, and they were getting so they lost the feeling in their legs, but they got well again. There were quite a few that had that same sort of a feeling.

This walrus that they ate had been shot by Idlout, a fellow that's at Cresswell Bay right now. It was a very very old walrus, with all sorts of scars on it, and while they were skinning that walrus they found seven or eight lead bullets in its hide. And when they were skinning farther, they found a harpoon head imbedded right through its hide into the fat and almost into the meat. They had that harpoon head there, and they gave it to us. I sent it out to Winnipeg so they could put it in the museum, and also to find out how old it was, because the people said that they themselves didn't make a harpoon like that for hunting walrus. We got a report back that it was the sort of harpoon that the Greenlanders used to use a hundred years earlier. They said that harpoon was at least a hundred years old.

Now then, about Kaymayook, the boy we shipped out to Edmonton, there is a followup story that gave me one of the best feelings I ever had in my life.

The next year, 1950, I was down in Edmonton and I went to

the Camsell Hospital to see the patients, any Eskimo that was in there that I could visit. I was talking to Dr. Davis, a friend of mine that had been in Spence to do X-ray surveys, and I was asking him how Kaymayook was, and said I wanted to go see him.

"Just wait a minute," he says, "you just wait here and I'll go get Kaymayook to see you."

And I says, "Well, I'll come down, don't wheel him out here."

He says, "You just wait here."

This was the old hospital, and there was one real long passage with rooms on each side of it. A door opened from one of the rooms down towards the end, and you know, I just couldn't believe my eyes — there came Kaymayook walking down this long passage, and without even a cane or anything. This was a little over a year after we'd put him on the plane so sick, and they had cut off both legs at the knees and given him artificial legs. Then we shook hands and he was really beaming all over, and so was I!

When Kaymayook left hospital in Edmonton he went to Cambridge Bay. They gave him a job there working in the nurses' station, and he worked at that for a couple of years, but he didn't like it. He said he didn't like working for the government and he wanted to get out on his own, hunting. Well, ever since that time he's been the best hunter in Cam Bay, he's the fellow that gets the most foxes, the most polar bears, and the most fish, everything. I see him quite often.

There's another interesting story about Kaymayook. When he was down in hospital, I think he was there almost two years, he learned to talk English — he couldn't speak a word of English before he left his camp — and the RCMP used to take him with them on trips all the time as an interpreter. The RCMP are very particular if they take anyone in a plane in the winter — they have to be really dressed warm in case the plane should be forced down anywhere. This particular time they were going down to Bathurst Inlet, I think it was, with the corporal in charge at Cambridge Bay. They had the Otter so full that the passengers couldn't get in the side door, and they all had to go through the pilot's door.

Kaymayook was the last to get in and he was dressed warm all right, but as he was going through the cockpit, the pilot noticed that he was just wearing oxfords, ordinary low-cut leather shoes, instead of boots, or *mukluks*. He grabbed Kaymayook by the leg and says, "Nope, you can't come like that," and Kaymayook says, "Why not, what's the matter?" Then the corporal that was going with them went up to see what the argument was about. So he told the pilot, "Kaymayook has oxfords on because that's all he wears all the time now. He has artificial legs up to his knees."

That was quite a joke. And I never was sure whether Kaymayook was pulling the pilot's leg or that pilot was pulling Kaymayook's leg.

Her son fixed the noose around her neck

When those two DC3s flew into Fort Ross with supplies for the camps, they had an RCMP corporal with them, Dick Mead, from Cambridge Bay. He came in to investigate a murder and I went along as interpreter for him.

Also on those planes was a letter for me about a tuberculosis X-ray project the government was setting up for Spence Bay in April. They wanted me to get in contact with all the camps in our area and try to get the people to come in to Spence for that time.

Well, this place we had to go see about the murder, Aveetochak, was about half way between Thom Bay and Fort Ross, and since there would be a doctor in Spence with the X-ray team, that's where we were to take the body for an autopsy. So it was fairly handy for me to contact most of these camps, or get word to them, about the X-raying at Spence while I was with the RCMP on his investigation, which of course we were doing by dog team. Besides the Netsilik and Thom Bay areas, there was about four camps around Spence Bay, and two brothers and their families right in Spence where they were helping to build the new post.

After we got straightened out from the plane wreck and everybody got away in a couple of days' time, Dick Mead and I and Jayko took two teams and went down to Aveetochak where we had heard that there was this woman they suspected had got murdered, though none of the people would come right out with it just that way.

Once this woman was dead, everyone had left that camp. There was no one at that camp at all when we arrived, though there had been about six families there earlier. So we had to find the body first thing. We were looking around, digging around, digging and digging, and we couldn't find it. We were there for about three days doing this. Three or four teams passed along during this time, and we'd go down and ask them where the body was, but no one wanted to show us. In those days the people were pretty superstitious about this kind of thing, as I've said — they didn't go for that at all.

We were getting kind of fed up, so the next team that came along was Kokiak, who lives at Spence Bay now. Dick Mead asked him if he knew where the body was, and he said, "Yes," but like the rest, he wouldn't show us. Well, Kokiak's kind of a nervous fellow anyway, and Dick Mead had to kind of threaten him. He said, "If you don't tell us where that body is, we'll have to arrest you." So Kokiak finally walked up and showed us where it was, and it was within about six feet of where we'd been digging; we'd been digging all around it. The body was buried in the ground, not on top of it under some rocks like they did sometimes, and also there was quite a lot of snow there and it was snowed over.

What had happened was that this old lady had been really sick; she was bedridden and thought she was a nuisance. So she told her son, Erkyoot, who lives here now in Spence Bay, that she wanted to be hung. He tied a sealskin thong around her throat — he hung the noose first through a hole in the snow house and then fixed it around her neck so that she could jump off the sleeping bench. That's what she did, and she hung there till she choked.

Erkyoot was arrested by Dick Mead and we took him, and his wife came along with us, to Spence Bay. Erkyoot said he'd asked another Eskimo, Ishakak, who lived in Spence, to help him with his mother's suicide, so Mead arrested Ishakak too.

We also took the mother's body down to Spence for the autopsy. It was wrapped up in deerskins and we put it in a coffin we made, and then we wrapped that in canvas. The doctor that did the autopsy found a thong around her neck, a harpoon thong which her son used for harpooning seals, and the steel harpoon was still attached to it. When they did the autopsy they took out pieces of her internal organs and put them in jars of fluid for the RCMP in Cambridge Bay.

Then we had to bury the body again, of course. Dick Mead and I wanted to do this without the people being around, so we just waited till night-time and took her up on the hill and buried her up under the rocks. She's up there right now, as a matter of fact, just up above my house here in Spence.

They had to wait in Spence until August — Erkyoot and his wife and Ishakak and the policeman — until a Canso came in to take them to Cambridge Bay. At the inquest in Cam Bay, the doctor said the autopsy showed the old woman was really sick and wouldn't have lived more than a few months anyway, so Erkyoot and Ishakak were charged with aiding in the commission of a suicide, and tried. Ishakak was found not guilty, but Erkyoot was convicted and sentenced to one year. When he came back to Spence Bay he was alone because his wife died in Cam Bay.

When we arrested this boy, we'd explained to him what the law was and what he had done wrong and why we had to take him out. I don't think he was worried about being arrested, or resented it, or even felt guilty, because what he'd done was a thing that they used to do from years and years back — if there was someone too old or sick that didn't want to live any more because they thought they were too much of a burden. They used to do this an awful lot.

I felt that this Erkyoot got fair treatment by what you call white justice. I mean, by this time they knew that it wasn't right to murder someone, but this wasn't murder in their minds. Some would even put it that he did this as a favour for his mother. But they did have to learn that what Erkyoot did was wrong now, and so I think it was right to arrest him and have a trial and a sentence.

In those days the people didn't really understand that they were Canadians, what that meant, or what the law was, and I think it was right to try and know how the people thought about these things so their punishment wouldn't be too hard on them. It's not like today, when they know what the law is.

This X-ray team that I've been mentioning had been flown in to Spence Bay from Edmonton to do the first ever survey of the people to find out who had tuberculosis. I was having to be interpreter for this medical team, and also for the RCMP, Dick Mead, at the same time. The X-ray team had a doctor, a dentist, and two technicians to run the machine. Ernie Boffa flew them in in an old Norseman, and he just stayed there while they did the X-raying, which took them about four days.

The Hudson's Bay post at Spence was not open yet; it was only partially built, and the only ones there were two Eskimo brothers and a carpenter. John Stanners flew in with the medical team to be post manager. The people that had come in for these X-rays were camped around the building for a few days, not in tents yet at that time of the year, it was all snow houses.

The X-ray team was using the HBC house, which was partially finished; there was a stove in the kitchen so it could be warm, and they had the machine in there, and the people would stand up against this X-ray screen.

The people didn't mind being X-rayed, they went along with that, but of course this was the first time that anyone was going to be shipped out for this disease. An awful lot were found with TB, not just from Spence but other places the X-ray team went, and the people didn't like that too much at all. They didn't like going out to the white man's country.

They didn't go out right then, of course; the X-ray film had to go back to Edmonton first before they could tell who had TB. Later they sent planes around to pick up those that had to go out to hospital. They took the people south by plane from Spence to Cam Bay in the Norseman, and then they took them in a bigger plane from Cambridge to Camsell Hospital in Edmonton.

When I'd say to them, "The doctor says you should go south to get treated," there was an awful lot of fuss kicked up, a lot of weeping and whatnot going on, and saying they wouldn't go, they'd rather commit suicide first, that sort of thing. I can remember two or three times when people that had to go out for TB treatment even tried to run away so they wouldn't have to go out.

Of course, when they had TB they had to leave, they were made to by the government, because there was an awful lot of TB around at the time and there was no way to treat them up here. I think there was about nine or ten shipped out from the Spence Bay area at that time, some young, some old, even some kids. And they were looking at staying away in the south like maybe a matter of years. They understood it was going to be a long time, but they couldn't see, I guess, why it had to be that way, that it would be serious to let this disease go on spreading that was killing so many people at the time.

We tried to explain to them what was wrong and why they had to go south, but of course they'd never heard of anything like this before. I mean, I don't think that they really understood the thing right. Oh, it used to make the people very sad, having the families split up. It was sad for us all, seeing something like that.

Well anyway, after the X-rays were finished, the medical team got stuck in Spence for four more days, they got weathered in. Before they left, some of the people in Spence, including myself, started to get a real bad influenza. As a matter of fact, I had a temperature of 106° and got so sick they put me to bed.

But as soon as the plane left, I got up and Jayko and I left because we had to make the trip back to Fort Ross. But I shouldn't have, and I was really sick on the way back, in fact both of us pretty near died on that trip and, to tell you the truth, I don't remember how long the trip took. It probably took us nine or ten days — I just can't recall because we were so sick.

We had our two teams, I had fourteen dogs and Jayko had twelve, and of course we had to feed them every night no matter how we felt. Before we left Ross we'd cut up bags of seal meat as usual to take for the dogs, but we had to buy some seal meat off the people at the camps, because while we were in Spence with the X-ray party we'd nearly run out of dog food.

We took the land route going back, and actually this was our big worry. When we left Ross we'd told our people that we'd be coming down the coastline on the sea ice, and that we'd be going back the same way. But now we thought we might save some time going straight across on the land instead. And then both of us got really sick and we thought we'd have to hole up, and if we didn't arrive the time we said we would, or near that time, they'd be out looking for us but they'd be looking on the coast instead of inland.

We knew what direction we had to go, and we were travelling through ravines and over frozen rivers and lakes most of the way. We didn't have to put the little boots that you may have heard about on the dogs at that time of year, because it's only later in the spring, when the ice gets candly, sharp, that you use them, like when it thaws in the day and freezes in the night. Ice like that can cut a dog's feet to pieces, and he can't travel without the little boots. It was a good thing we didn't have to bother with that.

We had to sit up on the sleds to see while we were travelling, as long as it was good going and not deep snow. When it was deep snow, of course, we had to do a lot of walking. We had to be giving the dogs directions all the time, so even when we were feeling really sick we couldn't just lay back and let the dogs take us home. Until we got nearer and the dogs knew the way, we had to sit up and watch what was going on all the time. This was the hard part for us.

It was the third day out of Spence and we'd got a long way up towards home when Jayko started to get sick. We were within maybe two days from home, going along this one morning, when Jayko said he was feeling so sick that he wanted to stop, and I was feeling really bad too.

By this time it was the end of April and into May. The weather was getting warm, and we were using a tent, and I remember that we couldn't stand up while we were putting up the tent — we were just crawling around — and we went right to bed, we didn't even feel like having tea or anything.

When I got in bed I told Jayko that I wouldn't lay clear down, I'd just sit up in the bed because if I went to sleep I didn't think I'd ever wake up! But I did go to sleep that way, and when I woke up early in the morning I was feeling really hungry. We had some caribou meat out on the sled with our grub, so I just went out and cut off a piece of frozen caribou and ate a whole lot of that, and then I started to feel some better, except that I was quite weak.

But all that day Jayko was really sick so we stayed there, and all the next day. The third morning Jayko figured he could travel so I thought we'd better get going. He was ahead of me, and I saw him fall off the sled, but he managed to catch the back part of the sled and got on it again, and then he stopped his dogs and told me he couldn't go any farther.

He was really bad, and I didn't know what to do. What I decided was to unload a lot of our stuff we didn't need, and I wrapped Jayko up in his sleeping bag and then wrapped a bear skin around him and lashed him on the sled. I put all our dogs together on the one sled, and I thought we could make it home that way. So for the last forty miles or so that I had Jayko on the sled, he seemed to be unconscious all the time.

When we were getting near home, about ten or fifteen miles away, the dogs' traces were all tangled up. They knew that they were getting home and were getting really excited, but I was quite weak and I didn't feel like untangling the dogs, so I just let them run. When we got home, Jayko couldn't even speak, so we just took him in, and they thought I was bringing a dead body home with me again!

The people at our camp were all pretty sick too when we got back, but Mr. Learmonth was at the post, he'd got back from Arctic Bay. Luckily a plane had got in with doctors and some medicine while Jayko and I were gone, and they left some penicillin with the idea that I could go on giving it to the people when I got back.

So Mr. Learmonth took Jayko into the post house and put him to bed and gave him this liquid penicillin — intramuscular, not in pill form. He also put me to bed and poked me at the same time, the first time ever I'd been poked with a needle. I was in bed only for a couple of days, but Jayko was laid up for over a week, he couldn't get up at all.

Spence Bay becomes home

When the Hudson's Bay Company was closing out Fort Ross and I took John Stanners out to Gjoa Haven, the idea was that they wanted to start a new post in a central location somewhere between Somerset Island and Pelly Bay to serve the people in the camps all around that area, and they'd asked me to recommend a location. The place I picked was Josephine Bay, about thirty-five miles northwest of Spence Bay, and that was where I'd expected to be going later that spring.

Then I got into all these other things I've been talking about and didn't get away from Ross, and in the meantime the Company started to build at Spence instead. Actually I didn't think much of Spence Bay as a location. It's good trapping and hunting in the general area, but right here in Spence itself it's a very very poor place for getting seals or whales or anything.

Anyway, after we'd got over the flu and when it was about time to leave Ross for the new post at Spence, I first took the whole family and we went over by dog team to Arctic Bay, and we just took our time. A whole lot of us went over, and we had a lot of foxes to trade. I didn't know what stuff they would have in Spence because they hadn't even finished building, so we loaded up on supplies, and I also bought a boat.

We got back to Fort Ross around the end of May, and on June 4, 1949 we left for Spence Bay. Napacheekadluk, Jayko, and Takolik and their families, and Kavavouk's family came south with me and my family, about twenty to twenty-five people altogether. Kavavouk wasn't with us as he'd flown out on the X-ray doctor's plane because he had a hernia that had to be fixed.

It was a real beautiful morning when we left, I think there were six teams of us all together. After travelling on the sea ice for part of that first day, when we hit the land it got really foggy and two of us got separated from the other teams. Another sled was following me, and since we didn't know where we were in all the fog, we decided we'd camp there that night. The next morning the fog was all gone, and we were surprised to find that we were right on top of a hill. How we got up there we still don't know, because it didn't seem as if we were climbing that much.

We were on Beacon Hill, just off Nudlak Bay, about thirty miles out of Fort Ross. That's where there used to be a lot of Netsilik Eskimos camped; there was a big fish river, and they had a big weir there for spearing fish, but at the time we came by there was no one there.

Anyhow, we knew then where we were. The rest of the teams had got back on the proper route, and they sat waiting for us until we finally caught up with them by noon. They knew we hadn't gone on ahead of them, so they figured we'd turn up, which we did, of course. From there on in, it wasn't too bad except when we were nearing Spence. There was a lot of water on top of the ice on the lakes, and coming across from Thom Bay we had a pretty hard time.

Coming in we couldn't see Spence Bay till we got right on top of it. All we could see was the roof of the one house on the post. But to me Spence seemed to be really flat, though actually you come down through quite a few hills and lakes and whatnot. But coming from Fort Ross where it's all high hills around — eleven or twelve hundred feet high — to something that only goes up to two and three hundred feet, it looked really flat.

It was on June 12, I remember that because it took us eight days to come down, when we arrived in Spence Bay at seven o'clock in the morning, just as the people there were going to work. Besides John Stanners who'd been there since the X-ray thing, there was one carpenter, a white man, and he had two Eskimo families helping him, Pelak and Anaija, that were brothers. Pelak's dead now but his son, Kootook, lives here and works at the HBC, and Anaija still lives here in Spence. They'd been there almost a year and they were all excited to have us coming in, for company and to help out. This carpenter was quite an old man, but he really had a lot of "go" in him. He was sixty-nine years old and his name was Joe Thorpe; he came from Nova Scotia.

When this carpenter and John Stanners saw us coming, they got the fire going and they put on a big breakfast for us. We had porridge, and then we had bacon and eggs, and coffee of course, and bread. It had been a long while since I'd had bacon and eggs. I hadn't seen an egg in three or four months, more than that probably. The policeman, Dick Mead, was still there too, and they took us all in and fed everybody.

When we'd had our breakfast we went out to put up our tents. All the men and the women used to help one another put up each tent. When the tents were up the women went inside, and the men passed in all the gear, the bedding and everything that went in, and the women stored things, fixed the tent inside the way they wanted it. That was their job.

The way to keep a tent taut if the ground's too hard to dig stakes into, which this was, is to carry over real big rocks and tie the tent down with those. For travelling we used about an 8 by 10 foot tent generally, but what we used here were great big ones, 10 by 14 feet. That's what we lived in all that summer.

Also we put our dogs away, tied them up to a rock. For that we always carried a rope with chains on it, as many as the dogs you had. You'd unharness your dogs, and they'd know they had to be tied up and each one would walk over to his own chain, and you'd just clip his chain on him.

Then it was work and more work, getting the post buildings so they'd be ready when the ship came in in late summer. Over the next two years John Stanners and I built the rest of the post buildings that's here.

The HBC's inspection plane came in early in August with the district manager, Pete Nichols. He came in on a Canso, an amphibious plane, and he also brought some mail, and Kavavouk came back with him. Nichols stayed two days. He just came in to check on the house and the store and part of the big warehouse that was finished. He brought a lot of invoices for stuff that was coming in by ship, and he went over those with Stanners. When the Canso went out after Nichols was through with all this, the carpenter went out too. Also the RCMP fellow, Dick Mead, went out on that plane and took Erkyoot and his wife and Ishakak to Cambridge Bay for that trial I told you about.

During the time we were waiting for the ship to come in, we got that big warehouse finished, and we also had to put up another little warehouse on top of the hill by the store to keep a stock of basics we might run out of in the store. That way we wouldn't have to go clear down the hill to bring merchandise up every time we wanted something.

The bay at Spence is actually quite big. Coming in from the southwest you come right in to what is called Spence Bay, and farther on you come up into what they used to call Spence Bay Harbour, which is a little harbour, quite narrow and about three-quarters of a mile long. It's now called the John Stanners Harbour. The Hudson's Bay post is on a little neck of land, a real nice place for building. It's about forty-five feet above sea level and the ship could come right in on the beach to unload, and the buildings are all overlooking the harbour out to sea.

When he was there Stanners was single, and of course he lived in the Company house. For the first year we were just living in a little shack built of frame with a canvas tent over it, which didn't give us a whole lot of room for five kids from eleven and a half down to a year and a half old — Bella, Bill, Barbara, Pat, and Betty. Johnny of course was with Kavavouk.

By this time we had radios. There was a two-way radio at the post, but we had an ordinary receiving set in our home too. What I liked listening to especially was any news about people in the north, Hudson's Bay people, things like that. Quite a few HBC men were working in Winnipeg and the station there would get them on and have them talking. Those were the sort of things I was interested in. Anything about the Mounties in the north, or anything at all to do with the north.

Because we had radios we used to take weather readings for the Department of Transport. We had two weather schedules a day in Spence, at six o'clock in the morning and the night one was at twelve o'clock. We'd get up about half past five and record the temperature, wind direction and velocity, the kinds of cloud formations, and that sort of thing. We'd send all that to Cam Bay and they'd send it on to Edmonton for the weather map there. We used to take turns weekly to do the weather and send messages.

We'd have breakfast at seven o'clock and start work. In those days I had to fill the water barrel for the post every second day, carrying it in buckets by hand from the lake, and also take coal up off the beach. The first year we used coal, but in the second year we had oil stoves installed. We didn't have the big oil tanks outside the houses like they have today. The staff house had a five-gallon tank just above the kitchen stove and a three-gallon tank in the sitting room over the heater. One of my jobs was to see that the stove tanks were kept filled all the time, which involved filling them up at night and then again in the morning.

The post manager, there or anywhere, didn't have to give me instructions unless there was something special that I had to do. I knew what I had to do, what my job was, and I used to have to do these chores before I'd do the ordinary trading or whatever.

We didn't have to wear a uniform for the HBC, but they did put out caps that we had to wear. They used to call them yachting caps and they were blue with a peak and were decorated according to how high you were in the Company. The junior clerk — and the interpreter, if they had just the interpreter and not a clerk — his cap would have just the HBC flag on it. The senior clerk's cap had the Bay flag with a cluster of gold leaves, and a gold band around the cap. The manager's cap had the flag and the cluster, and also a cluster of gold leaves on the peak. We were supposed to wear these all the time. Also the Company used to have blazers which you were supposed to wear, but they were so expensive I never could afford to buy one.

Well, to get back to those beginning times in Spence Bay, the ship arrived early in September that first year. *Niglik* was its name, and it wasn't as big as the *Nascopie*, I think it carried 120 tons all told, and that's what would bring all our stuff in, all the trade goods. Of course, then it was just essentials — there wasn't a big variety like they have now. The ship came from Tuktoyaktuk on the Beaufort Sea coast, over a thousand miles to the west, and it didn't stop off at other posts or settlements on the way; it came straight from Tuk to Spence because it could only carry enough to supply one post.

The ship had a captain, two mates, two engineers, and a crew of five, and they only stayed till they finished unloading, which was generally three or four days. They brought mail too, of course, but by this time we were getting planes coming in once in a while and they'd bring us mail too.

On the ship every year the Company sent a case of apples and a case of oranges and two cases of eggs. We used to try to keep some apples and oranges for Christmas time, but by then they were generally going bad. It wasn't like today — I mean, now the kids get to eat apples and oranges any time, but then they were so scarce we'd maybe give each of our kids a quarter of an apple, or a quarter of an orange, once a week or something like that.

We never had any sickness or trouble by not having much fresh fruit or other things like that to eat. The Company used to send up vitamin pills, they were always on the table, and we were supposed to take one every day. I don't know if they did any good or not — I've never taken one since I left the Bay, and I'm still okay. I haven't got any shorter or anything. Thank goodness.

I never met a policeman I didn't like

In lots and lots of places in the north, once the Hudson's Bay Company established a post, the RCMP would soon put in a detachment. They came in to Spence Bay in 1949 with the same boat that brought our supplies in. There were two policemen and they also had a special constable, an old man that came mostly as a cook, but he was a real handyman, too. Glen Sargent was in charge and there was Ray Johnson, another constable, and Rudy Johnson was the special.

They built their own buildings, just the three of them, they were building and building as soon as they arrived. They had all their buildings up by the time the first snow came that stayed, which was October 2. They built in another little harbour part of the bay, about a mile from the HBC post, and they picked a real good spot, a real good little beach, and they had a fresh water lake right behind them. Actually it was a better place for building than the HBC had.

When the police came to Spence they offered me a job as a special constable with the Force, but I didn't go with them because I liked my job with the Bay, and anyway I was always there to help as interpreter. As a matter of fact, I'd been offered a job with the Force as a marine engineer back in 1929, but it meant being sent out for a year's training, and I didn't want to go south for a year. I wanted to go farther north. Of course, as it turned out I went south that year after all — that's when I took sick with appendicitis.

There was an article in the October 1973 *RCMP Quarterly* that I'd like to quote a little bit here, and I hope it doesn't look like I'm bragging or anything, because it's just that I feel really lucky and proud that I could work so much with the RCMP.

The article was called "The Lyalls of the North" and it was

written by Corporal K.G. Huxter. He said, "There is one person living in the eastern part of the Arctic whose help probably extends over a longer period than any other individual. . . . During [his] years in the North, Ernie has helped judges, lawyers, accused persons, and members of the Force, especially due to the fact that he speaks Eskimo fluently. In the earlier years it was difficult to find anyone with a complete command of both English and Eskimo. In this aspect, Ernie has probably assisted more members of the RCMP than any other person living in this part of the North today."

Then he goes on to tell about my sons, about John being signed on as special constable in 1964, and Pat working for the Force for almost a year as a guard in Inuvik, and then three years after I became a Justice of the Peace in Spence, I swore in my son Charlie on June 1, 1973 as special constable investigator for the Spence Bay detachment. The article says, "This is the only known occasion where anyone in the Division has signed on his own son as a special constable when acting in the capacity as Justice of the Peace. It is a first for the Division where a man has two sons as special constables in the Force." That was a really big occasion for me, swearing in Charlie, and they printed a picture of that with the article.

When the RCMP established at Spence there was no crime, I'd say not until the last ten years or so, but they used to do a lot of patrolling out from Spence Bay with dog teams. They'd go south to Pelly Bay and Gjoa Haven and beyond, and they even made one patrol north right up to Resolute Bay, so it was like distances of up to three or four hundred miles.

They would leave here in the winter to go pick up the mail. The RCMP from Cambridge Bay would go to Sherman Inlet where the HBC had an outpost, about halfway between Cam Bay and Spence, and the RCMP team from here would go up and meet them there, probably around 250 miles. On their patrols they would check at the camps on just about anything really that was going on, like who was born and who had died and who'd got married. So the policemen weren't here so much for lawkeeping but more sort of representing the government, the outside. They didn't conduct any court trials in the small settlements in those days, they'd have to go out to Cam Bay or somewhere bigger for that.

By the time that first Spence detachment finished all their building it was too late to do any seal hunting, so they had to catch fish for their dogs' feed for the winter. The fishing that they had to do was no pleasure, because it was netting fish in the river, and at that time it was pretty blinking cold. When the fish were running they had about ten nets out and they had to keep those nets cleared all the time. But they had to get their fish to keep their dogs alive.

The first month they were there it really kept me going because they didn't have their own radio set up yet, and messages for them would come in at the Bay over our radio. I know one time I went from the post over to the RCMP place twelve times in one day just delivering messages. John Stanners was very efficient, and when a telegram would arrive we were supposed to deliver it right away. As soon as he got a telegram over the radio, I'd have to take it and walk over to the police, deliver it, wait for an answer, and bring it back. And that was a mile over and a mile back each time. Well, to tell you the truth, maybe it wasn't exactly twelve times, but I do know that going over there and back was about all I did that day.

One thing the RCMP had to do was issue family allowances. This was started in the north in 1945, but in some places like Spence Bay the first ones came later and included retroactive payments — my first one was over a thousand dollars.

When they first issued family allowance up here they didn't issue it by cheque, they had a ledger listing every family and how much they could get, and there were only certain things they could get on family allowance at that time. The police used to itemize what the people could get, and send a sheet over to the Bay, and the Bay would issue the stuff and send the statements back to the policeman and they'd send them out to Ottawa.

The RCMP also used to issue all the welfare, which wasn't very much in those days. For instance, I've got a record of what a family used to get for a month: fourteen pounds of flour, a pound of tea, three pounds of sugar, three pounds of rolled oats, two pounds of rice, six packages of Pablum, and a gallon of coal oil. And sometimes, for the widows, they'd let them have a tin of tobacco once a month. The people would go to the policeman and say that they had no grub, and the policeman would write a note over to the HBC and say, "Please issue one ration to so-and-such-a-person." And if it was someone that came in from a camp and they were hard-up, the policeman would probably tell us to issue them with two weekly rations.

Another thing, the RCMP used to have to handle a lot of the medicine at any settlement, and I was kind of lucky to learn quite a bit from them, because I used to go as an interpreter around the camps with them. There were hardly any doctors in the north in those days, and the police and the missionaries and the Hudson's Bay people all had to act almost like doctors sometimes. I'll say something more about that later on.

As far as the people were concerned, the RCMP guy was just another person, another white. The people liked them, there was never any hard feelings against the RCMP up this way; at least I never knew of any in those days. And myself, I've still to meet a policeman that I really didn't like — I mean, they were always courteous, friendly, always willing to help — and I've met a lot of policemen in my time. I sometimes pulled their legs the same as I would anyone else's. That's something I've found, the policeman is just human as far as I'm concerned.

We used to see the RCMP a lot. They were usually fairly young and generally single guys, and most every night I'd be over visiting them or they'd be over at the Bay post.

That reminds me, I've mentioned that people play a lot of cribbage in the north, and once when I was down at the RCMP place in Spence, I had a real standout of an evening at that game — this happened later on when the settlement was bigger. I've played a hang of a lot of crib myself, but this time was my real high point.

The RCMP plane had come in for an inspection. The pilot's name was Harry Heacock, and Inspector Mudge was on the plane, and he had two staff sergeants with him. So we were over there playing crib and I was playing with one of the RCMP boys, John Avison, and I was beating him pretty bad.

Almost at the end of the game, I had a really exciting hand which I counted as 28 points. At the end of the play when I counted out my hand out loud, the rest of the guys were really excited too, and then one of the sergeants pointed out that actually it was a 29-point hand, a perfect hand, which it's the dream of every cribbage player to get. It was a once in a lifetime experience!

Well, they wrote a little note saying I'd got this hand, and all these RCMP guys signed it, and when they went outside they sent it to a club down in the States that sends you a little membership card saying you've had a 29-point hand, and of course I still have that card!

"The chief kidnapper"

In the summer of 1950, before the ship came in, my seventh child Dennis was born, on June 29. Nipisha and I were out fishing, and we were walking along just this side of Middle Lake when she said that she had labour pains. So we walked home about four and a half miles and she went right to bed. I went down and got her mother, and the two of us delivered the baby. This was in the tent we lived in up on the ridge where the HBC post still is.

To Eskimo women in the north, any of them, it wasn't like down south when a woman was in labour. I mean, I've seen quite a few kids born, and the mother was never laying down. They always were just kneeling, sort of kneeling-up, on the sleeping platform. Then generally they had a man there that got behind the woman with his arms around her and squeezed her to help the delivery. Then they used to wipe the baby off, generally with a piece of flannelette cloth that they'd buy at the Bay. But if they were out at the camp and they were having a kid, they'd wrap it in a deerskin or a rabbit skin or something like that.

Having a baby was just a natural thing. I mean if there was anyone having a kid in a snow house or tent or wherever it was, and if people wanted to visit them or watch, they'd not think anything of it. It wasn't like women in the south, they wouldn't all rush around afterwards and gush or congratulate or bring presents or anything, there was no fuss at all. Maybe after the kid was born, someone might come in and visit, they might want to have a look at the baby.

I ought to know a little bit about this because, besides having our own kids, Nipisha and I midwifed some thirty-six kids in Spence Bay during the early years there.

Well, with my family growing so fast, three of my kids — Bella, Bill, and Barbara — were school age now and that was kind of a problem.

In those days the government had an education policy which most southerners know a little about: that was to build big schools in two or three of the larger settlements like Aklavik, that had a population of seven or eight hundred people then, and then fly the Eskimo kids from the little settlements and camps to those schools. I guess the government thought that made more sense than to try to build a lot of little schools in all the little settlements.

My three kids were the first to go out of Spence, along with one of Kakakoonik's kids, but it was five years before any of mine came back; I never saw them once, not even in the summers. They went out in 1950 and they never came back until 1955. The government did promise that they'd come back. The Catholics took kids out at the same time, and they brought them back for Christmas, besides bringing them back in the summer. They paid the cost of the airplanes. The government was supposed to do this too, but their program didn't seem to work.

My kids went to Aklavik which is over a thousand miles from Spence Bay. I would try to get them back but I couldn't do it. It just happened that the Commissioner of the Northwest Territories at that time, John Robertson, came up here, the first commissioner from Ottawa to ever come to Spence, and I went to him and asked him if there was any chance of my kids getting back for summer holidays. He said, "Where are they?" and I said, "They're in Aklavik." He says, "They haven't come home since they went there four years ago?" and I says, "No, they haven't come home once since they went there." So he says, "I'll make a point that they'll come home at Christmas time." Well, to give him credit, he did try to get them home then. They got as far as Coppermine, and then they were stuck there for nine days because of bad weather. Then they had to go back to Aklavik, so they never made it home for Christmas. But they did come back the following summer.

Kakakoonik's kid that went out with my kids, has never been home since, although her mother tried and tried and tried to get her to come home.

In some cases when the kids came back home they felt separated from their parents and couldn't even understand them, because a lot of the kids couldn't speak Eskimo any more. And when my kids came home they didn't think of us as their parents any more because the Holmans, the fellow in charge of the school and his wife, seemed more like their parents.

When my kids went out to school, they couldn't speak a word of English, none of them. My first two girls that went out, Barbara and Bella, did keep their Eskimo, but Bill, and later Pat, they lost it then, and I think that's too bad.

One thing I fought a heck of a lot over — and one of the things that I didn't win on, then — was that when the kids went out to school the people running the schools never wanted them to talk in Eskimo, and they didn't want the kids to write in Eskimo, even to write home. They just wanted them to use only English.

How the kids were supposed to write in English before they learned it, was one of my big beefs, and what they came up with was, "Well, we'll write a letter for them."

"Well," I says, "how is an Eskimo at home going to read it?" They said, "You can read the letters to them". And I said, "Well, how am I going to read letters to them, they're spread all over this part of the north!"

Actually, in 1954 or 1955 it came to be one of my jobs with the government to go around in planes in the summertime, dropping into camps and collecting these kids to be taken off to school. At that time it wasn't the Department of Education, it was the area administrator that had to make all the decisions — I was filling in for him in Spence for some while — and until years later, right up until when Spence Bay finally had a school, I used to have to go and pick up the kids.

We would send in a list to each settlement telling them what kids we had to pick up, and we had to get their parents to sign a form so the kids could go. They couldn't write English so they'd use syllabics to sign, and any of them that couldn't write syllabics would put a cross on and it would have to be witnessed by myself and another person. The ones that knew syllabics had learned this quite a long time back from the missionaries.

The government people running the program used to tell me, "Now we know that some of the parents are not going to want the kids to go, but it's up to you to tell them what benefits there will be if they do go, but you haven't got to tell the parents that the kids have got to go." The benefits I told them about was how things were going to change in the north, and if their kids went to school and got an education, they could get a job. That was supposed to be the benefits so they would want their kids to go to school.

At the start there were quite a few settlements that I was visiting in the summertime. I'd say we used to get around to eight or nine camps altogether, and I used to collect anywhere from twenty to twenty-eight kids — twenty-eight is the most I think we picked up one time. And in those days a lot of the kids didn't have any extra clothing, so when I'd get them here — we always overnighted in Spence — I used to get the ones that needed it an outfit of clothing.

It could be quite sad sometimes going into the camps, because the first thing, they'd say, "You're coming to take away our kids again." One of the pilots that flew the kids around a lot took to calling himself "the chief kidnapper". Sometimes the parents would want to go with the kids, even only just as far as Spence, and of course I had to try to explain to them, "Well, it's going to be just as hard for you then, because they're going to leave Spence tomorrow anyway." But we couldn't take them anyway because with the kids there was no room in the airplane.

Lots of the parents cried. Some people think Eskimos don't cry, but they sure do. I'm not sure if the parents really understood what this was all about, but I think in a way they did. The only thing we could do was explain why the kids were going — not that they had to go to school, the government didn't want us to say that. But still I had to put it in such a way that they'd want the kids to go. Some of them didn't want to refuse, because they figured that the whites might hold this against them, and in those days they wanted to do whatever pleased the white man.

One kind of funny thing happened when I was picking kids up for school one year. I had to go to Gjoa Haven, and to pick up kids from Back River and Sherman Inlet and some other places, so we had an awful lot of kids on board, and I had a list of them from each place. When I got into Cambridge Bay where the school was, the first thing the teacher said, "Here's the list of how many kids you're supposed to have — have you got any extras?" Sometimes I'd have two or three extra, but this time I didn't, so I said, "No."

So I was just having my supper when the principal came down and he said, "You've got this many kids on your list, but I've got one extra," and I said, "Well, where did that kid come from?" and he said, "He says he's from Gjoa Haven." Well, I'd picked up only the four kids on my list from Gjoa, but the principal says, "No, there's another little fellow from there, he's only about six years old." So I said, "You must have got one of your own kids mixed in or something," but he says, "Oh, no."

Well, I went up to see that young fellow, and what had happened at Gjoa was that two of the young kids going out were from the same family, and they had this little brother six years old, and while we were at their house collecting the two kids, he went down and hid away in the plane because he wanted to go with his brothers.

Sometimes though, some of the kids wouldn't want to go and the parents would make them go. But also I remember one year that we went right up as far as Cresswell Bay, at Somerset Island, and we only got one kid for the whole trip, no one else would let their kids go. That one was a young fellow that lives here in Spence Bay now, Kammimalik.

There were some things I didn't like about this system of flying kids out to school, as you can tell, and I could see where the people wouldn't like it, and how it sometimes wasn't good for them. But as a white myself, and working for the government on this, I thought that maybe it could help, and I'd never hold my own kids back, I made them go to school. I had quite a few fights with the wife when the kids didn't want to go, but I knew they had to go.

It was ten years after the Hudson's Bay Company founded the post at Spence Bay when we got our first school here. During that time, besides Dennis, we'd had four more children: Charlie, our eighth, was born on July 11, 1952; in 1954, Winnie who died when she was three years old; in 1957, Wilfred who died at nine months; and then Bobbie, our eleventh, was born on March 7, 1959.

Of course you might think that by now we were getting enough kids of our own that we could pretty near have had an Ernie Lyall School right at home in Spence, and I don't know but what you'd be close to right about that.

The plane was pouring out smoke

Before I tell about the first school in Spence Bay, I'd like to point out that with all the flying around to pick up the school kids, thousands of miles, we only had one crash, and fortunately no one was even hurt in that one. We've never had that many crashes in the north — the pilots have always been very careful — though of course there's been mishaps and some hairy situations. I think the crash this particular time was about June 1965. The kids that had been out to school in Inuvik had all been brought back to Spence, and from here we were flying them up to their different home camps. Don Hamilton was the pilot.

We'd already taken quite a few out, and this day we were heading out with six kids for a sealing camp about twenty or twenty-five miles from Thom Bay. The day before, we'd taken some kids to Cape North Hendon which was nearby, and we'd flown over this sealing camp place to have a look and Don thought it was safe for landing. We couldn't land right out on the sea ice any more at these places because there was a lot of water on the ice, so at this sealing camp we landed on the shore ice. Unluckily a crack had made there, I'd say about two or three feet wide; we were still going at about forty-five miles per hour after landing, and the front wheels went down into the crack and it took one engine off the plane. The plane tipped forward on its nose for a while, and then it tipped back, but as I say, fortunately no one was hurt at all.

We sent out a message on the plane's radio to the Bay in Spence and a bombardier from Spence came down to look for us. We could hear the bombardier, but we couldn't see it, and they didn't know exactly where we were and turned back. So next day we got three dog teams from the people at the camp and came back to Spence.

Later they flew in another engine and a couple of engineers to install it. We went back out to the plane and pulled it up off the ice higher onto the land — we picked the smoothest place we could, which wasn't very smooth. This was the only way the pilot figured he could get the plane out, anyway. He took off by himself, he wouldn't take any passengers or anyone, just in case something might happen. But nothing did, and he got it out to Yellowknife.

In those days the pilots learned to be real handy at figuring out how to deal with things they didn't expect or hadn't run into before. That reminds me of a story about Ernie Boffa. Ernie was one of the real old famous pilots in the north, one of the first, and he came into Spence one time in an old Norseman to bring the mail. We didn't know that he was coming in just at that time, and he didn't know if the ice was good or bad for landing, it was in November, so he buzzed the strip two or three times and then finally he threw out a ten-gallon drum of gasoline to test the ice. He said that seeing the ten gallons of gas didn't go through the ice, he figured it was safe to land on it, and that was what he did.

There was one time I was flying from Spence Bay up to Fort Ross, making an inspection tour of the camps and taking up some grub to the people. On these trips we always used to ask a nurse and the policeman if they wanted to go with us, which they always did. This time Paul Hagedorn was the pilot, the nurse was Kathy Ross, and Bill Pringle was the policeman. It was February, and very very cold, and we had an old single-engine Otter on skis. Well, we found there were quite a few sick people at Fort Ross so we stayed there longer than we'd figured we would, and every ten or fifteen minutes we had to go down and start up the plane so the thing wouldn't freeze up.

When we took off I was sitting up front with the pilot, and the oil or something had frozen after all and he blew a seal. The oil started leaking, spraying all over the windshield, and it was really hard to see. Paul figured it was pretty serious, so he radioed all the nearby DEW-line stations and Cambridge Bay and told them what was happening, and he said that he figured he wouldn't be able to make Spence — he figured he'd have to come down.

There were lots of lakes all along our route so Paul kept as close to them as he could in case we needed that smoother ice for landing. But finally when we got near Middle Lake, which is close to Spence, he knew that he was going to make it all the way in okay.

Paul thought he'd play a joke now, and he called Bill Pringle up front and told him he had one parachute aboard and where the parachute was, and he said, "Just for fun, I'll tell Kathy that someone will have to jump out of the plane."

He called Kathy up front and showed her the parachute, and gave her this big story about someone going to have to jump and said that since she was the only lady on board, she'd have the privilege of parachuting down. He told her that when she landed she'd only have to walk about three or four miles to get to Spence, and that when she got there she should tell them where she thought we'd come down.

Well, this scared her right on, of course. She got all excited about it and wanted someone else to jump instead of her, and then finally we told her it was all a joke.

After we got back, we got a sealskin mat made with a print on it of Kathy coming down on a parachute, and a polar bear standing up on his hind legs with his mouth open, waiting. Bill and Paul and myself also had a little plaque made and signed our names to it, and she still has that.

Now if that story sounds like something you've read before, then maybe you saw one like it in a book by Duncan Pryde* a few years ago. In it he wrote a story a lot like this that he said happened to him. Even though his story was quite a bit different from mine, it does seem kind of strange that the same thing would happen to both of us with the same pilot.

I got sort of anxious and worried during a plane ride in the summer of 1978. I'd flown out to Vancouver to be with Ed and Ruth Margaret Ogle and work on this book, and we got an invitation to take part in an air cadets' fly-past — this was part of a celebration down there in honour of Captain Cook.

They said that these planes would be flying around in formation over the city, and also over a bunch of ships — big ships with masts and sails, and a lot of small ones too, that would be sailing into the harbour. These air cadets were going to fly in little planes sort of low and we would go as passengers, so it seemed like a good way for me to see the city and the scenery down there. Besides, I like flying, and of course I'm used to planes, though I told Ed I sure would never go for any stunting around because that would make me really nervous. But he said there wouldn't be anything like that; they'd just fly close together in a pattern.

When Ed and I got to this small airfield near Vancouver, there were two small little stubby-winged biplanes painted up a bright fiery red with white trim, and a couple of nice young fellows to fly them. They called themselves the Canadian Reds and told us we'd be meeting up with the other seven planes, the air cadets' Bluebirds, in the air after take-off.

Well, they put us in the front seats in these little planes that just had open cockpits, and gave us big helmets to wear, and strapped us in like they were afraid we might fall out or some-

*Duncan Pryde, *Nunaga*, Hurtig Publishers (Edmonton, 1971).

thing, and then the two pilots got in the back seats and off we went.

Our Reds sure flew with the Bluebirds all right — as a matter of fact, we flew through them and above them and under them and all around them. Then all of a sudden I noticed that the other plane that had Ed in — it was just a few feet away from mine — was pouring out smoke and I was really worried because I figured they'd caught fire. When the smoke finally stopped, I was relieved that they'd got that fire out. Afterwards, I found out that my plane had been smoking like that too, and it was just part of their fancy flying! Well anyway, we were flying around so blinking fast I could hardly see the ships or the water or the city, or even the sky, for very long at a time as they turned this way and that, but it was all really exciting.

When we landed they asked me how I'd liked the little flight, and I said I'd got a really big kick out of it, but I said, "I'm sure glad you didn't do any loop-the-loops or that kind of a thing, because I'd have been scared to death." Then they were all grinning so much, I began to get suspicious, and my pilot says, "Why, Mr. Lyall, Ed told me you really wanted to do some stunting," and he says, "so just before we landed back here I did a couple of loops and rolls just for you."

And you know, I'm sure that I would have passed right out if I'd known about it at the time, but to be honest with you, it was one of the best times ever I've had in my whole life!

Once I was a baby

Well, to get back to Spence Bay, in 1959 we got a telegram saying that the government was going to establish a school here later that year, and to advise the people in the camps around that their kids should come in when it was ready, and that they'd lose their family allowance if they didn't. I was the one that had to tell the people about this, since I was the only interpreter here at the time.

Actually for three years before this, the Anglican missionary in Spence, Don Whitbread (he came in 1952, I think it was) was taking classes every day, just in the mornings. He had maybe six or eight regular kids but when the people came in to trade, they'd send their kids to him, so he might have as many as twenty-five kids at a time. He was just teaching the basics, and he wasn't teaching in English since he could speak Eskimo.

By this time there were quite a few permanent buildings in Spence — the HBC had six or seven, the RCMP about five, the Anglicans and Catholics one or two each. So in the summer of 1959 the government sent in the material for building the school and also for building a power house, and they flew in four people to build them, the first buildings put up in Spence Bay by the government.

There was a house for the teacher, and then there was a long one-room classroom, not attached to the house. The school was built maybe five or six hundred yards from the Bay post on the west side of the bay. The power house built at the same time was for directly heating the school, but I'll talk more about that later.

On December 18, 1958, it was right in the darkest days, I remember that, they flew the school teacher in; Isobel Pringle she now is, but her name then was Isobel Plaunt.

When she arrived it was quite exciting for us. Not many kids had come in to the settlement yet, so we started the next day and helped her unpack and get all organised for school days, and it was January 4, I think, when she first opened the school. The kids around were kind of excited about all this because some of them used to play with our kids, and ours were all looking forward to the teacher.

I think the first year Isobel was here she had something like fifteen to twenty-three kids from six years old up to as high as sixteen. Some teachers since then might wonder what all Isobel was doing. Well, it was an awful lot. For instance, there wasn't a kid here could speak English then except Adam Totalik, he'd been to school in Aklavik. So she had to teach them English right from the start, and maybe you can think how frustrating and hard that would be to teach a bunch of kids that couldn't speak your language and you couldn't speak theirs.

She used to have school all day, she started at nine o'clock in the morning and finished at four o'clock. And then she'd take the kindergarten kids, the little kids, three times a week in the afternoons. Besides that she used to take the women in for sewing and show them how to cook, and things like that. I'd like to see any other teacher come in and do the work that she did when that school was first starting up. It was awful tough for a white woman to come in to a settlement like this and start a school.

Today in the schools up here you've got interpreters, and you've got Eskimos that are teachers' assistants. But she was all alone, she never even had an interpreter, and she had to teach them starting from scratch. She taught until June, 1963 and when she left the number of kids had just about doubled — there were thirty-six kids her last year, and the school building had already been added to.

It was really interesting to see a school finally in this settlement that I'd had a hand in starting. I thought this was an important step, because I figured that if they had a school here the kids wouldn't be taken away from their parents. But as it turned out, it began to change the people's way of life, because it meant that they would stay more in the settlement. Before this there were very few people actually in the settlement, because they lived out at their hunting or trapping camps and just came in to trade. But they couldn't very well bring the kids in to school every day and back out to the camp again at night, with maybe twenty to fifty miles of round trips by dog team. So they began to move in.

Then as it turned out, having a teacher and a school in Spence Bay didn't mean that all the kids that had been going out to school could now stay home with their families. The ones that always had gone out still had to go, because at first the teacher was only taking the ones that the parents wouldn't let go out to school, or that they thought were too young to go. And the school only took kids through grade nine, so after that they had to go out to Yellowknife to high school anyway — which they still have to do.

Some of the kids that went out to school wanted to come back, and they'd write their parents — like before Christmas —

and say they wanted to come home. Of course the parents would get all upset about it, and I'd have to explain. I'd hear of any of these unhappy experiences through the parents, they'd come and tell me what their kids had written to them — the kids never did talk to me about it themselves. But I never did get any of the people saying, "Yes, we like the kids to go out, the kids are happy." Even when my kids, Charlie and Dennis, went out later on, and Pat — well Pat, I never heard him complain at all — but Charlie and Dennis were pretty unhappy too when they first went out. I mean, you expect this, of course, and we all know that they're going to get over it, but I think it was pretty hard for the kids.

There were quite a few parents that still wouldn't let their kids go to school in Spence either. Some of them let them go for one year, or not even a full year, and then they'd wind up back home out in their camps again before the school year was out. This wasn't so much because their parents needed them to help or anything, it was just the separation that they had no wish for. Whites, for years and years, had accepted that a kid would go away from home, to school or work, and live away from the family, but it was different altogether with the people. They never wanted their kids to go away from home for anything.

In the family Eskimo kids were treated different than white kids. The Eskimo kid was, and still is, let to do pretty well whatever he wants when he's very young; they'd never spank a kid or anything like this, and yet if he was told to do a thing, he'd do it right away. Kids really respected their parents, which is not the way it is today. The Eskimo family in the olden days was really close and the kids were very well looked after, and it was very much a loving happy family. And the man was always superior, though that much is still true today. To my mind, what brought on this business of the kids not doing as the parents ask, not respecting their parents, was going away from home, going out to the schools in bigger places. For instance, the kids in Spence never used to steal until they started going out to school.

As I said, when the school was built the government also built a power house. At that time there was no electricity, that is no general power, in Spence Bay, so they built a power house so they'd have electricity for the school. Later on this also provided light to the HBC and the police, but not that first year.

The Hudson's Bay Company still had its own power, they had a windmill and an engine plant just for the Company. It was the same for the RCMP — they also had a windmill and an engine plant. The windmill was a fairly good way of getting power, except if we got too many days of calm weather. We just had 32-volt batteries, and if we'd get about a week of calm, our batteries would run down, and then we'd have to use the Onan engine to re-charge them.

I looked after the school's power house — it wasn't the Company that did this, I was asked personally to do it. So I had to look after this power house in the evenings after I finished with the Company's work, and in the morning before I started my regular work. I used to get up about five o'clock to go down and check the engines, and go again at night. And for my four hours a day at this, the government paid me more than I was getting from the Bay for working twelve, fourteen, sometimes eighteen hours.

I knew a fair bit about engines, that was a hobby of mine right from when I was a kid, puttering around with engines. I guess they had a manual or a handbook for this power house, and the guy explained as he was installing it, but I could figure it out for myself actually. The first engines we got in were two 5-watt Listers, and then two years later we got in a 15-watt Lister. And then after that we got a 20-watt Cat.

These used to break down lots of times and fixing them could be pretty complicated. I used to have to pull the engines apart and fix them, and if we couldn't fix them we'd ask an engineer to come in. I remember that one time an engineer came in when we had the old 20-watt going, Jayko used to help me too at that time, and this engineer couldn't get it to go. He said he had to go out and get parts for it first, before he could do anything. In the meantime everyone was using lanterns and complaining, so Jayko and I pulled the thing down and we got it running again.

White people say that Eskimos have a special way with

engines, that they're mechanical magicians, and I know that this is very true. I think most any Eskimo can take a snowmobile or an outboard or any sort of motor, and if he sees it running for a while, he can always fix anything that's wrong with it. I don't know why, maybe they really do have a special mechanical ability. Take Jayko, he's still here now, he's been with the government for quite a long time, and I think he knows more about any of these — I don't say the power plants, but the Cats and the machinery the government has here — than some of the mechanics from outside.

To get back to the school again, they used to put on various program things, plays at Christmas, plays at Hallowe'en, this sort of stuff. Once I was a baby in a play at Hallowe'en. And there was a thing where I was a drum major. And once I was a patient in a shadow play, and my kids were crying because they thought my guts were being ripped out.

The first Hallowe'en the teacher was here, there was a costume party. A construction crew was here and they had a great big cook, so we got an Eskimo parka from one of the ladies and, because I'm small, I went as a baby in this cook's parka, in the hood. I had a bottle that I was sucking on, and it was supposed to have milk in it, but actually it was vodka. The cook got me in there and he took me out of his hood, and he told the teacher that I had to have my diapers changed, and Isobel had a sheet there so the cook changed my "diapers". The Eskimos got a real kick out of that. By the way, you maybe ought to know that I did have a pair of shorts on under the "diapers".

In the shadow play where I was the "patient" they brought me in all bandaged up on a stretcher, and the guy that was the "doctor" was carrying a mallet and butcher knives and whatnot. As they took me in the tent there were cries of "what's wrong with him, what's wrong with him," and someone explained that I was sick and they'd have to "operate" to take something out of me.

Now you've seen plays like this, where what the people do is behind a screen and it's lit up so the audience just sees the shadows of what's going on. So after we got in this tent was when the shadow part started. The "doctor" took his knife and made like he was cutting me open, and first he started to pull out my "guts", which of course were really a coil of rope, and that's when the kids started crying. Then they had a caribou heart in a basin which was full of "blood", and when he held up the old deer heart you could see the "blood" dripping off it. Halfway through I supposedly "came to" and sat up, and just as I sat up the "doctor" took this big mallet and made like he hit me over the head with it, and I flopped down and went back "to sleep" again.

For this drum major business, four of us were in kilts, and we went down to the school from the Bay post. It was blowing and really cold and we just about froze — somebody once asked if I'd had any children since that time! So we just went in and marched around and played different songs. The Eskimos thought it was really funny, they'd never seen anything like that before. They'd heard the bagpipes, though, because Eric Mitchell, the post manager, and John McDonald, a post clerk, used to play them outdoors just to entertain the Eskimos. I've got quite a few slides of them doing that.

So as you can see, we had plenty of ways of enjoying ourselves, it wasn't all cold and wind and hard work, we used to have a hang of a lot of fun. But there were a couple of funny stories around this same time that could have turned out serious.

There was one time when a crew of government people came in and they had a camp down about a mile from us; they were mapping the place at the time. One day Isobel Pringle invited the fellows over to have a little bit of a party, and we were there, and the RCMP, and there was this pilot, his name was Pretty, from Australia.

We were drinking overproof rum, and Pretty had had a few drinks and was getting a little bit high, and he said to us, "Did you ever see this 'flaming sword'?" — that was what he called it — and none of us had. So he takes a match and lights the rum in his glass, and he says, "To do this, you've got to take it all down in one gulp."

So he holds his glass up and says, "Here's to you," and we were all getting quite a kick out of all this, but unfortunately while he was trying to get the glass to his mouth, he hit his nose and splashed that burning rum all over the place, and his face was all on fire. He was laid up for five days with blisters all over his face. Of course then it wasn't funny — to him or to any of us.

Isobel reminded me about the first time the icebreaker *Camsell* came in to Spence Bay, and we were all invited aboard to have dinner.

At that time the RCMP were still living about a mile over on the other side of the bay. They were doing a lot of sealing at the time, and as we didn't have a canoe at the Bay to get out to the ship, the RCMP had left their canoe for Isobel and myself. It had some of their sealing gear still in it, like the harpoon, but they'd taken their rifle out of it.

Well, Isobel and I took that canoe. We were going around to pick up the two RCMP to go to the ship for dinner, and I was wearing a suit and Isobel was dressed in a long evening gown. And as we got halfway up the harbour we saw what we thought was a seal, and as we were getting closer to it, I said, "It looks like a wounded seal, Isobel, and we can get it for sure." I said, "You take over and just go where I tell you to go, and keep the kicker turning over and doing a good job." So I picked up the harpoon and Isobel was running the canoe and we were chasing this thing. There was three or four times when it came up pretty close to us, and then just as I would be about to throw the harpoon, it would dive.

This went on for quite a while, and we chased the thing all over the place, and I could see bubbles coming up so I thought it was wounded pretty badly. So we drove it in to shore in shallow water, and when I looked down all I could see was this great big yellow thing that rolled over, and it sure wasn't any seal. And lo and behold, it was a diver off the *Camsell* out trying to spear fish!

I just about fainted, because there was a couple of times — well, I was pretty good at throwing the harpoon in those days, and I'm sure I would have got him finally. And if I'd had the RCMP's rifle instead of the harpoon, there sure would have been one dead skindiver. We all got such a fright! And he got a real telling-off for going out there to skindive alone without telling anyone.

So I cut off his toes

In early 1960 a Hercules plane came in and started bringing the beginnings of a nursing station to Spence Bay. Quite a bit more stuff for the station came in on the Herc during the spring, and the rest of it came on the boat.

The people were very pleased about the nursing station coming. Before that there used to be a lot of talk with the Eskimos saying that they'd like to see a doctor come here, and I think what was in the back of their minds was that if they had a doctor or a nursing station, there wouldn't be so many people having to go out for treatment. So when they wanted to have a school and a nursing station, the whole point was that the people wanted the whites to come in for those things because they thought it would be better for them and would help keep their families together.

When the first nurse came in, although the nursing station wasn't ready at all, she was busy right away. Her name was Merle Pottinger, and she was from Jamaica. To start with they put her in a little shack built right down by the school, and that's where she'd see her patients and their babies and whatnot.

To show you how busy she was, I remember she wanted to go to that Hallowe'en party I mentioned earlier, and she was going to have a costume like a witch doctor from Africa. But about four o'clock that afternoon a lady came in to have her baby delivered, and she was there all night and Merle couldn't go to the party, which was really disappointing to all of us.

She had plenty to do, and believe me, she worked. The people would go to her — they weren't worried or afraid to show their sickness. And it wasn't all a case of the people going to the nurse's station, because when they had their snow houses or tents around here we used to have quite a walk to them any time there was someone too sick to go to her.

This first nurse didn't try to set up any sort of preventive medicine or clinics. Well, she did in the end, but after the first nurse they did set up a health committee to try and teach the people when they should report to the nurse, and that sort of thing.

One of the big things when Merle first came here was to teach the people cleanliness. The first two years of the nursing station, all the Eskimos had lice, for instance. There were a lot of lice, you'd see the Eskimos picking them off the kids' heads and eating them.

The first nursing station was a little smaller than it is now — another piece was added on around 1975. Originally it was a two-bed station, and the nurses mostly handled maternity cases and small sickness, any sickness going around, bad colds and this sort of thing. If somebody was seriously sick, they'd try to get a plane in to fly them south, but it seemed at the time of that first station it was hard to get planes to come in.

There were still people suffering from TB in 1960. After the first X-ray team in 1949, they used to come up every year and they would always take out five or six or seven more, for many years; but there doesn't seem to be very much TB here at all now.

When the people would come back home cured of TB, after maybe three years, or four or five, down south, I would be notified. It was my job to go down and give the good news to the people, and then the whole village would be down to meet this person when the plane came in. Sometimes the DEW-line plane would fly them in from Edmonton or Cambridge Bay — the DEW line was about fifty miles from here by dog team — and the RCMP would go over by dogs and bring them home.

But we had a very sad incident here one time when a man came back after four years in hospital. After he'd been away all that time a plane brought him in and they got here early in the afternoon, but his wife and kids were up at the Netsilik camp. He was all for starting out to walk up to that camp as soon as he arrived, but he was told that he shouldn't do that because he still was a little weak, and that in the morning a plane would take him up to his family. So he stayed overnight. In the morning the plane was getting ready, and this fellow walked into the propeller of the plane, and of course it killed him.

Before the nurse came in there was nothing, no medical help except what we could give — the Bay and the RCMP. A doctor never came in unless we had a real emergency, and then he would come from Cambridge Bay generally, or sometimes right from Edmonton. But only if it was a real emergency.

I remember one time at Spence there was Tulurialik, he had a snow house just across the bay. Unfortunately four or five kids had died around here from meningitis — the doctor had told us by radio what was wrong — and they had this little one in Tulurialik's snow house, and it was really sick. We used to take turns, the policeman and myself, staying up there to be with the kid all the time. We'd asked for a plane to come in for this little kid, but we had a real bad storm and the plane was held up, and just as it finally was coming in with a nurse from Cam Bay to pick up the kid, the kid died.

My family was pretty lucky about not having sickness, but one time there was a real bad epidemic of measles here in Spence, and a lot of people died. No people were actually living on the post but there were a lot of snow houses and tents right from the other side of where the RCMP was, about a mile away, down as far as the farthest point on the lake. When we had the measles epidemic it was just about break-up time, and no planes could get in either on skis or floats.

We'd been on the radio to the doctor, and we told him that just one policeman and myself were pretty sure we'd had measles, so he told us that the two of us should be the ones to go around and give the people penicillin shots. So we'd start off every morning to go and visit them and give all the people that were down sick three shots a day. I'd start off from the HBC point and come around one way, and the policeman would start from his side of the bay, and we'd meet sort of in the middle.

Well, one morning on our rounds we met at a fellow's snow house, this was Anaija who lives here in Spence now. The policeman, Doug Brown, told me he was feeling pretty sick himself, and he thought that maybe he was coming down with the measles after all.

Now Doug was really good at giving the needle, he could

take the needle and kind of throw it — I could never get on to doing it that way, I'd kind of have to press it in. The way they had us doing it, the doctors had told us where to make a cross on a person's buttock, and we had to put the needle in the upper left hand quadrant of that cross. And of course you held that place between your finger and your thumb where you were going to jab the needle in.

Well, Doug wanted to get home because he was feeling really sick, so he was in a hurry. He just made a jab with the needle, and he put that needle right through the skin between his thumb and his finger — it went right through him and into Anaija's buttock. But instead of pulling the needle out and doing it again, he just went ahead and gave him the shot with that needle still stuck in the flesh between his finger and thumb!

I don't know if most of these diseases were brought in, like some have said, by travelling whites. I know they had one epidemic in the spring of 1949 of some sort of influenza, which I've already mentioned, where a lot of people died, and some said that was brought in by that first X-ray party that was in here. That's the time Jayko and myself were so sick.

While I'm talking about sickness and nursing and doctoring and that sort of thing, when I first came to Spence and before there was any doctor or nurse, I used to pull teeth. As a matter of fact, when I was first with the Bay I was lucky enough to get some trips with the dentist by boat from Port Burwell, and we used to go around to all the camps in the summer, and he showed me how to pull a tooth. And he got me a whole set of forceps and everything that I'd need for this.

Some people I used to give injections first, but sometimes they never had any, because Eskimos are really good about taking pain. I remember one time I was pulling a tooth for old Tulurialik here and I had nothing to use as a painkiller, but that didn't matter to him. I just had him sit down on a rock outside his tent. I think it took me about an hour and a half before I got that tooth out, but he never even said "boo".

Pulling people's teeth is hard work. Like with Tulurialik, it was so hard that I had to have someone holding his head, bracing it for me. The way you do it is hard to explain, but you don't pull a tooth by putting the forceps on the tooth and then pulling out away from the gums. What you do is get the forceps on and push that tooth *into* the gum first, press in and wiggle it till you hear, you can almost feel, a crunch sometimes, and then you start to wiggle it loose and pull it out.

I found in those early days that the peoples' teeth weren't too bad, they weren't like the kids today that take so much candy and pop and get a lot of cavities. But I wouldn't say they exactly had good teeth. There was a lot of very old people that had all their teeth all right, but they were ground right down to the gums, especially the women who'd been used to chewing sealskin for making boots and that sort of thing. There used to be quite a lot of people with teeth that had to come out, though.

Earlier I was mentioning the HBC post medical kits that we always used to have, but I didn't really explain much about them. There'd be aspirins, splints, slings, bandages, milk of magnesia, cough medicine, nose drops, ear drops, iodine, fever pills, rubbing alcohol — I don't remember what-all else — and also a case of rum and scotch and brandy for medicine use. And antibiotics, when they came in — the sulphas, penicillin. And in the old days they even used to send morphine for any fellows that were in real pain. They taught us how to use morphine, which we had to do quite often.

The Company also had its own manual to go with all this, how to use the medicines and things, what to do, stuff about symptoms, and that sort of a thing. This medical kit was mainly for the employees' own use, but we used to get enough of these things that we could help out the Eskimos when any of them got sick or hurt, so this was a service to the people, too.

Also when I was going to school, training, I took a course in St. John Ambulance, and I knew a little about how to dress wounds and put splints on broken arms and legs, and things like that. Not too much, but it helped, and in time I also learned some things by experience.

We've had people at the house on the post being looked after — shot-up people, sick people, that we've taken out of their snow houses and brought in so we could look after them on the post right in the house. And unfortunately we've had people die in our kitchen because we didn't know enough, like a doctor, or have the right medicine, or we didn't get to them in time.

We just had this Company manual and we had these medicines and stuff, and then we just hoped for the best. It was a lot harder, of course, before we had radio to talk to the doctors, and before we could get planes in with doctors to help or take the people out.

I know we made mistakes sometimes, but I think about 95 per cent of the time we were doing a pretty good job. We were sure trying, anyway, to do our best. I remember one time, though, we had a person that was in real pain, and the post manager and myself agreed that we should give him some morphine. Both of us had done that before, but this time — and it was the only time that it happened that I know of — when we gave this person morphine, he died right there, and we felt pretty sure that we had done something wrong.

There were some humorous occasions when we were trying to offer somebody a pill and they thought we were trying to poison them or something, and they'd refuse to take it. Most of the people, before they were given medicine by us, had their own witch doctors, but the shamans never used to give them anything to take internally. So I think that was why they thought that by giving them pills we were trying to poison them. This didn't happen very often, but it did a few times.

So we were fighting the peoples' old ways sometimes in the very early days, but I never had an argument or a showdown with a shaman who would try and physically stop me from giving medicine. And if someone refused to take what we wanted them to, we'd just leave it for a while, and generally we would get them to take it eventually. Pills used to be the main thing we'd give, and then when penicillin came out in liquid form, of course we used to have to give them that by needle.

If somebody had a bullet in them, we'd try to see if we could get that out, and sometimes we could. But if we couldn't get it out, it could be bad. There was a case where one fellow was shot by accident in the thigh, and it was just with a .22 bullet and didn't seem too bad, but he died because we couldn't get it out. He got gangrene.

Taking a bullet out when the victim was in real pain was when we generally used to use the morphine. The Company supplied a scalpel to probe into wounds and try to get a bullet out, and they also supplied a saw for cutting off arms or legs, so you could saw through the bone. A couple of times I had to amputate.

Once in Port Leopold we had a fellow, Sanganee, that was coming in from his camp about sixty or seventy miles away, coming in with his family for Christmas. He got sick along the way and they had to hole up, and finally they got out of grub and were about starving, and their dogs died. But Sanganee was so sick they couldn't move him, and so his kids — his son Kitsualik and his daughters Soosie and Akina — they just had to walk in from about forty miles out to where we were, and they told us about this. I sent a team right away to pick up Sanganee, and when they brought him in, he was really sick, and he was cold and shivering. We asked him if his feet were cold and he said that no they weren't. Well, this struck Kavavouk as strange, so we took off his boots and found out his feet were frozen right up above his ankles, and so then I had to cut off some of his toes.

What we used to do when we amputated anything, we'd cut it so there'd be a flap of skin left, and then we could stitch it, sew the flap over. It was, I guess, what you'd call primitive surgery, but everyone used to do it, like the policemen too.

Sometimes the Eskimos had to do this for themselves — as a matter of fact an old fellow that I know cut off his own leg and made a wooden leg for himself with a muskox horn on the bottom of it. Right now that thing is in an Edmonton hospital in the office of one of the doctors. When the doctors gave him a new leg later on, they kept that old wooden one as a souvenir.

Jack of all trades

Now I'm getting up to the time when I left the Bay to go with the government, and so there's some things I'll add that I haven't said yet about the way we lived and worked in the early days in Spence, and even before that; and also there's some things I want to say especially about the Hudson's Bay Company.

The first year in Spence Bay our house on the post was a little one-room wooden frame shack with a tarp over it that I built myself. The house the Company built for me then, and of course I helped build that too, still was just a one-room house actually. I put up a partition so as to have a little kitchen, and in the back part is where we all used to sleep. But when the kids were home from school later on, there wasn't room in there for everyone to sleep, so we also had kids sleeping on the floor in the kitchen. Finally, I built three little bedrooms onto that with lumber I paid for myself, and that place is still used by the HBC as a storage shed.

At first we started off heating with coal and then they gave me a little heater, but for making tea and cooking, we used a primus stove. Lighting was with Coleman lanterns at first, but after three years we got power from a battery windcharger.

We had a collapsible rubber bathtub. The RCMP always used to get these fold-up rubber baths, and they'd given me one of them, so we used to have two days a week for the kids to have their baths. We had to heat the water on the stove, of course, and we had to haul all our own water in buckets from the lake. If the lake was frozen over, I'd cut a hole in the ice and keep that open for a while longer.

After the ice got about five inches or more thick, I used to cut blocks of ice with a saw and stack them outside by the house. Inside on the porch there was a barrel filled with water, and when we used some of that water I'd keep adding ice to it, and keep the barrel full that way. We did the same thing for the Bay staff house.

At first we had an outdoor toilet, but that wasn't all that great in the winter, so after a couple of years I built a little toilet in the house. We had a bucket in it that we used, and when a bucket would get full and had to be carried out, we'd just go out, winter or summer, and dump it on the post garbage heap about a hundred feet away. You might think we'd have got some kind of sickness from this, but we never did.

Saturday afternoons or Sundays if I was off work, I would take Pat out hunting with me when he was a kid, and I used to take Bella out with me all the time before she went off to school. When she wasn't any more than six years old, she used to go on the dog team with me, hunting seals.

We had games for the children to play, different sorts like tiddlywinks and snakes and ladders, and when they were old enough I taught them cribbage. Nipisha taught them Eskimo games, how to do the cat's cradle, that sort of thing. In the daytime the kids would be out sliding or playing outdoors, and then they used to go to bed at seven o'clock; we always had a rule that they'd go to bed at seven. It wasn't hard to get them to bed early; there were no other kids for them to play with because during our first few years here none of the people were living on the settlement at all. There was just the HBC and RCMP.

In the evening after we'd got the kids tucked in bed, I might sit and relax. I used to smoke a pipe before I lost my teeth. And I listened to the radio a lot. Both of us also visited the police quite often at night, we'd sit and talk and play crib with them. We liked the RCMP, as I've said.

Nipisha would be busy sewing most all the time, I mean evenings and all. Nipisha did a lot of sewing because she made our *kamiks* (boots), parkas, and mitts. She did all our sewing, except for the last few years when we've bought our things. Earlier she'd generally make me a new suit of deerskin clothing every year. She also taught the girls sewing and skin preparation. Bella was a real good seamstress — she used to make boots and parkas.

We all spoke Eskimo together, I always talked Eskimo to them. Until Isobel Pringle came here to teach, none of the kids spoke any English at home. Well, I shouldn't say that exactly, because John Stanners was very fond of kids, and he used to have them down at the post house, and he used to teach them a bit of English. But they didn't talk to me in English. I often think of it now, why the hang didn't I teach my kids English, but I never thought of it at that time at all because Nipisha didn't speak English. She understands English all right, but she'll still never talk English to me, just Eskimo.

What I used to eat was mostly like the Eskimos. When we could get it, I would put up enough caribou to eat for a long time in the winter; but it was hard to get caribou in Spence, they were really scarce and you had to go a long way to get them. We used to eat a lot of seal, and fish, and we'd get a lot of canned food from the store, but I couldn't afford to buy any fancy stuff.

I've already said that John Stanners and I were really busy with building here at Spence, getting the post established. After the carpenter left, for six months we worked right up until eleven o'clock every night, including Sundays, until we got all the building finished.

It used to be that any place you'd go where Hudson's Bay Company posts had been established, you'd be able to recognise them right away. All the buildings — the warehouses and store and living quarters — were painted the same at all the posts. They would be white, the corner trim would be green, the window frames all green, and the roof red. And you'd find that all the houses and warehouses were built the same basic way too.

The store would generally be an A-frame building and very very small compared to the big stores the Bay has up here now. The trading part would usually have a counter all the way around three sides of the store, with a little gate that was especially for the trading. The Bay clerk would go in there and shut the gate, and no one else was allowed behind the counter. There was no cash register because, as I've said before, we never dealt with cash in the early days, just the special HBC tokens. Since the early 1970s, the store is like any store in the south — people pick what they want off the shelves and pay at a cash register. There's no more trading like in the old days. Today you can get most anything you'd find in a store to the south — there's Pampers for the babies' diapers, and fancy dog food in cans and boxes for the dogs.

Only the post houses were heated in early times, none of the other buildings ever were. It was only the last year that I was with the Company that I worked in a heated store, and therefore there usually wasn't anyone in the store except whoever was trading. It would be too cold for just standing around. I used to wear deerskin clothing in the store, and it was so cold that we used to have to write with our mitts on.

The goods weren't on shelves in the center of the store like they are nowadays, they were all behind those counters on shelves, and so the people would have to ask, just point to the things and say they wanted this or that or the next thing. I've already talked about what we stocked, what the people could buy.

There were things hanging from the ceiling, like Coleman lanterns, lamps, and the like. That's the way we used to kind of decorate the store, from the ceiling. We'd have dog chains, dog webbing and that sort of thing hung around, and maybe have a canoe hung in the middle of the store.

The hours we worked were all according to how busy we were, how much trading there was. Sometimes we could be trading in the store for over twenty-four hours at a stretch without stopping. That would be at posts where the people would maybe only come in once a year, after the trapping season was over. That would be around the last of April or the beginning of May, and a bunch of them would come in with a whole lot of furs, and they'd want to get away as quick as they could. So we'd just have to trade with them until they were finished. Lots of times people would arrive in the night and say they wanted to leave the next morning, and so we'd have to go and trade with them.

There was no such a thing as a coffee break or a tea break during the day. We'd have our breakfast, and our next meal would be twelve o'clock and the next one would be at six, unless heavy trading upset that schedule. We used to get an hour off for a meal, and after I was married I generally used to go home for lunch.

We'd all be doing all sorts of heavy work. For instance, the hill here in Spence slopes down from the store to the water — it's forty-five feet above sea level. When Ralph Knight was here as post manager — there was just the two of us, and he was a real Hudson's Bay man — anything that we could do that we didn't absolutely have to hire done, we used to do it ourselves. When the ship came in we'd get all our fuel oil in 45-gallon drums, seventy-five of them for the Bay and twenty-five for my house. They'd all be out on the beach, and the two of us used to roll seventy-five of these heavy drums up by his house, up that hill, and twenty-five up by my house — besides carting all the other gas and stuff that had to go up the hill, up by the oil shed. We did all that by hand.

Most HBC posts were actually situated on a nice little piece of land overlooking a bay, so there was always some heaving up and down to the beach. When we used coal, before we had fuel oil, it would be dumped on the beach and we had to carry it up near the house, and that stuff used to come in 100-pound bags.

There was no such thing as voice-radio early on, so we had to learn to key. We started out with Morse code on the radio to send all our messages and to get them from other places. I forget how many years it was before they brought in the radio-telephone and we could talk instead of pounding a Morse code key. We sent all sorts of messages — any that had to go out. The Company had a lot of messages going back and forth, usually about trade, mostly business. At some places the police would have messages going back and forth, like here at Spence before they got their own radio, or at Fort Ross when they were around on investigations. The missions too, the nursing stations — I'd be sending messages for anybody that needed this, most any hour.

We never got any overtime for this sort of thing, of course, or for any of the extra work we did evenings or weekends. There was no such thing in those days. I was getting $120 a month when I started here in Spence in 1949, and when I left the HBC in

1962 it was $185, along with free rent and part of my fuel. I didn't feel that was low, I never even thought of it really, I guess, because I didn't have anything to compare it with.

The Company and the managers were strict. They had rules set down and they made sure that you went by the rules, some managers more than others, of course. I always used to get to work on time, it was eight o'clock then, but I remember I came in this one morning and this particular post manager came out and looked at his watch and said, "It's three minutes past eight and you're supposed to be here at eight o'clock. Don't let it happen again." He was really serious.

But I felt training like that helped a young person. I'm sure it did. I think anyone that had been trained by the HBC got a good training in other things too, like building, carpentry work, engines, book work, taking weather reports, knowing how to use radio — key or voice — everything like that. When you were working with the Bay in those times you had to be a jack of all trades.

It wasn't a dull job, there was plenty to learn and plenty to do, there was never a day you'd be idle, there was always something to do.

They opened up the North

When I was with them the Hudson's Bay Company in the north wasn't just a trading company, or just a bunch of whites that bought and sold things and that came up here to make money off the people. Because, you see, we were actually living among the people and the Company tried to help the people with their problems. I think it really did help the people, because if it hadn't, I figure the Company wouldn't still be here.

And the people, the Eskimos, trusted the Company. Here in Spence Bay, when the government first wanted to come in, the people said they didn't want the government to come in because they said the HBC had always looked after them. And the Bay really had always looked after them, I know from my own experience. They spent an awful lot of money helping the people out and getting nothing in return for it. That's what makes me so mad when outsiders say that the Bay just ripped the people off.

Some say that, well, the Eskimo lived for thousands of years in the north without the HBC, so what has the Bay given the people that they couldn't have got by without, maybe better. Well, outsiders that don't actually know about the old way of life get the idea that the old traditional ways of the people were the best life, but you have to stop and think. I mean they had to work really, really hard to trap and hunt and fish according to their old ways, just to get enough food to stay alive and have clothing, and they had to be always moving around to find good hunting for seals and caribou and fish and whatever.

Most of the old people alive today in the settlements, people who did live the old way, would tell you that they wouldn't want to go back to the old days, even if there are things that they didn't like, or don't like still, about the whites coming. A warm house and being able to buy some of your food and clothing sure beats the hang out of a snow house and shivering out on the ice somewhere hunting to keep your family and dogs from starving.

Look at it this way, if the HBC hadn't got things started up here, well, that old hard life would still be going on the same old way for the people.

The way I look at it is that the HBC, in three-hundred-odd years up here with the people, they're the ones that really opened up the north. Everybody else was scared to do anything in the north until the Bay came in. All through the north it was the HBC that opened up the settlements, that went in first, and if the other people came in it wasn't till after the Bay had started a post. A few free traders came to the north but mostly they couldn't make it, they've nearly always gone broke and had to get out. Even the missionaries and the RCMP waited to see how things worked out for the Bay.

From the first the HBC was able to help with an easier way of living for the people, because then they could get guns and ammunition and motor boats and better tools from the Bay. I've already told how the Company helped the people with medicines and things, and I've already told how, when the people were hard up, they sent us out with grub for them. They knew the people couldn't pay for it — the Bay paid for that — they wouldn't just let the people go and starve. And I've told how they would move the people to a better hunting and trapping area at their own expense. This is why the people had such respect for the HBC in the early days.

The Company used to give the people nets to go fishing, and to go seal hunting, and they used to give them traps to get foxes. Well, they didn't actually give the people these things, it was more a loan, but the people never had to buy nets or traps. Say a fellow would come in and he'd ask for two hundred traps, well they'd loan him the two hundred traps. When the season was over, he'd bring them back and they'd be hung up in the warehouse with his name on them so that next year he'd come back and he'd get the same traps. Sometimes the fellows would lose some of them — traps would get drifted under or they'd forget where they set them or something — sometimes they used to lose quite a few. Well, they didn't have to pay for the ones they lost, either. The Company would wipe that out as a bad debt sort of a thing.

Eskimo carving and art is such a big thing nowadays, but it didn't just happen that there was a market for that, it was the Bay that got a market started. Back in the days that I was in the east, around Lake Harbour and those places, the people used to bring beautiful carvings in — not this stuff you see today — really good stuff, and the Bay said to the people, "Look, give us carvings and we will pay you for them," so the HBC was encouraging carving and also giving the people another way to make some money. Not long after the government came here to Spence they started to buy carvings, and in other places they began to do this too. Actually in Spence I was the first one to start buying carvings on behalf of the government, because I'd had experience through the Company. The most I paid for the big carvings at that time was $45, but in later years, say around 1974, some Eskimos were getting a thousand dollars or more for the same kind of carvings, same size — that's over the counter at the store run then by the Department of Local Development.

Around here the Eskimos carve soapstone and whale bone. They used to go out and get the soapstone themselves, but now that it's got going in a big way, the government goes out and quarries it and brings in planeloads of soapstone. It's a very comfortable thing for a family to live on carving, some of them make an awful lot of money at it.

The HBC used to have what they called the district office reserve, which was stuff they brought up on the ships which wasn't for sale but was just for different things to help the people out. For instance at Lake Harbour, when I was there, the Company felt that the people weren't getting enough of the right kind of food, so when the ship came in there one year they brought in a great big marquee tent and a lot of dehydrated eggs and Klim (a kind of powdered whole milk). Of course the people hadn't seen this before, so we put up this big tent and in the mornings we used to go down at six o'clock and make milk and mix up eggs and feed these to the kids, so the people would know how to mix the milk right and how to cook the eggs for it to do them good. I don't know how much this sort of a thing cost the Company, but it must have been a tremendous expense, because they were doing this at this time at every settlement they went to when that ship was going around the north.

Of course some would say that the Company just did these sorts of things to help themselves, that they wanted to be sure the people were in good shape and could get plenty of furs and stuff to trade, and that this would be good for the Bay. Of course these things would be for the Bay's benefit as well as the benefit of the people. But I know that they really did have the people's good at heart, they liked to help the people out.

I don't know for sure what's meant when somebody talks about the HBC ripping the people off, but to me you rip people off when you pay them poor prices for what they're offering, and charge them high prices for what you offer. But I think that the prices the Bay offered for the skins, which was the main trading item, were fair; I don't think the Bay could have offered more. And I always thought the prices of the goods in the store were fair.

Today I criticise them myself because the stuff in the store here in Spence Bay is so expensive, but I know that everything costs a lot more today, in the south as well as here, and I don't think they could sell it any cheaper. After all, they're a business company and they've got to make money.

Some stores don't always make money, though. I know when I was at the Bay right here in Spence for twelve years, that all those twelve years they lost money. When I tell people this, they say, "Well, why did they stay there then?" Well, the way I see it, in some places the Bay was like a service someone had to provide, and sometimes it takes a while of being a service before they begin to make money. Also they've got so many stores, like down south too, that the Bay can probably afford to lose some in one or two of the posts in the north.

One of the big things the government and other whites and the people are trying to work out is a way for the people to have a chance to run their own stores in the north. They've tried to do this with a co-operative kind of store, and they've got those in some places. I think myself that if they could get a co-op running properly it would be a good thing, but the co-ops that I know of all go in debt, which is maybe because they don't have the experience the Bay has had for so long.

I think it could be a good thing if the co-op movement could get going, but I wouldn't want to see the Bay fading out in the north. I suppose, to be honest about it, maybe that's because I was a Bay man for so long.

I can't stand the cold any more

In 1962 I quit the Hudson's Bay Company after spending most of my life with them, though really I hadn't wanted to leave, and I was quite a while, several months actually, making up my mind to do this.

How it happened was that Jamie Bond, the first northern service officer at Cambridge Bay in 1960, came to Spence Bay to talk to the people about establishing government services in Spence, and I was the interpreter for him. Up to that time the

RCMP and HBC had been handling things like social assistance and family allowance for the government, but now the government wanted to take over all these things and be in charge of the settlement. They were also doing this in other settlements in the north.

Jamie came over to explain that, and then the next year he sent Mike Shand, who had been his assistant in Cam Bay, to be the first northern service officer in Spence, what they call a settlement manager today, and Mike wanted me to go with the government. At first he was talking about a job as interpreter for me, but eventually they offered me a job as equipment mechanic because it paid more wages than interpreter would, and because I'd been looking after the power plants.

So Mike said that the government would pay me $664 a month and give me a good house to live in, and that's where I first started to break down. As I've said, I was only making $185 with the Bay, and the house we had wasn't much. By now we'd had another daughter, Kathy, born at the nursing station in Cam Bay on March 10, 1961 which made five kids still at home at this time. Bella was working, and Barbara, Bill, and Pat were out for school.

I talked to Nipisha about this of course, but she was always asking me if there wasn't another job I could get where I could get more money — I guess I was the least paid that she knew of.

So finally I said to Mike Shand, "Okay, you promise me three things and stick by them, and I'll go with the government." One was that my wages would never be less than what he said, and he agreed and said not only that but he could guarantee that I'd get a raise each year. The second thing was that I'd get a good house to live in, which he also promised, and today we're living in a mansion compared to what I was living in when I was working for the Bay. And the third thing I got him to promise was that they were never to move me out of Spence Bay unless I wanted to go.

Because of the big difference in salary between what the government offered and what the Bay had been paying me, some might feel that maybe the Bay hadn't been doing right by me, but it never struck me that way at all when I was with the Company. I never thought of it that way, and I still don't really, to be honest about it, because I think they paid their people what they thought they were worth. When I was with the Bay I was satisfied. I was never used to getting big wages, and I had a happiness and security there. And I enjoyed the work, and that was the most important thing. I never did feel lonely or have any particular sense of isolation. Never did, never have. As far as I was concerned they treated me pretty well. But when I got this offer it was so much better and, well, there's things I look back on now that I kind of wonder about.

Anyway, when I'd decided to go with the government, the Bay had no notion I was thinking of leaving, and of course I had to give a month's notice, my contract with the Bay called for that. I wrote out a telegram one night to send to Winnipeg saying I was resigning, and took it down to the post to send. This was June 1, and I was planning to leave July 1.

Well, of course, the manager, Ralph Knight, was taken by surprise, and he didn't like it at all. He tried to talk me out of quitting, but I'd made up my mind. As it turned out, they asked me to stay on an additional two weeks until they got things squared up, because at that time we were right in the busy part of the year, painting and cleaning up the post and all this sort of a thing. So I agreed to stay on those two weeks more.

For a while things with the people in the Bay were strained a little bit. Some in the Company called me a traitor for leaving; I guess they really thought that when someone joined the Bay they ought to stay. But I didn't think there was any reason for name-calling or anything like that because I thought, and I still think, that I'd given them years and years of real good service. Finally, then on July 18, 1962 I left the Hudson's Bay Company and the post.

It had taken a couple of days for us to get all our stuff moved by dog team to our new place where we lived for nearly two years. There were no government staff houses built yet, but there was a construction crew in, twelve people, and they built a quonset hut for us which was used afterwards as a community hall and is now built into the co-op, and I used that free. It was fairly close to the school, where the government office is now, and it had four bedrooms and a big kitchen, and it even had enough room in it for our last baby, Sylvia, who was born in hospital in Edmonton on February 10, 1963.

After a couple years we moved to the house we have now. It has five bedrooms — three upstairs and two down — and one end of the big sitting room is the dining room, and there's lots of cupboards and closets. We have a phone and six different radios — short wave and long wave — and two television sets, one black and white and one colour. There are four different record players around the house, and we have a clothes washer and dryer, a dishwasher, a slide projector, the kitchen stove is electric, and we have all those appliances like a blender and toaster and this sort of a thing. I don't think people in the south have anything much that we don't have except maybe a car — and that wouldn't be as much use here as the snowmobile that we do have.

Things sure have changed from the old days — and so have I! For one thing I never used to get cold, but nowadays after sitting in an office for years and years, any time I go out I have to dress up in a lot of stuff, and I still get cold. I can't stand the cold any more.

Well anyway, in this new job I got as equipment mechanic I had to see that all the equipment was in good shape; I had to see that the power plants kept going, and if they broke down we had to repair them. Very fortunately, the year after I joined the government, Jayko also joined as a handyman, and he was very very good at repairing engines, tractors, or any of the vehicles we had, and he still does this today. Also he could look after the power plant as well as I could.

This new job gave me more free time evenings and weekends to do what I wanted to do, be with my family or whatever, because the hours weren't as long as what I put in at Bay posts. With the government, mostly we could get any day off we wanted to, if there wasn't too much doing. I had this job for four or five years.

As I'd been in Spence Bay since 1949 when it was founded, just as a little HBC trading post, I'd seen quite a lot of changes in the settlement. I've already talked about how the people began to move in more after the coming of the school, and you know about the nursing station, and we had the Bay and the RCMP of course, and the Anglican and Catholic missions had come in. And in 1962 the government came. So there were quite a few whites beginning to be around besides the people.

Up to this time there were no changes that I didn't like okay. As far as I was concerned everything was great — except one thing: after the government came in I think things moved too quick. Too much was given to the people all of a sudden.

The nursing station, the school, the police — all that wasn't too much too quick, but what I'm getting at is that after the government came in here they gave them so much so fast, like fuel oil, good houses, welfare — it was all really just handouts — that the people didn't really have to do anything to earn. When I first was issuing relief to the people, they were willing to work, they wanted to work, and they'd ask, "Have you got some work for me?" We could always find them some work to pay off $40 or $50 or whatever the amount of relief was that we issued them. But then I was told they weren't *supposed* to work out their relief amounts, that this wasn't legal! So, of course, I had to quit doing that, and there wasn't anything for them to do but just take the government handouts.

The government had started a housing project in 1956, low-rental it was called. This was houses for Eskimo employees of the government. The first three houses were for Jayko, David Tucktoo who at that time helped at the nursing station and now is the local housing foreman, and there was another nursing station helper. They were called "matchbox houses", and they weren't as good as the ones that are built today for Eskimos. As a matter of fact, some of the early housing for government employees wasn't as good as the Eskimo housing is now — the big difference is that all houses built now have flush toilets instead of honey buckets like the rest.

The material for these low-rental houses arrived on the barge in the fall and they sent in a crew to build the houses, the same as they'd done for building the nursing station and school. The carpenters generally used to find work for any of the people that wanted to work helping build the houses. These were about the only jobs available then to Eskimos, except for janitor work. Jayko drove the Cat to clear ice and did any land clearing that had to be done. He also scraped up gravel pads for houses to be built on, and my son Dennis helped to clear some of the roads and take some of the rocks away.

In the beginning when there were just a few houses we all got our own water the way I described earlier, from the lake and ice blocks, and just emptied our honey buckets into a garbage dump. Later when there were a lot more houses, Jayko and myself, and Mangnik, who was the school janitor at the time, started hauling the water around to the houses. In the winter we'd saw up enough ice blocks for the government buildings and the school and places like that, and we'd cut enough ice so that the people could come and get it too. And we used to dig a great big pit in the spring, and we'd get the garbage and honey buckets hauled away to that for everybody, and then have the tractor-Cat bury it all.

About these honey buckets,—for anyone that doesn't know about them — when they began building houses they put in bathrooms with toilets, but of course there wasn't any proper sewage system for flush toilets yet. So these toilets were sort of like a bigger version of a kitchen garbage can, but with a regular seat and lid on, and a vent pipe, and there was this removable bucket inside, the honey bucket. When that got full, it had to be carried out and emptied. Later we got big plastic bags for liners, which were cleaner and easier to handle.

We got movies fairly early on. The Catholic mission used to show them on a regular basis in the community hall, the old cook shack, for a long time before the school ever showed any — they've been shown in the school to raise money for special things. And then a movie club was formed and they used to order movies every month.

The first snowmobile was one that the HBC brought in — I

think it must have been around 1956 — it was called an Auto-boggan, and I bought it. Ralph Knight was here at the time, and one Sunday afternoon when the first snow came and the ice was good, he and Mrs. Knight and myself took that Autoboggan out just to test it, out to Middle Lake. Coming back, as we got near the post we noticed some nuts and bolts on the ice, and we decided we'd better check on this and we went back, and it took us about three hours picking up nuts and bolts for about two miles back!

The second snowmobile was bought by Father Laverge and this was running until 1977. The third one was bought by one of the RCMP. After that it built up, and everybody started ordering them by the late sixties and using them instead of dog teams.

In 1970 Prime Minister Trudeau flew in to Spence Bay with the then-commissioner Stuart Hodgson in a Twin Otter. There was a meeting with the government officials in Spence, and the prime minister stayed here for most of the day and then they left again that evening.

I had quite a long talk with the prime minister. The area administrator had some business with the commissioner, so Mr. Hodgson asked me if I'd take the PM over to my house for a cup of coffee, and he stayed for about an hour and a half. We chatted away and had a real good time. Mr. Trudeau seemed to be quite interested in my life and experiences in the north. He asked what I thought about changes in the north, and I told him I agreed with his policies, and I said I thought it was good what the commissioner was trying to do.

At the plane at departure time the PM said, "If you ever come to Ottawa, be sure and come and see me." I know that he probably was just saying that, but if he's prime minister when I do get to Ottawa, maybe it's not proper but I'm going to go up and see if I really can see him, just to see what they'll do to me!

At the time the prime minister was here, there would have been close to four hundred people living in Spence, with quite a few people living in shacks around the shore — there were only a couple of camps still existing out of Spence on the land. So the prime minister saw a pretty civilised kind of settlement with, like

I've said, houses and movies and honey buckets and water service, and snowmobiles everywhere.

A couple of years later Judy McGrath came in here and started the craft shop, which I think is one of the best things that they've ever had going here. Mrs. McGrath came here with her husband who was an economic development officer. Everything they do in that shop is all done with stuff from the country around here. They even dye their own wool, make their dyes out of the different flowers and plants they have here. Everything they make is all stuff from the country around here, except they have to get the wool from outside.

The things they make in the shop, the coats and mittens and things, are mostly for selling to visitors and to people down south. This gives a lot of work for the women, and they get paid very well, they've made a lot of money on it. When Mrs. McGrath — she's in the Labrador now — got them going, she'd tell the women what kinds of things were wanted, and then she'd tell them to do their own designs. In the end there was a lot of women coming in with really good designs, different than anything that had been done before. Angnaya Alookee, Judy's chief designer, designed a lot of things that were never done before, and she helps run the shop now with Eva Strickler.

This was the kind of a thing that was good because it showed the people they could use what was right around them, something new that they hadn't done before.

Justice, Soosie, and Mr. Mowat

I've been talking about changes around Spence Bay since it started as the Hudson's Bay Company post. The law is an important thing in the north — how the white man's law works with the people — and that's been changing quite a bit too. I've already mentioned some cases where I was interpreting for the police, and what I thought about whether the people were treated fair or not, and there's one more case I want to talk a little bit about.

Mr. Justice Jack Sissons, when he was circuit court judge up here years ago, used to say that justice didn't always work out when the whites from the south tried to force their laws on the Eskimos. In the Eskimo language there wasn't any word for "guilty" so in his court he wouldn't let any lawyers ask an Eskimo if he was guilty or not guilty; they had to ask, "Did you do this thing?" And sometimes it was something that yes, the Eskimo had done, but as far as the people were concerned, according to their ways there was nothing wrong about it. So Judge Sissons used to always try to understand the people's ways so as to be fair in their trials, and not give such stiff sentences as for whites that were used to the laws.

This was the judge that came to Spence Bay in 1966 for the Soosie trial. I was interpreter on that case and also at the murder trial, and it was written up in newspapers in the south, and Farley Mowat also wrote about that trial in his story about Soosie and the people in his book that I've already mentioned several times. What he wrote had a lot that wasn't correct, but before I get to that, I'll tell you what really did happen.

Soosie wasn't the one that was on trial, she was the one that got killed. You might remember the story I told about the Josie case when I was in Fort Ross back in 1941, and how, at the end of it, Soosie was married to Josie when he killed himself. By the time of this story she was married to Napacheekadluk.

So to start at the beginning, what happened in the Soosie case was this. In the fall of 1965 a pilot and myself and an RCMP fellow were flying about picking up kids to take them to school, and one of the settlements where we stopped was up by Fort Ross at Levesque Harbour where Napacheekadluk and Soosie lived. We'd been up there in June to take a kid that belonged to Napacheekadluk and Soosie back home to them from school, and everything was all right then. But in the fall, when we landed there to pick up this kid again, everyone came down to meet the plane the way they always did, and I saw that Soosie wasn't there. I asked Napacheekadluk if Soosie was sick and he said, "No, she's dead." I says, "When did she die?" He took a little notebook out of his pocket and he looked at it and told me the date in July — the eighth is what I think he said, but I'm not sure of that. Napacheekadluk said Soosie had gone crazy, and then he handed me this notebook and said, "Here's all what happened."

So I took the notebook — it was written in syllabics — and I interpreted Napacheekadluk's notes and handed it over to the RCMP. Napacheekadluk told everything that had happened right from the day Soosie went crazy until they had shot her.

Soosie had gone berserk, she went right off her head, and the people at the camp were so scared of her that they left the camp and went out on a little island to get away from her. The way they said they knew she was crazy was that she was going after them, that she used to, as they say, "blow her breath" at them, trying to make the people the same as she was. She had also been throwing rocks at the kids and trying to harm them. That's when the people got scared and ran away from her out to this island.

This was at that time of the year when they couldn't make a trip down here to Spence to get help, they couldn't travel by dogs because there was too much ice floating around.

They were out there on that island for quite a long while, and with a telescope they watched Soosie up where the camp was. She tore all the tents down and she was doing all sorts of crazy things like breaking up all their equipment around the place. They said she was possessed with the devil.

They were really scared of her, and they were all beginning to get hungry because they were afraid to go hunting, so they decided that they'd have to kill her. If they didn't do away with her, it would be a case of her killing the rest of the people if they died of starvation because of her — and they had quite a lot of children with them at the time.

So they decided that it was better to do away with her if they had to, and they picked two fellows, Shooyook and Aiyout, for this. Aiyout was Napacheekadluk's and Soosie's son, and Shooyook was Aiyout's cousin. Shooyook's father was Kadloo.

The idea was that Shooyook and Aiyout would go in with a dog team, stop at the shoreline, and then walk up to where Soosie was. If Soosie tried to run away, they would try to catch her, but if she came after them, threatening them, they would shoot her. So when they went on shore, when they were walking up, they called to Soosie. She was doing what they called witch-doctoring, and she came after them. They fired about three shots, not trying to hit her, just trying to get her to stop. But she wouldn't stop, she came on after them. That's when they decided they'd shoot her.

And they did, they shot her dead.

Well, the policeman couldn't do anything about all this right then, so we went ahead and took the school kids out. After the policeman got back to RCMP headquarters in Spence Bay, he reported all this, and the RCMP in charge there went up in the winter and arrested Shooyook and Aiyout and brought them down to Spence and charged them with murder. The territorial circuit court party came in and they had a jury trial that lasted two days, April 15 and 16. The outcome of that trial was that Shooyook was found guilty of manslaughter only, and given a year's suspended sentence, and Aiyout was found not guilty. So actually they were let right off, they didn't get any punishment compared to what whites would probably get for something like that.

Mr. Mowat, in his Soosie story, wrote this all up like it was such a terrible, terrible thing, all that happened to Soosie and the people, and also like it was all the white man's fault from way way back that Soosie had terrible times and went crazy. I don't know, maybe he thought Shooyook and Aiyout shouldn't even have been arrested or had any trial or anything. Well, he's got a right to make a great big deal about things and people according to the way he thinks about them, like when he thinks that the people have been treated wrong. But what I don't think he's got any right to do, as I said before, is write a story like the one about Soosie that shows dates and names and places that make it look like it's all really a hundred per cent real, at least not if it's just one of his made-up stories like some of the others in that book. I mean, in another story that he called "The Woman and the Wolf", I don't suppose anybody would expect Mr. Mowat would know for sure what a wolf and a pregnant husky bitch are thinking.

But anybody reading his story about Soosie and the people would come out thinking by the end that a lot of things in it were true when they weren't. I know they weren't true, and so do a lot of other people — such as RCMP and Hudson's Bay people and the Eskimos themselves — that are up here now or that were up here in earlier times when some other parts of his Soosie story were supposed to have happened. I guess getting things wrong like this is why, in a lot of places up here, I've heard Mr. Farley Mowat called "Mr. Hardly Know-It".

Anyway, he wrote that after Soosie was killed, Shooyook and Aiyout came down to Spence to buy ammunition and that's where Shooyook was arrested, and that Shooyook was flown to Yellowknife to jail, which he certainly wasn't, and that Aiyout was co-charged only an hour before the trial began. Baloney.

Then he says that by the end of the trial Napacheekadluk "had become a shambling, incoherent travesty of a man whose mind dwelt only in the past", that Shooyook's father Kadloo (Mowat called him Kadluk) "tried to drown himself in the swirling waters of Bellot Strait not far from the ruins of Fort Ross," and that Aiyout and Shooyook "were now themselves forever broken. Some of the people would survive in the flesh a little while longer, but the spirit within them was dead."

Oh my goodness, what baloney! Kadloo didn't try to drown himself. Napacheekadluk is now sixty-seven years old and living in Spence. Kadloo and Shooyook both live in Arctic Bay. And Aiyout is here in Spence — he drives machinery and is mechanic for the co-op. And I can tell you there's a hang of a lot of "spirit" left in the lot of them — and always was.

I read somewhere, maybe on the outside of this book of Mr. Mowat's, that he is called a "great Canadian storyteller". Well, there's stories, and then there's stories.

I was appointed Justice of the Peace and Coroner in 1970, and as a JP, sometimes I've had to bend the law a little bit because some of the law that's made for down south still kind of conflicts with circumstances up here. I try to be fair and try to think the way people are thinking. One thing I get a lot of static for, at times, is that when white people come up before me I generally give them stiffer sentences, because I think that they've known the laws longer and they should know better, where sometimes I feel that the people still don't know the law thoroughly enough.

But the way the people are these days, the way that they've come to feel, they want to live the same as the white people down south, have the same kind of houses and clothes and food and movies, jobs and vacations — that sort of a thing — and I think if they're going to be like white people, then instead of bending a little bit backwards for them, I think they should be treated like white people as far as the law goes.

Actually the law is generally applied the same up here as down south, except for some things in the game law. People up here have the privilege of shooting game out of season. But the bird act should be changed, the people should be able to shoot ducks and geese out of season too, because by the time the season opens, the birds are all going south for the people down there to shoot. I mean, the Eskimos don't get any benefit from that law, so therefore I don't see why they should prosecute anyone for shooting a few birds for fresh meat.

One of the big problems up here, of course, is alcohol. I think seventy-five per cent of all the crime that's committed — not just here in Spence but other places also, because I've had to go to different places to hold court — is almost always caused by liquor nowadays. It causes theft, it causes violence, and many times it even causes people getting killed.

I wouldn't completely prohibit alcohol — I drink, myself — but I don't know what they can do about it. Maybe it's partly a matter of time and learning about the effects of liquor, but the people have been drinking quite a long time now, and it still doesn't get any better. They know it causes trouble, but it still doesn't seem to make any difference. I don't know if it's getting any worse.

Thievery's getting worse, there's a lot more theft than there used to be. If you could put a fellow in jail in his own town I think that would work, like for theft, drinking, fighting, and that sort of a thing, because you've got to do something about this. But here in Spence all we can do is hold someone temporarily for a short time; there's nowhere to keep a fellow in jail for any length of time.

You can give them a big fine — well, that doesn't hurt them, they always pay their fine and then they go and do the same thing right over again. Sending them down to Yellowknife to jail, the way we have to do, is no good either. When we send them to Yellowknife to the Correctional Institute, that's just a holiday, they don't mind that at all. They've got everything there, they've got television, they're let out to see ball games, and all this sort of thing, they just have one heck of a good time.

What's being done now in some places is to give them an intermittent sentence — that's putting them in over weekends. We did do that to one fellow here, and we haven't had anyone that we've put in jail since. So I think that's going to work.

There's another thing that's being done some places which has come into force just recently, which I had asked about doing here quite a long time ago. That is, instead of sending offenders down to Yellowknife to jail, or fining them, to put them to work in the community, let them work for so many days. If you sentence them to thirty days, instead of just putting them in jail, let them work every day without pay helping in the community. If the nurse at the nursing station has a job she wants done, the police if they wanted, or any of the government departments, or even the people themselves that had chores to be done — let the prisoner work eight hours a day the same as we all do, but without pay. And I think this might be an answer. I'm talking here about minor crimes only, of course.

Some people feel that the RCMP, as a white organisation, shouldn't have a place up here any longer and would like to see more Eskimos as RCMP officers, and not just as special assistants. But to be honest, it will be hard to have Eskimos as RCMP until they get a lot better education than most of them have, so they can be trained outside and know enough about the law.

The percentage of Eskimos that break the law or get in trouble with the law in the north is a hang of a lot higher than the percentage of Eskimos to whites, and because of that, sometimes I'm asked if maybe this is because it's the whites that are enforcing the laws. I don't think so. And I don't see any feeling against the whites when an Eskimo is sentenced by a court. He accepts that. He doesn't say, "Here are the whites again pushing me around." From talking to other Justices of the Peace, I think we all try to make the law as fair to the people as to the whites, to everybody.

A new breed of Eskimos

A brand new school was finally finished here in Spence Bay in 1975 and it's having its effect on the settlement all right, a big effect on the community, and I think that's for the good. Now they've got this big school and they've got everything in it, work-shops, labs, everything you can think of.

The grades run from kindergarten through nine; for high school the kids still have to go outside, mostly to Yellowknife. The teachers are six whites and one Eskimo, and they've got four Eskimo assistants, what they call teachers' aides. In kindergarten and grade one they teach the kids entirely in Eskimo now, but that cuts down as they go along, and by grade nine they get two hours a week of Eskimo. They've got all the ordinary school subjects like any school, and they also have got subjects like law, government, astronomy, typing, painting, shop, that sort of thing.

In 1976, for the first time, there was an exchange between some of the school kids here and some in Toronto, and I think that was really good for everybody. This was set up by Nick Newbery, now one of our teachers here, but he was working in Toronto then. Fifteen kids went down from Spence to Toronto for two weeks and lived with people down there, and a bunch of Toronto kids came up here and lived in Spence for two weeks and learned what life's like in an Arctic settlement. The kids that went down there got a real kick out of it. The kids that came up here certainly did too, and so did all the Spence people — well, everyone got a kick out of it. I think they thought that was a real good thing, especially the students that came here from Toronto staying with different families, and the people here thought it was great to have the white kids staying with them.

My daughter Kathy was one of those that went to Toronto. There was a lot of things that she was really thrilled with there. And it was more than just being interested and curious, just going and learning *about* the white people in the south. As far as Kathy was concerned, and some of the other kids that went down there also, I feel pretty sure that they'd like to go and live there for a while. I know Kathy would. Of course this is partly just being young and wanting to do something different. But Kathy's the same as the other kids up here, because all her life she's lived up north. Of course her background is a little different, because I know the south a little better and speak their language, and she's always heard me talk a lot about the times I went outside. This maybe is what got her more interested than the average Eskimo kid.

In the old days it was an awful hard job, like I've said, to get the people to go down south, even to a hospital to be cured of TB or whatever, but today people are getting really interested in the south. Nowadays, it looks to me like every chance they can get, the people will go down south. I don't mean the elderly people, but people up to say thirty-five or forty years old — the older people don't want too much change. But it seems to me the younger people don't feel any more that they are just Eskimos, they're beginning to have a little bit of a feeling of being Canadians too.

The big thing around here in these times, of course, is the question of a pipeline, the possibility of a polar gas pipeline that would probably come very close to Spence Bay. A lot of natural gas has already been discovered in the Arctic islands north of us, and the feeling is that some day they're going to have to get that gas south for the people there to use. A lot of people feel, and their feelings are very strong about this, that this would be a good thing, but also there are some that think it might be dangerous for different reasons.

I don't see anything dangerous in it at all, myself. I think it would be all for the good of the people. I can see where these old people might not want it, for the simple reason that I don't think they understand the thing. But for the younger people, I think the pipeline would be good, because we've got to think twenty or thirty years ahead, and this could bring a lot of employment for the younger generation that's coming up.

I don't think that the work would simply be temporary and then after a short while they'd be left with no jobs again — like some people say — because it's such a vast thing I think there'll be jobs for a long time.

There are young fellows here today that I think could go down south and work on the pipeline or do other work and have real good jobs, but they don't want to move down there — I mean to live there for good.

Some young people here in Spence have jobs with the oil companies that are drilling in the north for the natural gas. The young fellows get real good pay and they work in the field for twenty days and get ten days off with full pay, and the company flies them home and picks them up again. They'd like to have jobs like that right here in Spence Bay so they wouldn't have to leave.

The Inuit Taparisat of Canada (ITC), which is an Eskimo brotherhood, has been saying a lot about the pipeline and that the people don't want it, that it would be dangerous, and they're talking about land claims and self-government. But they don't represent all of the people, at least I don't think so, and going by what ITC is telling the people, I'm pretty sure that the people here don't understand what it's all about.

The ITC say that the people have the right to claim money for the loss of their land, but I don't think this is right, because I don't think the people would be actually losing their land. The people never believed, in times back, that this was their land, as a property they owned sort of thing. They didn't think about the land that way, so how can they lose it?

And self-government, I don't think they are ready to handle that. I know they couldn't here — I'm speaking about Spence Bay because I'm not qualified to speak about other places. But in my own mind, I know they couldn't run Spence on their own, not yet. And I feel that there's no way that the Eskimos can take over the Northwest Territories, not at this stage of the game. Maybe the young generation coming up, if they go out and get good enough learning, then I think that they probably could; but not this generation, not now. I don't deny the possibility that some day, some time in the future, the Eskimos might be able to run the Northwest Territories under some sort of provincial government of their own, but it's going to be a long, long time away if they do do it.

Some say the people that run the NWT government just live in Yellowknife and don't know what the hang is going on in the rest of the place, but I think that's quite wrong. For one thing, Mr. Hodgson, who was the commissioner for over twelve years, visited every settlement in the NWT, most of them twice a year, and talked to the people. And the present commissioner, Mr. John Parker, has also gone around all the settlements. And I feel pretty sure that all these people the commissioner has working for him, especially in the territorial council, keep him advised enough about what's going on. So I think that any commissioner would know what the problems in the north are. Maybe he won't be able to solve all of them, but I'm sure he knows what's going on.

Mr. Hodgson came in in 1967 when the Northwest Territories got its capital in Yellowknife. He's been criticised because some think he went overboard a bit, and others don't think he did all that much for the NWT, but anybody can see what's going on today, what the difference is. A lot of people from the south — the Hudson's Bay people, the RCMP, the missionaries, and even some government people — tried through the years to do things to really help the people, but it was nothing like what was done after Mr. Hodgson came in. When he came in, that's really the time that the government started to do things to help the people.

233

It used to be that people from the south just saw the north as a place where they could take whatever they could get from the country, like gas and oil and gold and furs, and leave the Eskimo alone. But I don't believe they think that way any more, and it's people like Mr. Hodgson that's changed their way of thinking. I think they're trying to develop the north now, and I sincerely think that they're interested in the people as well.

Mr. Hodgson tried to get the people so they can help themselves, begin to run things themselves. Under the new education ordinance he was trying to let the people run their own education system, decide what kind of education they really want. Running the whole thing themselves is what I think he was looking at.

When Mr. Justice Tom Berger killed the gas pipeline for the Mackenzie Valley he said that the native people ought to go hunting and trapping and live that way more. Well, already now the people are not really hunters and trappers any more, not anything like they used to be. And they won't ever be, again, like in the old days.

I think the truth is, in spite of what some would like to think, that they can't keep their culture. They can't go back to the old ways; I don't think they can ever do that even if they wanted to. There's going to be a new breed of Eskimos eventually.

The people now are used to nice houses and they just don't want to go out in the cold and live in a snow house for a couple weeks or months of hunting and trapping. That's if they could even build a snow house any more, which a lot couldn't do. Of course you can find quite a lot of people around here with frozen caribou carcasses outside their houses, because they're going out hunting with snowmobiles; they can go out and be back in two or three days at the most. You don't see people going out now caribou hunting and staying out for two or three weeks at a time the way they used to.

The best hunters here, the fellows that get most of the game, are weekenders — people that work for the government and can only get out on the weekend. And these are the fellows that take foxes, for instance, the only people that bring in any amount of foxes. The snowmobile has made hunting more of a weekend occupation now.

When the people want caribou, they go out and they can always get enough. The caribou are not, as some keep saying, decreasing, there are more and more all the time, more now than ever before, they're coming handier. But when the people are hunting caribou now, they're not trying to make a livelihood and it's not a life and death sort of thing like it used to be. They go out for caribou because they get hungry for the taste of that meat, what they've been used to eating. It's not a case now like it used to be, when they had to get everything they could for themselves just to stay alive and feed their dogs and that sort of a thing.

Like I say, they're just not interested in old style hunting, and I don't think that half of the people here are interested in trapping any more. As the game officer since 1975 I know the figures and statistics in this town. Trapping and hunting have gone down, very much so. They're not bringing in anything like as many foxes as they would have ten years ago, my goodness no. When I was working for the Bay, if we didn't have a thousand foxes here by the middle of the trapping season, that's about Christmas, we'd think it was a poor year. Now I don't think there's a thousand foxes sent out of here in the entire year.

The people are definitely staying home more, and they're not training their young people to go out on the land as much. If you had to train a fellow to go out trapping, for instance, you'd have to take him out on a trap line, have him out there and show him how to do it, not just put a few traps out here and there and then jump into your snowmobile and come back the same night. That's not trapping.

Yes, things are going to change a lot, they're changing already, now that the older ways of hunting and trapping aren't necessary any more. Look at the young people that are sitting around in town here not going to school, not working at jobs, not going trapping. They know they're not going to go hungry, they know that if they don't get any grub, they're going to get it from welfare anyway.

I think probably that the idea of training and working at a job is something that may be hard for some of the older Eskimo families to grasp. A white man goes to school, gets his education, and he thinks of a job — his job is the thing that will support him, not a handout from somebody. That's something that's still hard for some Eskimos to grasp when they used to have their whole life on the land. That *was* their job — living, hunting, trapping, and the rest of it. But that life they had before just had to change — I mean, there's no two ways about it, they weren't going to live forever like that.

My background was different, of course, so with my own kids what's been pounded into them is — get to school, get your learning, so you can get out and get jobs. I'm happy the way my kids are because, fortunately, all of them are working; they've all got jobs except the two still in school. So for the record, here's a rundown of my eleven kids now and what they're doing.

Bella's a housewife and she's married to a Ministry of Transport inspector in Newfoundland. Johnny is an RCMP special constable. Bill is a member of the territorial council. Barbara stays home and works in Spence. Pat's home at present, but he's had a job ever since he got out of school, at different things — fire inspector, for one, and polar gas expediter. Betty lives in Yellowknife and works for the Co-op Federation; before that she was in Cambridge Bay and was the commissioner's personal interpreter. Dennis has been working ever since he got out of school — he worked for Panarctic different places where they were drilling for oil and gas in the islands, he's also been a pipeline worker and expediter, and at present is in Fort Smith working as a mechanic. Charlie was special constable with the RCMP, and is now working as the field service officer in Coppermine. Bobby goes out to Yellowknife at times, gets jobs, until he comes back home again. Kathy and Sylvia are going to school in Yellowknife.

Also I might mention that now that the kids are just about all grown up, Nipisha has more time so at present she's a member of the territorial committee on land claims.

There are families in Spence that are gradually changing a little bit. You take, for instance, James Eetoolook, the settlement economic development officer here, he's thirty years old. I don't know why, but he's the only one here that I think could go out and, in business or anything, get a good job at any time he wanted it, which he has done. He's had a job ever since he got out of school.

I think it's mostly a question of time before the people really come around to going for the job and going for the school idea — but I don't think it 'll be in the very near future. I think most of the young people, right at present, don't understand the situation. They've got to start to realise that things are changing so much, it's not like it used to be. They're going to have to move out of the settlements, or be more willing to move out for periods of time. I don't really see a future for a young person, actually right in the settlements, in the next ten or fifteen years. I don't think the north can offer much to a young person yet.

That's why I don't understand people's objections about the pipeline business. I mean, this is one thing that could develop the country so much, where there could be jobs and the people could learn to weld, and be electricians, they could get a really good training. But if it goes on like it is now, I don't know what the north is going to come to.

I think it's going to take a whole generation of young people going through the school system and getting the job idea before *their* kids will really grasp the changes that have come about. And I'm sure that those kids a generation away are not going to want to hunt and fish, except for the sport of it, for the excitement of it. But not for making a living.

Some day I think that some of the younger generation of Eskimos may be the type, the new breed of Eskimos, that goes south to get work down there, and they'll get used to living and being down south, and I think some of them might want to stay in the south.

Now I see the communities where already the older people are tending to live more like whites, the younger people even more so, and that doesn't distress me at all as a man that lived as an Eskimo and enjoyed it at the time. But to be honest about it, it makes me feel disappointed that, having schools for so long now, the younger people are so far behind, and not grasping the things that they should be grasping about changes.

A lot of what they teach the kids in school here is about the south. As a matter of fact some people think that there's too much about the south being taught, but I don't agree with that. I mean, we have to face it, within the next twenty or thirty years I don't think there's going to be any Eskimo-speaking people. Already now on the streets around here you hear the kids speaking together in English — they don't talk to each other in Eskimo anything like as much as they used to.

But I do feel that for the time being, for a while yet, the people should keep their own language. I said earlier that I was really unhappy about it when they started sending the kids off to school and wouldn't let them speak or even write home in Eskimo, but that was nearly thirty years ago. Before too much longer it's not going to matter that much, because the people that they have to communicate with now in Eskimo are older people, very old people, and they're not going to be here forever.

So I think we're going to lose the Eskimo language, like for everyday use, and just talk the same up here as down south. I think that it's in the interest of the Eskimos not only to know the language of the south but to know as much about the south as possible. At least I think that it *should* be, because how else are they going to get jobs and work along with whites and live among them, either up here or down south?

Back a couple years or so ago when Nick Newbery and I were taping all this stuff you've been reading, Nick said, "Ernie, you've lived all this long time in the north and you still seem to be in pretty good condition. Is it all that activity and clean living, and the fun you've had, that's kept you healthy?" I guess I kind of glared at him, and I said, "Well, I'm not *that* old, I'm only sixty-eight!" And maybe I had to grin a little bit about the "clean living" part of it.

But yes, I think the fun has sure helped, and I know all the activity has, because ever since I was a kid at home, right from when I was growing up in Port Burwell, we would get up early and start working. I was always hard-working, getting up early in the morning. But I worry some about maybe starting to feel a little bit old pretty soon now, because the last seven or eight years I've been sitting in an office and not getting any exercise or anything.

And by now, well, I could also say that trying to get a book ready to print is even more sitting around and even less exercise. It's sit and talk into the tape recorder, sit and read what's been typed, and sit and talk some more to correct things that we got wrong or mixed up, or that got left out, about what I used to be doing back in the early days, or what have you.

And to tell you the truth, I'm just about "sat-out" after all this. Right now.

About the author

Born in 1910 in a little place near Hopedale on the Labrador coast, Ernie Lyall was one of 19 children. His father was Scottish, a cooper by trade, and both father and grandfather had worked for the Hudson's Bay Company. He learned his ABCs from a Mountie, Sergeant Jim Wright, who boarded with his family.

At seventeen, Ernie joined the Bay as a clerk and spent the next 30 years working for the company in various parts of the Arctic. When he settled down in Fort Ross, in the Arctic Islands, he married an Inuit woman, Nipisha, and immediately became part of her extended family. Fluently bilingual in Inuktitut and English, Ernie was many times the point of contact between the Inuit and Canadian officialdom.

Ernie and Nipisha now live in Spence Bay, on the Boothia Peninsula.

Ernie wrote this book by narrating it into a tape recorder, and then editing it down so that it became exactly the story he wanted to tell — an intimate, insider's account of life in the Arctic.

Other Canadian Lives you'll enjoy reading

Canadian Lives is a paperback reprint series which presents the best in Canadian biography chosen from the lists of Canada's many publishing houses. Here is a selection of titles in the series. Watch for more Canadian Lives every season, from Goodread Biographies. Ask for them at your local bookstore.

Something Hidden: A Biography of Wilder Penfield
Jefferson Lewis

The life story of a world-famous Canadian surgeon and scientist — written by his journalist grandson who has portrayed both the public and the private sides of Penfield's extraordinary life of achievement.

"One of the most valuable and fascinating biographies I have read in many years." — Hugh MacLennan

Canadian Lives 1   0-88780-101-3

Within the Barbed Wire Fence
Takeo Nakano

The moving story of a young Japanese man, torn from his family in 1942 and sent with hundreds of others to a labour camp in the B.C. interior.

"A poet's story of a man trapped by history and events far beyond his control." — *Canadian Press*

Canadian Lives 2   0-88780-102-1

The Patricks: Hockey's Royal Family
Eric Whitehead

A first-rate chronicle of the four-generation family of lively Irish-Canadians who have played a key role in the history of hockey for more than 70 years.

"A damn good story." — Jack Dulmage, *The Windsor Star*

Canadian Lives 3   0-88780-103-X

Nathan Cohen: The Making of a Critic
Wayne Edmonstone

A giant of a man, a legend, Cohen had a vision of what Canadians could achieve in the arts and entertainment — and he convinced both audiences and artists that Canadian work should and could equal the world's best.

"A man of vision, prophecy and insight." — *Ottawa Revue*

Canadian Lives 8   0-88780-108-0

The Wheel of Things: A Biography of L.M. Montgomery
Mollie Gillen

The remarkable double life of the woman who created Canada's best-loved heroine, Anne of Green Gables.

"A perceptive and sympathetic portrait of a complex personality." — Ottawa *Journal*

Canadian Lives 9   0-88780-109-9

Walter Gordon: A Political Memoir
Walter Gordon

The gentle, passionate patriot who became an Ottawa insider and fought for his principles in a cabinet of politicians all too ready to abandon theirs.

"Valuable insight into our political history and a revealing portrait of the man himself."
— CBC newsman Norman Depoe

Canadian Lives 10   0-88780-110-2

Troublemaker!
James Gray

The memoirs of a witty, warm-hearted, irreverent newspaperman who witnessed the golden age of Western Canada, 1935-1955.

"A book of great immediacy and appeal — wise and extraordinarily revealing about ourselves." — Jamie Portman, Southam News Services

Canadian Lives 11   0-88780-111-0

When I Was Young

Raymond Massey

One of Canada's most distinguished actors tells the story of his aristocratic youth as the offspring of the most Establishment family of Toronto. The first of his two-volume memoirs.

"An urbane, humour-inflected and sensitive recollection."
— *Victoria Times-Colonist*

Canadian Lives 12   0-88780-112-9

Having trouble finding a copy of a book in this series?

If you're having difficulty finding a copy of a book in Goodread Biographies' Canadian Lives series, send us a stamped, self-addressed envelope and we'll put you in touch with a bookstore that stocks all titles in the series.

Write to:

    Goodread Biographies
    333 - 1657 Barrington Street
    Halifax, Nova Scotia
    B3J 2A1

Be sure to enclose a stamped, self-addressed envelope with your letter.

Printed in Canada